THE UNSHAKEABLE ENTREPRENEUR

BTD Studios

B.T.D
Studios
PUBLISHING

Concept, Design, Layout & Publishing

First Published in Great Britain in 2025
By BTD Studios

Copyright © BTD Studios 2025

BTD Studios reserves the moral right to be identified as the author of this
work in accordance with the Copyright, Designs and Patents Act 1988.

Dedication

In a "quirky" move, I want to dedicate this book to a feeling rather than a person. The moment when your heart beats too fast, your stomach drops, the fear/disappointment or sadness grabs you, and you experience despair. The type that you didn't see coming, the type you know you don't deserve.

When you have worked so so hard, for so so long and you find yourself at the short end of the deal. When you know you have put your heart and soul into something just for it to be either mismanaged, disrespected, misunderstood or missed entirely. For in those moments when it seems too hard and not worth it. When you have to walk away from your computer, the table, the office and have a cry. For every time a client can't muster the energy to speak to you with respect, for every chargeback that wasn't valid or just. For every refund request that was neither morally or legally sound. For every invoice that went unpaid by someone who just assumed "you were good for it". For every time you became scared to open your emails.

For the moments when the bills feel too high, when the workload is too much or you feel utterly and totally alone. I hope you grab this book, make yourself a cuppa (or a wine) and go and sit in a beautiful smelling bubble bath to read it. Cry it out if you must, surrender for one evening in it but know that you are not alone.

Successful entrepreneurs are not clean-smelling of roses after walking a red carpet; we crawled our way here in the mud. But please know - most of the time it really is much easier than many other paths, there is a light to this and it is wonderful. We reveal the dark side of the moon only so you can experience the full and truest potential of entrepreneurship, with the joy and wonder it really deserves. Because when is good - its fucking magic.

CONTENTS

Chapter 1 - 1
THIS WILL ONLY HURT FOR A MOMENT

Chapter 2 - 28
'HER CE0 SHOES' 3 SIMPLE STEPS TO FREEDOM

Chapter 3 - 54
BREATH. REGULATE. RISE: 13 STEPS TO ALIGNED
SUCCESS

Chapter 4 - 72
INCREASED COMPETITION & MARKET
SATURATION

Chapter 5 - 94
ONE POST, £2000. THE BUYER JOURNEY THAT
CHANGED EVERYTHING.

Chapter 6 - 118
IT STARTED WITH A DREAM AND NOW YOU'RE
FEELING PRESSURE

Chapter 7 - 148
FROM STORY TO SOLD.

Chapter 8 - 158
HOW TO BE THE BEST SELLER IN YOUR INDUSTRY

Chapter 9 - 188
AI FOR THE REST OF US: DESMISTIFY AI

Chapter 10 - 216
WHEN YOU'RE THE BACKUP PLAN, THE SAFETY
NET, AND THE CEO

Chapter 11 - 240
THE COMPARISON TRAP: GUARDING YOUR
MENTAL HEALTH IN THE AGE OF 'SUCCESS PORN'

Chapter 12 - 268
TEAM MATTERS: STRATEGIC HIRING, SCALING,
AND RETENTION FOR LASTING SUCCESS

Chapter 13 - 296
CASHFLOW - HOW TO PREDICT, PREPARE
AND PROSPER

Chapter 14 - 322
BURNOUT BE GONE

Chapter 15 - 350
SHE WAS FOUND IN OVERWHELM

Chapter 16 - 362
BE KIND TO YOURSELF, IT'S TRICKY BEING HUMAN

Preface
By Dawn Baxter

Within the Chapters of this book, there is a gift held tightly. The greatest gift I could perhaps ever give you as a reader, as a visionary, as a leader, as a business owner, as someone who has looked inside the smoke-filled mouth of the dragon of self-employment and thought "game on".

Throughout my time as a multipotentialite entrepreneur, I have had the pleasure to work with and know some of the best minds in the business. The conversations I have had in the direct messaging section of Meta, around dinner tables with wine and within the sweet squares of Zoom rooms are nothing short of extraordinary.

They have undoubtedly shaped my journey towards success in a way that nothing else could claim to have the same impact.

In digital business entrepreneur land, real life is somewhat gatekept. The kitchen table business woman weeping into her coffee because invoices haven't been paid, or struggling to feel worthy of fighting a sea of competition for clients, isn't sexy; it doesn't sell courses or services. It can be all together too real. It is hidden and huddled in scared, brief whispers by the brave during networking meetings, over coffee with friends, in the doubt-filled shake of your voice as you admit to your partner that "this isn't working".

The thing is, behind closed doors, with their most trusted contacts, the big, successful, shiny entrepreneurs you follow on socials are opening up about their struggles too. Yes, new level, new devil, etc, but each of us has scars and crosses to bear from the time we have spent in the trenches of this crazy, beautiful, stressful, ridiculous life we have chosen. None of us got out unscathed, we walked through the fire and we are all at different levels of sooty and scorched. We hide it well - especially during launches, but it is there if you look closely enough.

You are just like them, just like us, and that's not a bad thing. We have an opportunity that we have grabbed with both hands with this book, the opportunity to turn around and outstretch a hand to you to help you up, too.

What if we could be your tour guide through the landmine field? What if we could tell you all about the devil on your back and the next one you are about to meet?

What if, in the time that ground level opportunity and global economic uncertainty got married and decided to have wild babies, I could gift you astute minds of stability, security and sexy supportive practice.

What if I could gift you a low-cost pass into the minds who survive, thrive and dive headfirst into their next challenge with the confidence of completing the last still lingering in their aura.

What if I presented the modern-day business equivalent to Hercules' seven challenges in a simple way, with a guide on how to overcome each one?

What if, from the comfort of your chair, I could give you a supportive circle of experts who have helped me, my clients, their clients and will probably be revered by your clients and you too.

Settle in for a mind-blowing all-in-one type experience, or pick this book up by the chapter as needed, like business owners' medication to increase belief, resilience, idea generation, efficiency, wellbeing and more and more and more.

One of the highest indicators of survival of a brand, in difficult times, is the ability to adapt. Which is almost always accompanied by a person of significant control at the helm who can continue learning, to process new opinions and thoughts and find merit in them, for themselves.

You may absorb or reject ideas, but you are open to considering them and bending them to your own super-specific need. By buying this book, you have already proven this skill and solidified the likelihood of potential continued and found success.

This is a love letter from your peers, it is a chant at the football pitch line of cheerleaders with big foam finger hands, it is a gentle knowing that you are up and coming and holding your hand whilst you step into yourself, it is an open door and an invitation to come sit in our company and break bread with us. It is a warm hug on a cold night and a sweet pat down after a fall.

Enjoy the wisdom, the comedy, the insight and more importantly, the way individual expertise held together like this redefines the word value.

This is the 42 of all business books, the teseract of good energy and the multiverse of entrepreneurship.

Dive in, it's your turn now & we have made the water safe and warm.

Dawni
X ♡ X

Beyond The Dawn of Business podcast

Instagram - @dawnbaxterofficial

Facebook - Dawni Beth Baxter

Dawni Baxter

Dawn is a neurodiverse multipotentialite entrepreneur, angel investor, and bestselling author who built multiple businesses from the ground up. She's a certified social media expert, passionate about ethical marketing, meaningful connection, and supporting self-employed creatives.

This will only hurt for a moment

JBB, JB,BB,AB,. - without you there would be no point in it all. I love you with my whole heart.

EN,NUE,LPD - I will never not be grateful for you and your presence in my life, not just work, but definitely work included. Thank you!

AA,GG SG,SP,JP,JD,LP,CM,CM - For loving me enough to always be there, you are the type of friends books are written about.

THIS WILL ONLY HURT FOR A MOMENT

If you look at my online presence at the time of me writing this chapter, you will see a ton of very luxurious pictures of me looking well, on the beautiful island of Ibiza. You will notice multiple entrepreneurial pursuits such as products, events, podcasts, funny short-form videos and much more. You would also find a lot of love for me online. Testimonials, words of support and people who will quite literally stop you mid-scroll to explain how I have improved their life for the better. It is all wonderful, and despite what I am about to tell you, there very much is a realness to it, I promise! When I dive in, though, it is going to lift the 'veil' of business a bit and, like letting you behind the Wizard of Oz's curtain, you won't ever be able to unsee what you see here. It is the truth on a level most business books will never allow themselves to enter into.

In the space of self-employment, there are stages that most of us go through, much like when we are in a new relationship. The dreamy stage where everything is exciting and possibility, the realistic stage when the honeymoon is over and there are some elements of difficulty to face, choose or overcome and then there is perceived to the disillusioned stage where everything feels like utter dog shit and you start daydreaming about a steady wage and stacking shelves.

I did not intend for this book to be an exposé of the truth behind the scenes or to debunk the dreamy stage of business; it is very much intended to provide you with real, valuable tools and tips to help you sustain your dream, even in the hardest of circumstances. To provide a guide and resource that holds the phrase strong, "The only way to fail is to quit". But in doing so, we do have to put a neon arrow light above the pitfalls and areas you could find more difficulty in.

For many, reading these pages will evoke a nod, a long moment of understanding, perhaps a slight playful snigger of knowing. For many this book will sound nothing like anything they have consumed before and might feel a bit like a kick up the arse. Good. Let it. Then come and find us online so we can soothe you with community and care, and empathy after. Lessons are very rarely licked onto your skin by kittens whilst someone strokes your hair and feeds you grapes. They are tattooed on you with painful needles whilst the universe holds you down with all its might. In the chapters of this book, you will find personal experiences, expert tips and fountains of future-proofing knowledge to support you in seeing the elements that are not easily seen, but being prepared for them and more in a way that many of the authors of this book were not.

We are the ones who have had bad money months and survived. We have had awful clients, legal battles, difficulty balancing our personal life and the business, we have cried over work we have done, clients or opportunities lost. We are also the ones celebrating invoices paid during economic downturns, winning awards when 60% of the businesses that started the same month as us fold for good. We are taking the trips abroad with our families and teams. We are the ones doing things differently and making our own rules whilst following some fundamental pathways that support the side of business that is difficult to know about until you are up to the neck in it.

One of my favourite Marvel movies is Captain Marvel. It is seemingly one of the most hated out of the franchise, but I have a few key moments from the film that hit me personally. It helps that it hits my age bracket right between the eyes with references such as Nirvana being the soundtrack to fuzzy memories and a quick trip into Blockbuster. I love the character and the way she holds herself all the way through, she is a little disruptive, but holds a powerful silence despite being confused, unsure and trying to put the puzzle of who she is together throughout. For someone like me, who can't hold her water, and is extremely open about all things, watching steely strength like that is inspiring. But more than anything, at the poignant moment of the film, when the odds are against her and she has her hands tied down, she is accused of being "Only Human" and the Kree tell her "without us, you are weak". It replays her memory in that moment of her as a young child right up to a young woman, before the morning that she was changed. Her memory shows that the bumped, bruised, bloody, tired and shaken girl hit the ground in multiple underdog circumstances; she falls down. Hard. And then in a beautiful honouring of her memory replays every single time she got back up. Shaky legged, worse for wear, beaten and hurt, she stood back up and faced it head on.

Although some of the things I speak about here are going to be a bit meh and not the shiny side of the moon, know that I am knocking it down with the intention of strengthening your awareness and comfort in "getting back up".

The mental game for successful people is where it is at, not just because you have the power to manifest your dreams (you do). But because your brain, more specifically your limbic system, plays a central role in administering both your emotions and your hormones. This is integral to the moves you make, how quickly and with what underlying motivation you make them.

Sometimes an experience is a rubber hammer to your knee, and the reaction you have as default can't be an immediate kick out. Your brain holds the key to everything first, and this is where we will administer some of this survival knowledge.

In case you didn't already know, your brain will support or hold you back in these four mental locations.

Your Amygdala - processes fear, aggression and some memory - often tied to emotional memory.

Your Hyppocampus - takes your current situations and stores them by linking them up to new emotions.

Your Prefrontal cortex - helps regulate emotional responses, calm down and get back to baseline (she's the queen who we will be invoking a lot throughout our tools here together)

Your Hypothalamus - reads the emotions and links them up with a physical response, such as making your heart thump like a speeding freight train through the night when you get a customer complaint or refund request.

There are also your endocrine system and pituitary gland to consider, but let's stop there before I get too deep into my favourite subject, which is the way that Science and psychology shape people and our businesses alike! You wouldn't make it out of that book alive, nor would I.

Knowing the threat and knowing how to deal with it internally (your body) and then operationally (within your business) is key. But how many entrepreneurs do you know who are adding their mental and emotional well-being into their SOPs?

In SME world hardly non and in corporate land absolutely fucking no one but the top cheese and even he is pretending he isn't to look relatable to the constantly churning employees below who are being bolt on micro managed daily just to keep the wheels turning.

The thing is, many of us thought that life would be simple and that notoriety would create more business, audience and visibility would bring more money and that we would at some point be able to hire our replacement and reap the rewards of working for passion rather than for pay. The truth is that there are so many other experiences involved in that journey that you just don't know you don't know, until you have learned about them. The road isn't smooth, it's rocky as hell, and it will cut your feet and watch you bleed while you tentatively take your next steps.

I hate horror movies, I don't see the point in flooding my brain with information about pain and suffering and fear. I have always cultivated my thoughts and beliefs towards happy, positive outcomes, and this has served me really, really well in the first few years of business. More and more however I am realising that you cannot look away, you cannot hide, and you should not bury your head in the sand when it comes to protecting your life, your loves and your business.

Most of us want an "easy" life, and that's fine, but self-employment or entrepreneurialism is not the place to find that. It will be a "good", sometimes absolutely incredible, life. But ease got taken out the back and executed between the eyes the moment you decided to do this. Understanding that is a massive part of your success going forward.

Here are some truths for you. The more visible you get, the truer they become. The more clients you take on, the more likely statistically you will come across them. Good news - there are ways to handle them all, and well, so you can do what you came to do when you started this thing!

- You can hire your replacement but you will need more than money to make that work. Talent is not easily found. Even with the most talented entrepreneurs you will find out there will be a key element lacking. That's why you should take a look at the talent acquisition pages in this book - you won't ever be able to fully step away if you don't have competent people who actually care and will weather the responsibility the way you do (or better).

- You can make money while you sleep, have sex, sit on a yacht sipping champagne, but all of the things that bring you money in like this require upfront graft and continued maintenance. "I filled my membership with 100 people and made 10k months just from this" is great, but you will experience churn, and how do you keep those 100 people or get more people in all the time? Be prepared to launch over and over, forever and ever or to spend years and years growing audiences. Again, totally fine as long as you are aware.

- Your business can be brilliant and fulfilling without being loud, but personal brands that show up will always have more power in growth.

- People will screw you over. I am so sorry - it hurts me too, I still cry about it myself when it happens. If you are particularly heart-led and have a business that holds a direction of supporting others for their good, this will sting like a mo'fo.

- Your superfans can and often do turn into megatrolls. I know - fucking wild isn't it. The person who adores the ground you walk on can turn, but know there is always a reason, and it will often involve money!

- People steal. Just accept that. Your ideas, your copy, your pics, your identity, your offers, etc, etc - Protecting them and having systems in place to defend yourself are critical.

- If you look like you are making money, people will come after it. People do mad things in the pursuit of money, and often will throw out moral and ethical standing.

- They will look at you like competition, not everyone on the scene has the emotional maturity to realise there are enough clients for us all.

- Business relationships and collaborations will fail.

- People are flaky and don't do what they say they will. You, too, sometimes.

- Some people will not like you, often their reasons will be shit and unfounded but that's non of your business.

Most of the issues you will have in your business that will feel soul-destroying will be down to

People and Money. This sucks because to make money you need people and to help people you need people and to keep your business running you need money. It is the snake's tail that eats itself.

That being said, **all businesses** have the same issues you have or are about to have; it is just that the painful stuff that might make a reputation look bad and a PR and Marketing team need crisis control is gatekept away for secret board meetings and non-disclosure discussions.

It is time we lift the lid and tell the total truth. So here goes.

Failure is necessary and it should feel shit
The best entrepreneurs out there have messed up massively, and you would never know.

You, too, are going to fail.

Little daily fails and sometimes Big Fat Public, fall on your face, arse in the air level fails.

Repeatedly, hopefully not at the same thing repeatedly, but you will ultimately find ways to fail over and over. You will spend to much. Hire the wrong person for the job. Exceed reasonable expectations on that VA, Course, or product you have purchased. You will ultimately get things wrong.

Failure will feel like shit and it is supposed to. **In walks your Amygdala.** If this lesson didn't feel like utter crud, you would likely forget it. It wouldn't be significant enough for you to hold onto the memory and learn from long-term. The emotional significance of fear and threat is absolutely necessary for you to hold on to.

Now Amy (we will call Amygdala Amy and apologise to all other Amy's for this) is just trying to make this experience stick. Much like you riffling through your phone photos and videos trying to decide which picture of your dinner is the best one to keep and which ones can be deleted permanently to relieve storage space on your iPhone, it is your brains job to filter out things that are not important to you and to hold onto the ones that are.

Remember, our brains are wired for survival, not happiness. We have to understand the survival and manually input the happiness ourselves.

I never want to feel bad or for you to feel bad. I wasn't put together in that way. That being said, scientifically and in business strategy, us all occasionally feeling bad is incredibly valuable.

What isn't valuable is the knock-on effect to your core needs, your ability to rest, your mental health thereafter and what a storm of all of those things can do to your relationships and productivity. This is when the brain creates a situation which your energy has to shift. If the bad experience is required, your

8

energy is your filter - it needs to take the bad and allow it to be without poisoning the rest of you.

There are tools to remember when you fail.

Firstly, everyone does, some more than others, but definitely everyone.

There is honour in owning it. In this day and age, honour and valour aren't spoken about much. The civilisation codes of those amongst us who are considered role models have shifted.

If I could highlight two areas of your moral compass as a business owner in this world that will make you stand out and secure areas of long-term success for you it would be

1. Honour and 2. Valor.

Fuck up. Face it. Forgive yourself. Change it. But hold yourself accountable and don't hide from it. Stand up.

You will have bad clients
This one sucks for me to admit because I have spent years online praising my client base. I have worshipped them as much if not more than they have me and I was incredibly cocky in stating that MY clients were in fact the best of the business ever ever. For the majority, this is still true.

To me, a 97% chunk of my clients are the most innovative, inspirational, kind and caring human beings with real skill and value to offer the world. They work hard, they get themselves out there, they appreciate work and people and hold exceptionally wise and understanding ideals over the way to treat people and conduct themselves. They are intelligent, reasonable and open-minded legends.

I'd never recover.

The 2%, however, look the same as the above, which is why it is so difficult to spot them and weed them out beforehand. They present as all of those things (good personal marketing), and they allow for you to trust they belong to the 97% because it benefits them greatly if you do.

Then there is the 1%, and these are damaging lessons in business or the lack of professionalism that you can find in the business world sometimes. These look okay at first, but you get a gut feeling early on - If you continue forward from that point (you shouldn't,) they will become an absolute nightmare and steal your mental health, emotional wellbeing and hurt your business financially and in productivity and efficiency - if you let them.

When they turn, it can be dramatic or it can be subtle. Sadly, by the time they turn, if you don't have a system in place, it can be too late. When looking for the 3% not great clients, you should consider the below.

Example: Silvie is a virtual assistant and her post in a group I am in reads like this: "In the last 6 months, one of my clients, whom I have worked for, for four years, screamed at me down the telephone and made me cry. He has always been demanding and condescending. He often forces me to work evenings or weekends to get stuff done, and he is almost never happy with the work, but he has paid his invoice on time every month, and I need the money. I started going to therapy a few months back to get some emotional support for my outbursts, perhaps I should increase my prices to cover it?"

Just no.

The lesson here is to never let a relationship get to this level. In business, of course, but I would also suggest anywhere in your life.

Friendships, relations, relationships and work connections can all be toxic and when they are, you need to cut and run as fast as you can. Sadly, when money and contracts are involved, it's not always that easy. Every business cut and run feels like a divorce.

Look out for

- **Scope push.** Clients love bargains of course, and also have dined at the table of "if you don't ask, you don't get". That being said, you can tell the difference between a cheeky ask and someone who is entirely unreasonable. Maybe they message at midnight. Maybe they take your words and spin them to mean something you didn't offer, and then get offended when you re-establish a boundary.

- **Accusatory, rude or overtly dramatic communication.** If the world is ending and you have ruined someone's entire business prospects because of a typo - RUN. If a client tells you on a call they are "picky" or "particular" on a discovery call, find out more. Like a bad romance when the guy says "I don't want to hurt you" and you can translate that to "I am definitely going to hurt you." You can pick up on when a prospective client says something like "I can be a little bit picky" not always, but often this can be a declaration more like "I don't trust people, I need to micromanage everything and I will pick your work apart"... also look out for ANY slagging off of the hired help before you. You are likely watching in real time what will be said to your replacement in three months' time, despite your performance.

11

- **Blatant disrespect of your time.** Booking your third meeting this month after no show at the previous two? Don't bother. People who don't show up for you (or themselves) are wasting people's time in order to look and feel important themselves - check out the ways we abandon ourselves in business a little further down in this chapter.

- **They don't want to do their side of the work, or "you can't do anything right".** Expectations in business relationships are everything. Sometimes there are genuine misunderstandings, and the odd meeting doesn't occur; this is true of everyone, but multiple times in a row is an indicator that someone doesn't respect your time. Another example of this, sadly, is the "I hired you, why do you keep bothering me" side of the equation. Unfortunately, unless your business is in clairvoyance, most of us are not mind readers and we do need input, support and communication from the clients we work with. One of the biggest red flags is the person who makes you feel like an inconvenience when needing their input to support them. The more you have their input early on, the better you can work with them in every single capacity.

Don't rely on the income of a client until you have worked with them for 6 months or more and if they show signs of being difficult, remove their financial income from your stable finance forecasting. Be prepared to end a contract early or use their finances to support yourself in court or other necessary paperwork proceedings. If you are sitting here thinking, "I can't afford to do the work and not rely on this income", then you have two operational issues to face.

1. You aren't charging enough. Your business prices should not be what your household bills are and wages need to be split into division by the number of clients you have. You must consider

taxes, bad client admin spend, bills, unexpected costs and savings of 6-12 months of wages in your cost. When you work that out if might only be an extra £50 quid per client (depending on your needs) but you don't negotiate on that because when the shit hits the fan, no one will negotiate with you! On top of that should also be profit, and remember that what you want for profit needs 20% added to it for the Sheriff of Nottingham, aka corporation tax. Keep an eye on the following chapters that will support you further in both sales and financing.

2. You are not realising the power in closing one door to open 20 more. Sure, business is a numbers game and the more clients you get, the more likely you are to get stung, but know this: YOU GET TO CHOOSE who you work with, and if there is one person satisfied and a good fit, there will be thousands more. Like a bad date, cut it off quickly and move on.

Radical responsibility in business

Have you heard of it? Radical responsibility is where you look at the information before you and you allow yourself to fully own it. You don't allow yourself to make excuses that flip the lid and make everyone else the bad guy. This takes mastery, as this is not something we were ever taught in school, and it often gets lost under the "accountability" label of self-awareness.

Radical responsibility includes action. It doesn't hold its hands up in "OK you got me", it takes the information and uses it to do things better, without someone else having to ask you to.

The main reason I love Radical responsibility is that it takes away something I have a love/hate relationship with. I hear "feedback is the breakfast of kings", and I love the sentiment. The problem is, as a previous corporate worker, I have been fed feedback that should have been labelled "Yoghurt of the one I need to pin this on" or " Toast of my own insecurity and lack". You only need to be fed a few poisoned feedback breakfasts before you start to doubt its legitimacy. Radical responsibility takes your power back so you aren't force fed someone else's unfactual opinions in an attempt to shift something of theirs that doesn't belong to you. It allows you to welcome the feedback door and to look at the information objectively.

If you are, in fact very self-aware and hold yourself to radical responsibility, you will likely never be fully shocked by feedback; you will, in essence, be aware already and be working to improve the best you can. At this level of self-confidence, you can then take the nectar of feedback in the parts only that you couldn't see yourself, the blind spots if you will. Then you can really take action and make a difference.

I am a recovering people pleaser and excuse maker. In fact, if making excuses for myself and others was a viable career path, I could have pursued this with vigour. I won't just excuse myself for that 12th spoonful of sugar I put in my mouth (it's okay because I didn't sleep well and it's been a hard day), but I will easily make excuses for others. Its probably that "the best possible behaviour that would be excusable is entered here" and that person is not in fact a knob.

Making excuses soothes you with lies. Pretty, sweet-smelling, warm, fluffy, convenient half and devoid of truths. They fake you into feeling okay, burying the experience away and making it right. The problem is they don't. An issue that arises and is excused will arise again and again and again until it is addressed with an action that stops it from happening. There is nothing more frustrating than seeing, naming, voicing and airing a problem, creating a solution and watching the same problem return. You are left knowing you didn't follow it through properly, and that helps no one!

Practice radical responsibility, not to beat yourself with a yardstick, but to give yourself the answers to how you can do this better.

You can't do anything right. (damned if you do, damned if you don't).

Sometimes you will meet a rare type of client. The type that looks like they want your help, they trust your expertise, and they are excited to work with you. These are dangerous people because, like a narcissist about to love bomb you, they fill you with immediate excitement at the work you are going to do together. If you are heart-led like me, these are by far the most dangerous type of clients for both your nervous system and your bank account.

You will notice that not one piece of work or session or event wasn't right and that nothing is ever quite right. You will take instruction and bend over backwards, you may abandon your boundaries in fear of upsetting this client, they may hold fear over you, they may hold back money, they may threaten legal action, they may turn into a refund troll. No matter what they do, you have noticed that whether you follow your skills and expertise to support them in the best way for them, or you have followed their instructions to the letter, it is never good enough.

This is hard once you have fallen into the "we are sorry, we will fix it" category, because exceptional customer care will be used against you to abuse you further. The more you bend, the more will be wrong and ultimately, the relationship will break down, and it was always going to, no matter what you did.

I didn't understand this behaviour until I started learning psychology. It has almost always nothing to do with you, and you are a victim of someone who is trying to do three things.

1. They don't know what they want in business, but they want to feel important. They ask for things they don't fully understand and refuse to listen to experts because they aren't able to admit what they don't know. Ego and pride will be visible with these clients.

2. They need to make it look like they are trying to be successful. Maybe to their partner, kids, old school friends on Facebook - who knows. They want the notoriety and low-key local fame, but they aren't actually in it to do the work.

3. They feel powerful over you because they believe they have "bought" you. Money psychology is wild. You will notice this when you encounter clients who hold a "I paid for you, slave" mentality. Somewhere deep down, they can't differentiate between hiring an expert with buying a product from a shop. They have a consumer mindset, not a commercial one. You are not a "thing" to be bought. You are a paid collaborator brought in to help them do what they were already supposed to be doing without you.

It is not your responsibility for someone else's success, and I don't care what it is you offer.

Sales coaches do not make the sale.
Virtual Assistants do not convert the client.
Life Coaches don't live their clients' lives for them.
Therapists don't do the inner healing work for their clients.

Remember what your role is and don't let someone "own you" from an inferior human perspective because of money. For those of us who have had to heal our money mindset, this is one of the real reasons we had a problem with money in the first place.

One of the most liberating ideas can be that the problem is never money. It is the desperation and bad behaviour that humans will stoop to in order to have, gain or increase their money. This comes from a moral standpoint. Not everyone out there has morals when it comes to money. Be aware of that with everyone you meet, and don't do what so many of us (definitely me) did and immediately trust everyone on face value.

Mind your circle - depressed and sad energy loves company, and it is easy to absorb the flow of the people around you. You will be altered by the people you work with, the events you attend and the masterminds you join. I joined a mastermind once on the basis that the other people in it were "bigger than me". They had a big following, great market placement, looked to have great systems and websites and pictures, etc, etc, and they all had just enough money to pay for that level of mastermind and to look like they were 5 leagues ahead of what they actually were. I went into that room to be inspired and take 4 leaps myself, and found that everyone in the room was just like me or worse (in regards to their reasons for being in business).

I was in the room to gain insights like the ones in this book. To learn about trends and survival tips - how to secure my business in longevity, how to grow, but in a way that didn't scorch me, so I could be slightly uncomfortable but not out of my depth entirely.

They were in the room because being seen in that room would highlight them as more successful than they were to their potential clients. It was entirely social scaling. If I get a picture with this person, then by association, I am considered at that level. The only person who wins in that scenario is the mastermind host, and the people who lose are every other person wanting to learn for real in that room and the audiences of those who are using social climbing as a marketing tool to take money without substance.

I have since always only joined (and hosted) more quiet masterminds - those who will not tell you who is already in them before you sign up. If you work in a mastermind with me, you sign up for me, and the other who signed for themselves will be my gift to you. You will never see me using a big name to sell my offer. You will never see me tagging in someone irrelevant but well business famous in a post just to boost my own "street cred" it is not the way to do it. It is using people and their success to further yourself. Visibility and collaboration are wonderful social climbing is the biggest business ick and it won't do you any good long term.

The popular club only care about what they get from you or maintaining relationships well enough to not expose themselves as the popular club, and it ultimately falls down because once you stop being useful, you stop being invited, and once they can't get anything from you, you stop being part of the crowd.

Now don't think I am saying that when you spot a group of populars, rich and famous that you have animosity towards them because that's ridiculous too. My loving suggestion is to be kind and open, and honest about who you are and what you do in business. In a way that you don't get sucked in and tossed out but you have a chance to make real connections and support from whatever close proximity you are comfy with. But please don't pay 20k + and think you are buying friends, you may make friends (I hope you do), but you are buying into a hierarchy of business. Business fame is a pyramid scheme, and it is not the same as visibility.

If someone is friends with you because of what you can provide for them that isn't a connection. It's a transaction. Everyone is trying to make money. Not everyone is your friend.

The glamour of working from anywhere

I remember in 2020 posting a picture of me on a boat with my family in Fuerteventura. I had taken them out on a holiday in the half term, and I had gotten word from a friend at the BBC that they were going to report that day on another UK shutdown. Covid times. I made the decision that with a purchase of a Spanish laptop and somewhere to stay that had good Wi-Fi, there was no real need to come back to the UK if the kids were going to work from home anyway. The flights in and out of the UK started getting sketchy, and I saw an opportunity to stay in the warm weather and experience something so many of my nomad freelancers have every day. Working from anywhere in the world! Now I had a team on the ground who helped for me to do this (remember - someone's managing it), but I also wanted to see whether life could be enhanced by working this way.

I posted about sitting on a boat and paying off a 10k+ invoice to my team, and I felt incredible. My team worked hard and did well, and here I am, lady muck in the sunshine, in the med, bubbles in one hand and sending money to payroll with the other on my phone.

Only when you break down that moment, I was working. I was thinking about the money and sending it right, not looking at the islands that I was passing on that boat. I was taking the "perfect" selfie that showed the world what a fabulous moment it was (it was), rather than taking it in and enjoying the actual moment.

Don't get me wrong, as I sit here in sweat pants watching the rain roll down my window, it was an epic moment and only 5 to 20 minutes out of what was a three hour experience but you need to realise that when you are mixing business with pleasure it will tip back and fourth and not always in your favour.

Sure, whilst abroad relaxing you can weather a few work WhatsApp messages but what about 11.30 pm when you are trying to help your children feel well from a fever or when you go on actual holiday that isn't meant to be for business and you have your family roll their eyes at the prospect of another snap for mums Facebook page.

There is a truth behind the glamour of working from anywhere, and it is that once you open that door, you are accessible from anywhere too. But like all the pitfalls here there are ways to work this in your favour.

- Have boundaries. On this trip, on Wednesday from 10 - 3pm is working - the rest of the trip is not.

- Don't open messages late at night / have a separate work phone (more business tips from drug dealers should be considered legit - organised crime is at least organised!)

- Understand what you are giving up for marketing and make sacrifices that feel right.

- Don't stop yourself from sharing if you enjoy it (sometimes we love sharing, and that is a business benefit)

- Remember that you sharing your light is for you - if you sense for a moment that the motivation deep down is to make someone else feel less than or shit about themselves - don't do it. There is real, understandable human emotion in those feelings, but fight them and do some shadow work to heal parts of you that feel more worthy when others are "put down". Radical responsibility style.

Maybe make yourself less accessible, like, in general. Energy is the current and the currency (need to get that on a t-shirt). It is more valuable than money, and it is deeply connected with your experience of time. If you are giving too much energy, you will feel like time has sped up to x2. Making yourself consciously less available when you have the opportunity to rest, pause or be is very powerful and will support all the mental frameworks we have discussed. You don't owe anyone your energy to the point where it makes you frantic, unwell or empty. No money - no person deserves that from you. You will however, have to be completely in control of this yourself. Other people don't realise how draining they are, they don't know what your energetic reserves are like - we don't have battery depletion icons on our heads like mobile phones.

The ways you secretly kill opportunity and abandon yourself. This one is going to sting, and you might want to go back up and re-read Radical Responsibility ahead of this one. There are many subtle ways you undermine yourself every single day. I know that is rough, but it is true. I, for instance, am constantly worrying about my health, but I allow myself to eat sugar much more than any healthy person should. To some degree, there will always be some of this, but it is a slippery slope that many of us don't recognise in ourselves because we are excusing it. You know the times you plan something with friends, and the day comes around and you cannot be bothered. You know, once you get there, you will enjoy it, but you can't be bothered getting ready and going out and socialising, so you tell a little white lie in the group chat about a dodgy chicken sandwich you had earlier, and you cancel going. If you did that regularly, the invites would stop coming over to you. No point messaging her, she never comes to anything anyway. The same happens for business, only worse.

Often, the things you don't show up for, you have already paid for. You can tell yourself you are trying to get out there more and network and watch the money leave your account for that networking event, allowing it to soothe you. But you aren't really trying to network because that would require turning up to the

21

Zoom meeting or getting up and heading out in the car to a different town, etc. You tell yourself a little lie like you aren't feeling your best, it's not viable considering how busy the week turned out to be or that it is too much hassle for your home life, childcare, do, the neighbour's dog, etc. This subtle undermining is self-sabotage.

The reason you joined the gym was to use the membership. You're not going again tonight is you're not choosing you. It is you choosing the exact same version of things that you have right now without change, and using your "paid membership" as an emotional plaster excuse for someone who "intended" to do the thing. "Trying to" and "intended to" are where many businesses and dreams go to die. Doing and actioning are the only elements that move. Networking may have been for more clients. You might not have too much problem with that now, but in a few years' time, the connections you didn't make today won't bloom. That opportunity that you set on its journey never started.

You might undermine your own success by ignoring emails, deciding that you can't be bothered marketing that offer, by not showing up for other people in terms of comments, likes, DM's, reviews, testimonials, events, etc.
It's all going business backwards, and the sooner you can identify the areas of business you are "playing at" and the ones you are taking seriously, the better.

You need agency.

Agency means the capacity of individuals to act independently and make their own free choices.

- Example: "She took back her agency after years of feeling powerless."

- It's about autonomy, self-direction, and control over your own actions.

You have to be able to look at the possibilities and make your own decisions and actions without blaming anyone else around you. You get to choose what you do with information, and holding agency is the most powerful move you can have in your own life and business. It is very easy when the "chips are down" to scour the horizon for someone to blame. The problem with this is that it allows for you to throw situations that very much are/ were in your control out to someone else. Agency is being able to evaluate, understand and solve without their being blame. It also means you look at the crowd of online sheep all jumping off the same cliff and turn and walk the other way, not just because you see that the sheep are falling to their death but very much because you have complete and utter confidence in making the choices so many would not, based on your belief in yourself. You are the director of your life and you don't need anyone else's permission!

Leadership comes from being able to have that strength and it is beyond the simple "business owner" or "entrepreneur". It's a role in itself that you can embody that changes all things.

You don't have to absorb others ideas. Even this chapter, you are able to read this and think "Dawn's talking bollocks there" and as long as you're sure why and have good reason then good for you!

You have to decide your belief system and follow facts that are helpful to you and allow you to do what you want for your business and your life.

You can self qualify your agency in yourself, you're in charge of your business, your career and ultimately your life.

The hurt mirror. When you take a metaphorical business bullet, it can be difficult not to want to seek some kind of revenge or to get into game playing. Someone didn't pay your invoice on time, well maybe you will just hold onto your cash a bit longer too. You got a court letter, well then let's roll up the sleeves and go after everyone. This is totally normal and quite human. Because sometimes the biggest issues in business and especially in economic downturns or global strife, feel like war. That comes from the need of more people feeling the difficulties and challenges and choosing bloody, messy survival over professional and kind conduct. Which when backed into a corner we can all understand. That being said - it is horrendous when you are unexpectedly the victim of someone else's need to "recoup" finances.

Choosing not to mirror the ways in which the world (ahem, money and people) have hurt you is called integrity. You will find that word used a lot in language and not so much in action. Be one of the people who actions it. Over and over. Time and time again. Give people chances to back out of their threats. Give people space to evaluate their behaviour. Then, if you have to (and sadly you will) be prepared to fight for what's right. But never ever embody the behaviour to others, like a chain reaction of pain. Much like breaking ancestral linage of curses, true leaders sometimes are the buck stop for bad behaviour, shoddy business practice and lack of professionalism. It is your cross to bear. Think of yourself as Buffy the business knobhead slayer - grab yourself a Scooby gang of support and get to work on fighting each demon one at a time so they can't go on to hurt anyone else. But don't allow the pain to turn you into a demon.

Be discerning with your response. Be calculated in hope and kindness in your attempts to engage with those who are just totally out of fucking order.

In recent times I have had the pleasure of many different situations dragging me by the hair into learnings that are so valuable and at the same time totally heartbreaking. The type of situations when you can see that things are not fair, justice isn't in the building and yet you have to deal with them just the same. Sometimes broken and tired you have to stand up.

Some people will be totally unreasonable, ethically redundant and totally in the wrong. Do not be one of those people, no matter how many punches you take. You are putting yourself in the place to encounter them every time you deploy opportunities to take on new clients.

I tell you this because over 250 clients at the same time have paid into one of my companies, received goods and services and loved every second and the handful of bad apples will have no effect on our wider legacy. We have been able to grow our group by 2 and we are delivering a higher quality service than ever before. We have won awards and been praised from here to Timbuktu.... And we couldn't have had a moment of that joy or success alongside the issues if we didn't adopt the values I have shared with you in this chapter. We could have failed a million times over from just one really bad situation. We have weathered multiple and as your business begins to grow you will need to, too.

Every single punch makes you stronger but you must know that you don't have to take all the punches alone. That in your corner, giving you a warm encouraging hug and letting you know the fight pattern of your next opponent are people like each author in this book.

Not enough focus is given to knowing these difficulties and having plans in place to ensure that in your darkest moments you have the tools to continue.

We want you to win , please use all of this information to your own benefit like a beautiful entrepreneurial buffet and pop the things you don't yet need in a draw so you can come back to them when they are relevant, but know that you have it inside you to win but it's not going to look like how anyone else won before you. You're building your own unique path and we are lovingly rooting for you.

Go be great and change the your world and the wider world for the better for us all .... Together.

You can do it.

Check out Dawns best selling book Audience Attraction.

Kellie Williams

Kellie has over 20 years' experience in sales, marketing, coaching, recruitment and outsourcing. She has been running her six figure VA Agency and VA Mentoring business since 2019. Kellie scaled to six figures within 18 months, and her passion is supporting her clients in creating money and freedom.

'Her CEO Shoes' 3 Simple Steps to Freedom

Thanks to my dad Richard Grace, Serial Entrepreneur for teaching me - "Experience is what you get when you don't get what you want!" And for inspiring me to become the entrepreneur I was always meant to be.

Linkedin - kellievamentor

'HER CE0 SHOES' 3 SIMPLE STEPS TO FREEDOM

Introduction: Why Freedom is the Goal

I worked in the family businesses whilst I was growing up and I developed a real interest in business and most of all people and communication. My mum was a Dancer, and my dad left corporate to run his own businesses, he was a born entrepreneur.

From an early age I'd help in my parents' photocopy shop and factory then as a teenager I used to help train the sales force in their inks recycling business. I loved it! I remember my dad used to give me business books to read like 'The One Minute Manager' by Kenneth Blanchard & Spencer Johnson. But my favourite was 'How to Win Friends & Influence People' by Dale Carnigie.

This book was a revelation to me, and I knew that alongside my love of Dancing and wanting to become a professional Dancer I also had a calling in business. I think my dad always knew that I was going to be an entrepreneur one day. They say you're a product of your parents and your upbringing and it turns out this is definitely true of me.

When I left school, I followed my dreams and went to dance college. I wanted a life of freedom and travel whilst doing something I loved. I was so lucky that I got to travel the world and get paid for it. I worked in Dubai, America, Mexico, Holland, Ireland, the Greek Islands for big holiday companies and cruise lines like First Choice, Stena Line and Carnival Cruises. Entertaining the audiences was amazing. Having the chance to see different countries and experience their cultures really enriched my life experience and shaped me as a person.

Following my dancing career, I reluctantly joined the workforce and "normal" 9-5 employment. Why is there such an outdated expectation on people to do the daily grind of the 9-5? Not everyone can fit in a box, some people are creative and need to thrive in a different type of environment.

I have to say I'm surprised I excelled for as long as I did. What worked was that I really enjoyed talking to people and I had a natural ability to sell. My career took off when I found recruitment which was the perfect mix of people and selling! I was trained as a Head-hunter/Search Consultant, and I ended up running recruitment branches and divisions until I realised I had lost my freedom and given up on my dreams. I don't regret it though because I learnt so much and gained masses of experience.

I never really fitted in though, I knew I was meant for something else, and I've always had the entrepreneurial bug! It's in my DNA.

My children were 11 and 7 years old and I was consumed by my job as well as supporting the care of my dad who had been diagnosed with Dementia. Things were tough. There was a daily juggle, and it was starting to take its toll. I was time poor and I had no flexibility. So, one day in 2019 something had to give! I drove to the office and put the keys through the letterbox. I had no idea what I was going to do but within 24 hours I had created a business plan and came up with a business name. I started to work on my goal of freedom and flexibility. Within 2 years I had a business supporting women who had the same dream. I couldn't be prouder of the business I have created and the amazing women around me. I now help women start and scale their businesses with the goal of freedom and flexibility.

The business was going really well but then… in 2023 I was diagnosed with a heart condition and then after visiting a neurologist for a tremor in my head I was told I had a brain tumour. My world could have come crashing down but I had an amazing team of women around me in the business and a supportive family. I spent the year making sure the business would run like clockwork without me, and I also embarked on a fitness journey for my body and mind. I knew I needed to be as fit as I could possibly be going into such a difficult operation. Mentally this is how I coped by building business and fitness into my daily life. I removed myself from the day-to-day workings of the business. I organised, automated and delegated. I created freedom so that I could take 3 months off. I stepped into my CEO shoes!

In this chapter I am going to give you tools to implement my freedom formula- you will have the secret but simple steps for putting in place your own 'Her CEO Shoes' formula that will see you find the flexibility, calm and readiness needed for a future proof business.

Why 'Her CEO Shoes' 3 simple steps to freedom?

All the business owners and entrepreneurs that I know have a why and they're all on the hunt for freedom, flexibility, and a way to make money in the easiest way possible. Along the way I have helped many people including:

- Mums who want more time with their children
- Business owners that want more income streams to support their family
- People who have caring responsibilities for family members
- Entrepreneurs with health conditions
- Employees fed up with the 9-5
- Those who just want to make more money through passive or semi-passive income

They all had these things in common: a why, a need and the drive to succeed. Plus, they were open to advice, help and new ways of thinking to be able to realise their dream. I have multiple whys'. I started my business because I needed more flexibility to help look after my dad as his dementia was getting worse and it was hard to juggle being a mum, having a career and caring responsibilities. My dad is now in a nursing home so my why is a little different. My why is now to have freedom to be able to take my son to football training and matches when I need to. Another why is my health. Having been diagnosed with a heart condition and navigating life with a brain tumour made it essential to take time for self care, not to get burnt out and to enjoy life as well as building a freedom business.

Does any of this resonate with you? Are you a parent, do you have caring responsibilities, or do you have a disability or health condition? Having an end goal of your dream business supporting your lifestyle goals is brilliant but even better if you have a need and a why to make it work. Always come back to the why and remind yourself the reasons why you are dining this.

If you fall into any of these categories then this 3-step formula will help you make sure you don't become the bottleneck in your business, understand the power of delegation for growth and make a plan using 'Her CEO Shoes' 3 simple steps to freedom to help you start working on your business rather than in it.

Are you ready to hear about 'Her CEO Shoes' 3 simple steps to freedom?

Let's break down into 3 manageable steps:
1. Organise
2. Automate
3. Delegate

I'm going to go into this in a lot more detail through this chapter but, for now, I want these 3 words to be etched in your mind:

1. Organise
2. Automate
3. Delegate

Write these down and put them on your vision board because these are the keys to your ultimate freedom formula.

Let's go!

Step 1: Organise

To be able to step into your CEO shoes and start working on your business rather than in it, your business needs to run like clockwork. Step 1 is all about deciding what you want, visualising your life and business goals and reviewing your current business structure, processes and systems to identify what you can improve.

You wouldn't go on a trip without planning your route or using a SatNav and business is the same. Organise, automate and delegate.

Vision

So, let's start with that first key step: Start with your lifestyle goals and then fit your business around them.

Lifestyle Vision Task:

Take time to think about what you want your lifestyle to look like and write it down. Include:

- Number of working hours you would ideally work
- Flexibility
- Freedom
- Salary, dividends, pension
- Family
- House/home
- Car
- Holidays
- Wellness & health

Sit comfortably, close your eyes and imagine your best life. Imagine how it looks and how you feel. Are you ambitious? Do you want to run a successful business that makes lots of money? Are you more interested in the freedom a business could give you? Do you want to do something worthwhile, to give back and make a difference?

This exercise is so helpful. You may even want to put together a vision board. I find this really helps me focus on my goals. I have a digital version on my phone and on my desktop. I'd definitely recommend making one in Canva.

A vision board is a powerful tool used to help you clarify, concentrate on, and maintain focus on your goals and dreams.

Imagine a collage of images, words, and quotes that represent the things you want to achieve or experience in your life, whether that's related to your career, health, relationships, home, travel, or personal growth. That's essentially what a vision board is.

Here's how it works:

- You collect pictures from magazines, printouts, or online sources that reflect your goals. (You can also do this digitally)
- You add inspiring words or affirmations that motivate you.

- You arrange them on a board (physical or digital) and place it somewhere you'll see regularly.

The idea is that by visualising your goals daily, you stay inspired and more focused on making them a reality. It taps into the principle that what you focus on, grows. A vision board is your visual reminder of what you want in life, it helps keep your dreams front and centre. I've had a vision board since 2020. It has always helped me focus on my goals and reminds me to keep working towards them. I am a big believer in manifestation and the law of attraction. Our thoughts and emotions are powerful energy fields that can help us attract and realise our dreams.

Business Vision task:

Spend time mapping out your business vision. Here are some ideas on what to include:

- Business Vision Statement. Who you help, how you help them. Get as specific as possible
- Scaling goals
- What does success look like for you?
- Revenue goals
- Size of your business, what do you want it to become and achieve?
- Becoming the 'go to expert' and authority in your niche or industry
- CEO Shoes. What does this look like to you to step into your CEO shoes?

Developing your goals and building a strategy is key to being able to focus on, work towards and achieve your dreams.

The best advice I can give you is to do one thing every day to improve your business and take a step forward.

Working in your 'Zone of Genius' task:

'Zone of genius' refers to the area of work in which you excel and have natural talents and passions and that you gain most satisfaction from doing. It's the sweet spot where:

- **You're doing something you're exceptionally good at**
- **You enjoy it deeply, it feels energising and not draining**
- **It feels effortless or intuitive to you, even if it's challenging for others**
- **You create the most value for others while feeling most like yourself**

This is a crucial part of 'Her CEO Shoes' 3 simple steps to freedom. You need to know what your 'zone of genius' is and be strict with yourself to stick to it. This is how you're going to build and scale your business and create the life of your dreams.

For example – If you're a Coach you should only be coaching. You should be automating and delegating everything else like admin, invoicing, tech, diary management, website updates, marketing and social media.

Sit comfortably, close your eyes and really think about your work, where you excel and what brings you the most satisfaction and pride. Imagine how your business would look, how successful it would be and how calm and fulfilled your life would be if you were focussing on this and automating and delegating the other parts of your business.

Take a breath and write down what you have visualised. This is your zone of genius. Add to this more detail about what you are the expert in and what makes you the authority in this niche.

You need to focus on this, automate and delegate the rest! Having this focus will help you step into your CEO shoes and realise your dreams.

Task sorting task:

To be able to step in to your CEO role, scale your business and create your freedom you need to be able to sort all of the business tasks into categories:

1. Delegate: Identify tasks that can be completed by someone else and that don't require your specific skill set and time. For example you can delegate admin, social media, blog writing, building landing pages or setting up funnels.
2. Only I can do: Identify tasks that can only be done by you. For example if you are a coach then only you can host your 121 coaching sessions.

Working only in your 'zone of genius' and delegating the rest of the tasks is absolutely the smart way to scale! To work out how to do this, list all of the tasks and responsibilities in your business and put a 1 or 2 next to each of them. The number 1 list to delegate should be the longer one.

Systems task:

Having the right systems in place can help you save time and money.

The best advice I can give you is to:

• Minimise the number of systems that are used in your business
• Have systems which are fit for purpose
• Choose scalable platforms
• Be aware of increasing costs as your business grows

- Have SOP's in place
- Implement intuitive systems
- Identify potential areas to use automation.

Essentially your current systems should have the ability to automate as much as possible and run like clockwork to save you time and make more money. If this isn't the case, you need to review and implement new platforms.

1. List your current systems i.e. Accounting software, CRM, Online course platform, marketing platforms, scheduling systems, Google sheets, spreadsheets
2. What is the full cost of these systems?
3. Could you minimise these systems by looking at an all-in-one platform?
4. What difficulties or niggles do you find with these systems
5. Are these platforms scalable in terms of functionality and cost?
6. Be aware of increasing costs as your business grows
7. If you were suddenly out of the business would a VA be able to take over by viewing your SOP's and are your systems intuitive?

Outsourcing & Delegating

Outsourcing and delegating was a game changer for me. I realised that I couldn't wear all of the hats if I wanted to scale my business, so I hired my first VA in 2020. Yes, I was nervous about the monthly outgoings, but I very quickly recognised that it was an investment. This move was a game changer for me!

The return on investment (ROI) can be direct or indirect. For example, if you are outsourcing lead generation and business development to a Virtual Assistant and they are having a visible impact on your revenue this is direct ROI, it is an investment, not a cost.

Delegating to a Virtual Assistant who frees up your time by doing the repetitive, time consuming, non-revenue generating tasks like admin, email & calendar management, tech etc. would be classed as indirect ROI. This would mean that you can concentrate on working solely in your zone of genius.

In the first year of having a VA I halved my pressure and doubled my revenue. This move had "such" a direct impact on my business that within 12 months I had hit the VAT threshold of £85,000 revenue. My agency model is now built on outsourcing and delegating so there is no income ceiling.

Task

Conduct a review of your list of tasks and identify what you can outsource, and I promise you'll be able to outsource most of it! I help my clients with this all the time, and they're amazed at what they can delegate to a Virtual Assistant or Online Business Manager.

Strategy

Use my free resources to put together your strategy. This will include:
• Lifestyle Vision
• Business Vision & Goals
• Business Overview and Offers
• Systems Audit
• Systems Implementation
• Automation Plan
• Marketing, Visibility & PR
• Delegation List

- Outsourcing Plan

Download my free resources here:

Step 2: Automation and Systems

The more you prepare and plan in your business, the more efficient it will be. Designing and implementing processes, producing SOP's and setting up the right systems will save you time and money!

Looking back, I was just watching my business evolve and it wasn't until things started to get really busy in 2020 that I realised I needed to implement systems and processes. I knew I had reached this point because it became difficult to track what was happening with each client when I'd reached 50 clients and around 20 freelancers. So, I started to look at all the tasks that needed to be done and where I was having difficulties which could pose a risk to the business. I had just been focused on building and moving forward and I had let things evolve organically. I quickly realised that I was missing some of the basics. I didn't have a CRM system in place, and I didn't have a process for the freelancers to upload their invoices and for me to track and know what payments needed to be made.

It was time for me to start creating 'Her CEO Shoes' 3 simple steps to freedom. I reviewed all tasks, processes, SOP's, systems and automations. I created a plan and started to implement it.

Here is a list of processes and documents that I would recommend you have in place in your business:

- General processes
- SOP's
- Documents, contracts and T&C's
- Onboarding and offboarding process
- Customer journey
- Finance & Admin process
- Client delivery
- Client Communication
- Sales, marketing & PR (lead workflow and bus dev pipeline)
- Meeting and calendar management
- Technology and security

Your Business on Autopilot

My aim is to help you implement 'Her CEO Shoes' 3 simple steps to freedom by systemising and automating your business so that you can work in your zone of genius, step into your role as CEO and find your freedom.

Identify potential areas to use automation.

For example: marketing, invoicing, payment reminders, recurring payments, appointment scheduling, email sorting & auto responders, contracts, workflows, proposals, data entry, social media scheduling and email marketing.
There are so many different automations and systems/ platforms you can use so if you need support feel free to get in touch with me.
Here are some examples of the automations I have in my business. Hopefully this will get you thinking about automations you could implement in your business

CRM Systems

Many small business owners will initially use an Excel spreadsheet to manually hold client data. As you scale, I would recommend a CRM system. Before you decide which one, make sure you know what functionality you need now and what you're likely to need in the future.

Think about your business how it is now and your growth plans and the types of tasks and functionality you'd like to see in a system. Here is an example list of functionality:

- Contact management: Storing customer details and contact history
- Lead and sales management: Track and nurture leads and sales
- Task and activity management: set reminders and follow ups
- Email marketing: communication with potential and existing clients
- Customer support and service: log and track tickets
- Reporting and analytics: activity, performance and forecasting
- Workflow and process automation: automating contracts, terms and conditions and onboarding
- Calendar and scheduling: sync with calendars to schedule calls and meetings
- Integration with other tools: connect accounting software
- Document and file management: Store contracts and other key documents

Communication

Using Gmail or Outlook for communicating with potential and existing clients may not be the most effective use of platforms. This communication could happen through a CRM. This way you have everything in one place and you can easily access the contact history of each client or potential client. Depending on the CRM system you could also use it for email marketing, host courses, memberships and lead magnets. This would have the potential to transform your business, build relationships with clients, generate leads, improve client retention and increase sales.

Contracts & T&Cs

Rather than having to manually send contracts and then downloading and saving them you could choose a CRM that will automatically do all of this for you. Like Dubsado for instance. You can have your contracts in the system and workflows to automate your onboarding process. This is great for time saving and also to reduce the risk of human error.

Booking meetings

Instead of manually booking client meetings you can use Calendly. This can link to your calendar and to Zoom so clients can click the link and book in. This makes things so much easier and saves time trying to coordinate diaries.

Tracking Payments

If you have a growing team and you need to track and pay freelancers, this can be done in Airtable. The table can be customised in a similar way to a Google sheet. You send a link to your freelancers, and they upload their invoice, so things are all in one place and all records are kept there. This makes things much more efficient and minimises risk.

Using Airtable to track freelancer payments is more efficient because it centralises all invoices, payment statuses, and communication in one easily accessible platform. Instead of searching through emails or scattered documents, you can view everything at a glance, saving time and reducing admin tasks. It also minimises risk by creating a clear, time-stamped record of invoices and payments, helping you avoid missed payments, duplicate payouts, or disputes. With everything stored securely in one place, it ensures greater transparency and accountability across your team. This has helped me minimise the risk of mistakes in my business.

Once you have all your processes, documents, SOP's, systems and automations you will start to see a real difference in your business, and it will be much easier to outsource to freelancers or delegate to employees.

In the first 2 years of my business, I found it very hard to take time off and go on holiday. Since I've implemented 'Her CEO Shoes' 3 simple steps to freedom, everything runs like clockwork!

Download my free resources here:

Step 3: Delegation

The Mindset Shift - From Doer to Delegator

Thinking back to my corporate career in recruitment. I will admit that I was terrible at delegating. I believe this was for several reasons. First of all, let's face it, I am naturally a control freak. It's just part of my personality; I literally want to control everything! As a Manager I used to struggle delegating tasks to my team. I either believed I could do it better or I felt guilty and thought I should be doing it myself. It took me years to realise that I was holding myself and others back and it was only when I started to understand the power of delegation that I started to become a great leader.

My teams enjoyed working with me, they felt trusted, empowered and my recruitment branches became so successful they would run like a well-oiled machine even without me there every day. Earlier in my career I would have worried that I wasn't needed but I realised that this was success for me. Being able to go to a regional meeting, take days off or go on holiday knowing that my branch would tick over nicely made me feel like I'd really achieved something. Little did I know at the time that I'd go on to run a six-figure agency based on outsourcing and delegating and train and mentor business owners and freelancers to do the same.

So here comes the mindset shift. I have known multiple business owners who worry about spending money on hiring freelancers and outsourcing. They continue to do all the things and wear all the hats thinking that is the way to scale their business. Well, I promise you it's not. You can't wear all the hats and scale, but you can invest in outsourcing and delegating. This will free up your time and you will be able to step into your CEO shoes and work on your business not in it.

Will you stay stuck where you are with an income ceiling based on you doing all the things? Or are you going to smash through that income ceiling by moving from doer to delegator?

The moment I started to outsource and delegate, the magic happened. In less than a year from hiring my first VA Associate I had reached the VAT threshold of £85k and my business went from strength to strength. The freedom that I created was amazing.

Cost vs Investment

So many entrepreneurs and small business owners struggle to let go. Your business is your baby, you've started it, and you've been nurturing it. I get it so don't worry you can take baby steps, start small and get comfortable before letting everything go.

The key to changing your mindset around cost vs investment is to talk to the freelancer or virtual assistant that you're thinking of working with. Communication is key to building these relationships. Make sure you talk about your expectations and goals on the discovery call before you make any agreement or sign a contract. Once you have agreed and signed a contract make sure you have a project management board like Trello or Asana to make plans on and communicate and set up regular review meetings.

You're right in thinking "No one can do it like me" but you may actually find that the right virtual assistant can do certain tasks much quicker and more efficiently.

Start embracing the CEO mindset: clarity, trust, and leadership

Finding the perfect match of Virtual Assistant or Freelancer.

In my experience there are some key boxes to tick when finding your perfect match. It is vital that you

*   Decide what would you like to delegate
*   Think about how you work best, your personality

- The best VA personality fit to work with you
- What experience will they need
- What capabilities will they have

All VA's have different skills and experience, you may not want a general VA unless you only want to delegate admin tasks. If you want marketing support, then you need a VA who specialises in marketing. If you want to launch courses and products a tech VA who is also creative may be the right fit or it may be that you need an Executive Assistant/ PA to support, you.

All these different niches exist in the VA world; it's just finding them which is the tricky bit! But that's where I come in. As a VA agency owner and virtual assistant mentor I have a team of experienced VA's in all areas of business support so if you need anything please don't hesitate to get in touch kellie@ atthedropofahat.co.uk. I will save you time and provide you with excellent support.

The key to a successful partnership with a VA or Freelancer

The key to a successful partnership with a VA or Freelancer is communication, communication, communication! Please don't forget that VA's do the doing. You need to tell them what you need, what the tasks are and set your expectations in terms of the work and the timeline. Remember they own their own business, and they are a service provider, not an employee. If you remember these key points, then you are more likely to have a great relationship with your VA/Freelancer. If you are not sure about some of their work or you don't like it or it doesn't meet your expectations, then speak with your VA. They will be more than happy to get it how you want it. This can easily happen when you first start working together as you don't know each other yet. You need to get used to working together and the VA needs to learn you voice and how you like things done.

Here are my top 5 tips when working with a VA

- Communicate
- Build a rapport
- Respect your VA
- Discuss and set expectations
- Use a communication platform/project management system

Onboarding for Success - Setting Expectations and Systems

It is essential to have an onboarding meeting over Zoom. This meeting should be at least an hour – but this is just the beginning of the onboarding process. Think about this as an induction just like larger businesses conduct with employees.

Here are the areas that need to be discussed and agreed:

- All about your business
- Goals, plans and expectations
- Regular tasks daily, weekly, monthly projects
- Choose a project management board Trello/Asana
- Communication methods (Mainly Trello, regular zoom meetings)
- Logins & passwords for systems (They should be creating in your systems not their own.

Don't expect the VA to know everything after the onboarding meeting. Make sure they know that they can check in with you and ask questions any time they need to.

I've seen so many clients just expect that because they are busy, they can just hire a VA, and the VA will just know exactly what they want. These clients want to free up their time because they are busy but if you are going to make your relationship work with your VA you do need to take the time to get to know them, build a rapport, delegate, support and explain things.

Happy VA, happy client - How to retain your team

Retaining good team members is about being respectful and making sure you communicate with them. Check in and make sure they're happy, ask if it's working for them. All VA's want to feel useful, productive and appreciated. Don't forget they are a business owner too.

Why good VA's and freelancers leave - and how to stop it

VA's and Freelancers may leave a client relationship for various reasons. It could be personal life or health. But in many cases in my experience over the last 6 years of managing teams and mentoring VA's it comes down to communication.

When VA's set up their business it's usually to gain freedom and with that comes the idea that they won't need to work many hours. Then comes the thought that they need to earn more money and they start selling time for money. They sometimes let clients negotiate on their prices and this will never end well as they then have to take on more and more clients to have the chance of reaching their income goals.

Before they know it, they're too busy, burnt out and unfortunately starting to resent the client work they are doing for the lower paying clients even if they do like the client. When I'm mentoring VA's I always discuss this and make sure they understand what effects discounting their prices will have further down the line and that I advise them to avoid doing this.

So please consider this when you are thinking of hiring a VA. But if you work with www.atthedropofahat.co.uk I will manage all of this for you.

Building a culture of appreciation, clarity, and collaboration

"A person who feels appreciated will always do more than what is expected." Francis Flynn, Professor of Organisational Behaviour at Stanford. This is a favourite quote of mine and it's so true.

Make sure you are clear in your instructions. Say what the outcome is that you want. Discuss and agree on a timeline. Be on hand to answer questions. Communicate well and collaborate with your VA/Freelancer. Make sure you thank them and that they feel appreciated.

Regular check-ins and reviews

Your VA will want to maximise the time that you're paying for as much as possible so using a project management board is really useful but having regular meetings will help you make sure you are both on the same page, build your relationship and also minimise the risk on wasted hours in case a piece of work doesn't turn out the way you'd planned or imagined

Creating win-win relationships

The relationship between you and your VA needs to be a mutually beneficial one. You need to be happy with the standard of work produced and the VA needs to feel appreciated and useful.

Delegating doesn't have to feel like losing control

I get it, your business is your baby, and you may feel that nobody can do any of your tasks as well as you. It is possible you're a control freak like me! But to be able to scale and step into your CEO shoes you need to work in your 'zone of genius' and outsource the rest.

- Make sure you hire your perfect match
- Set expectations
- Communicate but don't micromanage
- Show appreciation and thanks
- Use a project management system
- Trust, monitor and refine the process

The Recap

Here it is… Her CEO Shoes - 3 simple steps to freedom

Organise

To truly step into your CEO shoes and create a life of freedom, you need a clear strategy that brings structure, focus, and direction to your business. Start by defining your lifestyle vision and aligning your business goals to support it. Map out your offers, audit your current

systems, and create an implementation and automation plan to streamline operations. Review your tasks to determine what can be delegated or outsourced, so you can work in your zone of genius. Finally, boost your marketing, visibility, and PR efforts to attract aligned clients and grow with purpose.

Automate

By implementing 'Her CEO Shoes' 3 simple steps to freedom, reviewing and systemising every area of my business I transformed the way I work. I moved from chaos and manual tasks to streamlined systems, automations, and clear processes, which made it easier to manage clients, support freelancers, and scale efficiently. From using a CRM for communication, contracts, and onboarding, to tracking payments in Airtable and automating admin tasks like invoicing and scheduling, my business now runs smoothly behind the scenes. The best part is that I can finally take time off knowing everything continues to flow giving me the freedom I once only dreamed of.

Delegate

Delegating effectively is all about making a mindset shift from being the doer of everything to stepping confidently into your role as CEO. It means letting go of control, identifying the right tasks to outsource, and hiring the perfect match who aligns with your working style, personality and business needs. Clear communication, mutual respect, and well-structured onboarding processes are essential for building a strong, collaborative relationship.

By using project management tools, setting expectations, offering appreciation, and staying involved without micromanaging, you create a perfect environment where both you and your VA/Freelancer can thrive. This will free up your time so you can focus on the growth of your business whilst only working in your zone of genius.

This is your time to go from doer to delegator and start creating the business of your dreams whilst becoming a calm, capable and successful CEO.

I'm Kellie Williams, six-figure VA Agency Owner, VA Mentor, and Business Strategist. I can't wait to see you step into your CEO shoes and scale your business. You can find all my free resources here:

I'd love to support you and help support your business so to thank you for reading my chapter I'd like to offer you a free 30 minute consultation: https://calendly.com/atdoah/client-consultation

Amber Doughty

Breathwork. Coaching. Wellbeing. Burnout Disruptor. Parent support.

Breathe. Regulate. Rise: 13 Steps to Aligned Success

E. The one who's always watching & my biggest why. X

amberdoughty.co.uk

BREATH. REGULATE. RISE:
13 STEPS TO ALIGNED SUCCESS

Redefining success your way!

Hello my lovely! I'm so glad to have you join me here for this very important conversation today. One that is going to be transformational for you, and those who watch you rise & thrive.

I'm all for success. Success for me, you, everyone (…well not quite everyone, but that's for another book).

However, I have a problem with what success is deemed to be, & how the pressure of it can affect us. All too often we can tie our own self worth to this thing called success, & it can leave us feeling fragile, depleted & burned out, feeling not worthy… & just not enough.

Does that resonate?

I think it's important to hold a conversations not only define clearly what success actually is, but what is it that we are all chasing? How can we create & experience real, sustainable success that encompasses much more to each of us and have it mean something deeper than what we have been perceived to believe success is on the outside.

We're living in a world that, for all its progress, is quietly stealing our joy, our health, and our happiness. On the surface, everything might look fine, but underneath? There's a silent pandemic affecting us all: chronic stress, burnout,and rising mental health challenges. And it's not just us anymore. We're watching it filter down to our children, and that - more than anything - is the loudest red flag of all. Something has to shift. And that shift doesn't start with policy or systems. It starts with us. With you. With me. With each of us choosing something better.

So let's not sugar-coat it. Let's dive in and start making meaningful change.

Now, you might be wondering, what does this have to do with business advice? You're here juggling a hundred things, multitasking like a pro, spinning plates while chasing goals. But here's the thing: even in the business world, you're still being influenced by outdated, harmful beliefs about what success should look like. The hustle. The grind. The myth that exhaustion equals achievement.

If you're feeling overwhelmed, disconnected, or stuck, it's not a personal failure. It's a symptom of a bigger problem. And it's time we did something about it.

Terms of success have become a standard, despite being outdated and associated with "burn out" via a patriarchal lens. This has been accepted and it is dangerous because not only is this deemed normal but it is widely seen as part and parcel of the only pathway to achieving this accepted standard of success. You can almost expect a good pat on the back or a knowing not of acceptance, that yep, you did it and now everyone is proud.

You only deserve the success because you have clearly sacrificed your wellbeing and therefore get a free backstage VIP pass into the club. A brutal initiation process, the amount you are willing to give up and to prove how much you really want it.

But, is all of this sacrifice really the key to achieving?

Normalised exhaustion is the world we live in where ill health, overstretching until we are dangerously thin, and carrying so much weight is completely standard. "Once I have achieved ((insert goal)), then I will be ((insert positive emotion))". The truth is, this toxic practise is so deeply ingrained in our culture most of us don't even realise that it is there, or that it is the auto pilot constantly pushing us to do more.

We have learned to place conditions upon ourselves before we earn experiences of the emotional state we wish to experience.

Today we have more freedom, more choice, and more possibilities available to us than any generation of women that came before us. As much as this is a genuine privilege, it can also hold a weight of expectation and added pressure.

This message is filtered through to us everywhere. Through the media, films, TV, and schooling. In fact don't even get me started on schooling!
One example that springs to mind is an episode of Friends where we are given a glimpse at what a 'successful' Phoebe would be like, stressed, having a heart attack, but it was okay because she had lots of money.

Was this what real success looks like? Why couldn't she be seen as being a success, in her life, filled with friends, love, connection and a business following her own path, aligned to her values?

This chapter is going to unpick the norms of success as we've been conditioned to know it, and uncover the options of another way.

Success through the lens of YOU. Your values, needs & desires, but most importantly of all this through your nervous system.

This chapter is designed to support you to both nurture your ambition AND your wellbeing, and therefore redefine what

57

success means to YOU, as well as leading the way for more of us who are ready to thrive!

It all changed for me when I was laying on the floor of a basement in a hotel. I was surrounded by around a hundred other coaches. I was attending a Full Moon Ceremony and we were about to take a journey through what is called a "Concious Connected Breathe". I had dabbled in breathwork previously, albeit only briefly. I had loved what I had experienced but there was no way for me to know how life-changing this event would be and that I was about to receive my "next level".

I went deeply inside myself, reconnecting to an energy I didn't know lay dormant within me. I experienced a level of peace I couldn't even recognise having ever felt before. My whole body knew. In that moment, this work, was exactly what had been the missing piece. My journey began.

At that point in my life I had been recovering from another period of burn out that had just occurred quite recently. As an accredited coach I knew my mindset knowledge but here I still was, feeling like a failure. This new experience helped me to feel the possibility of another way to live, right through my entire body. The power of another version of success, via breathwork!

I knew in that moment that this message was not just about me. This work needed to be shared. We all have this incredible power within, and my mission was clear, to support as many others as possible, to lead from a regulated space.

To change the narrative for generations to come.

And so here I am, having this important conversation with you.

It comes with a gentle warning however, that once you have realised that your version of success is available, you will not want to return.

The world is ready for more regulated & heart led leaders, so my lovely this is your time to step up. And I'm here to hold you along the way.

I want you to first consider these questions and become really deeply honest with yourself.

First lets look at what it means to be "Values driven".
What's important to you?

What gets your finger wagging at the screen when scrolling?
What gets your goat?

What lights you up?

All of these answers are clues about what values are driving you towards your version of your best possible self.

Your body is the best guide to detect when you are following a strategy, or doing something in your business that is out of alignment with your values. More often than not, we have been conditioned to turn the volume down on this intuition because values driven people are inconvenient and powerful and loud at times when the world wishes us to be quiet.

So this is where I start with clients. Stepping into a place of connection each day. A Deepening of your senses felt

Now let's consider Burnout and the 'Patriarchal Blueprint' for success.

Burnout is a huge issue impacting & limiting many of us. It affects our wellbeing, our income, our lives, confidence & relationships. It is a buzzword on line and it is something we are not nearly as worried about as we should be.

Burnout is defined by **WHO** (World Health Organisation) as; "Burn-out is a syndrome conceptualised as resulting from chronic workplace stress that has not been successfully managed. It is characterised by three dimensions:

- Feeling of energy depletion or exhaustion,
- Increased mental distance from one's job, or feelings of negativism or cynicism related to one's job.
- Reduced professional efficiency."

Any of these relatable?

The blueprint of success now that drives much of society towards this path of burnout is underpinned by the messages of constant hustle in order to achieve.

Recognise any of these?

- Productivity over presence
- Competition over collaboration
- Achievement over alignment
- Logic over intuition
- Doing over Being.

This model of success we have been drip fed throughout our lives, often without even realising, from school to the noise out in the world of 'personal development' today.

Personal development should be about you making your way home to yourself. Not adding to the never-ending pile of "things" that you have to do to make you "worthy".

These patriarchal values are still filtering through into our lives & businesses to keep us playing small. It is time for a new way forward.

Now I have to say there is a place for taking action, without this the success you desire isn't going to land in your lap. However, I believe that the action you take needs to be aligned to YOUR values and at your pace. The consideration for your life, your capacity, your resources and your emotional health needs to be considered first.

Success is framed in this model as fast, external reward, and linear in its focus. Rewarding the constant striving, pushing, the long hours spent slogging, striving, sacrificing & suppression of every other thing.

These are traits that were historically essential in a male-dominated world that are deeply out of sync with relational, cyclical, and more embodied ways of being.

Those that don't fit this pressured mould find themselves contorting to try and fold to achieve. Doing this, is nothing short of dangerous.

Burnout that leads to disconnection. A deep sense of losing themselves in the process.

In the pursuit of external success, the validation, the approval, the sense of being accepted, something often begins to fade. The spark. That unique gift within you. The purpose that once lit you up and had the potential to inspire and uplift others starts to dim. It doesn't vanish overnight. It gets buried under pressure, under expectations, under a relentless push to keep going.

Burnout isn't just tiredness. It's a deep soul-weariness. A fatigue that comes from years of trying to be seen and valued in systems that were never designed to hold your full humanity. Systems that have long demanded we be palatable, productive, pleasing, and perpetually grateful, no matter the cost.

We've inherited a narrative that tells us we must earn our worth by contorting ourselves into an outdated blueprint of success, one shaped by patriarchal ideals and built to reward constant output. And when does that effort become too much? We're hit with guilt for even needing rest. So, often, we don't rest.

We push through. We override the signals. And our nervous systems, shaped by experience and reinforced beliefs, learn that it isn't safe to slow down. That stillness equals failure. That softness is weakness. And in doing so, we gaslight our own needs.

This isn't just a women's issue, though women feel the weight of it in profound ways. It's a human issue. A collective inheritance that asks us to do more, be more, prove more, without ever questioning who set the rules in the first place.

But knowledge brings power. And awareness is where transformation begins.

So let's take a breath. Let's pause long enough to reflect on the impact of these silent stories we've been living by. You don't have to keep striving within a model that was never built with you in mind. We get to rewrite the rules. Reclaim success on our terms.

Not just for ourselves, but for our children. For our communities. For the generations that will follow our lead.

A new way is not only possible. It's already beginning. One breath, one brave step at a time.

The Dawn of a New Way.

Burnout doesn't always come crashing in with a big sign. It can also creep up, silently, as if from nowhere.

But we now get to choose that burnout doesn't have to be a loop we remain stuck in. We can break the loop, step out of the cycles to start another way.

We can choose to see burnout as a wake up call. An invitation, that we can actually choose to opt out of this system if we like. It can grant us back the power to choose differently.

That all sounds good, but how do we even do that?
It starts on the inside first.

Reconnection to yourself, beyond the shoulds. Beyond the subtle conditioning you have taken onboard your entire life. Starting to turn the volume up on your intuition instead.

Remembering and reconnecting to YOUR needs and YOUR values. Its about coming home to you.

I'm going to run through 13 steps to support you through this process. 13 because, well it was the patriarchy who decided to promote 13 as bad luck, when in truth it is a sacred feminine number.

The number of cycles for women, the number of moon cycles & much more. Plus, the inner rebel in me is wanting to stick up 2 fingers to the patriarchy in any way possible…. and it's a good amount of steps to ease you through gently.

The following 13 keys are designed to open up more choice & freedom on your path to building sustainable success for you & your family, and breaking free from these old restrictive ways of being.

Ready?

The first two go deep so lets start there first:

1. The Burnout Myth's...an invitation to unpack your old story...

So many myths & stories we have internalised to shape the way we view burnout. But also, in what we believe to be true & possible for us as we map out our own version of success.

This is an invitation to unpack what you know, feel & believe around burnout. Have you normalised exhaustion as a state that you accept?
Is running on coffee essential to get through the day?

Do you believe it is selfish to take time to rest?

When was the last time you allowed yourself space to be? What feelings & thoughts came up for you?

What are the stories you telling yourself why you cannot rest?
Are any of these beliefs or stories being passed down from parents, or from other people?

Our lives are shaped by what we believe to be true, sometimes this is held deep in the subconscious & we aren't even aware. So this first step to get curious.

Without blame or shame, simply allow yourself to explore through these journal prompts what comes up for you? What do you notice?

Breathwork has supported me in my own practice & with clients to dig into our own truth. Allowing yourself space to connect to the clarity you seek.

Try, in a space where it is safe for you to do so, closing your eyes breathing through the nose to deep into your belly, slowing the breath down as much as feels safe to do. Then ask yourself some of the above questions, note down whatever comes up for you.

I'd love to hear what comes up for you, so share this with me on socials or drop me a message - I would love to hear from you.

2. Nervous System Wisdom.

This is possibly THE most important key to success you need to learn about. A regulated nervous system is one of the most underrated assets for leaders & entrepreneurs alike. Leading the way towards success by prioritising regulation enables expansion, connection, growth, as well as supporting your overall wellbeing.

"You can't be a leader if you're constantly triggered. Regulate your nervous system first." -Dr Nicole LePera (The Holistic Psychologist).

Success, & by that I mean the kind of success, that lights you up, connects you to a feeling of purpose, connection, happiness & freedom all come from a space where you have regulated your nervous system.

Now this doesn't mean you are always in a zen, calm state. It simply means that your body is responding in an appropriate & measurable way in accordance with the external experience.
Your nervous system's key role is to support keeping you alive. In Polyvagal Theory, it speaks of your nervous system as if it is a ladder. This ladder has three states that we travel between throughout our daily lives.

Look out for the state of chronic stress, perhaps due to lack of rest, constantly being 'on',with the phone pinging constantly with emails that needs responding too, difficult clients to manage, pressing deadlines etc. When you realise these things take our nervous system into 'fight/flight/fawn' response you can make yourself aware of what it is doing to your body.

These chronic stress signals to the body that we are in danger. And when these experiences are constant, without utilising tools such as breathwork to regulate ourselves, we can find that we are live in a perpetual state chronic stress. Which is a prolonged amount of time spent with our body in this fight/flight state, which is designed for short-term activations to keep us safe and not at all meant to be sustained for a long period.

The body is an incredible system that responds by redistributing blood flow only to essential areas needed to support us to run/fight etc. This shuts down our ability to problem solve, our creativity, to respond instead of react, it overloads our body with cortisol (stress hormone), our breath becomes more shallow, stopping our lungs from activating the diaphragm to detoxify our body, as it is designed to. Our body is designed to be in this state for short bursts in order to survive. Long term, it is incredibly damaging.

Did you ever have a boss, or teacher that just used to snap, or yell out of nowhere? This is probably what they were experiencing in their body, & you will know first-hand how this doesn't make for positive leadership.

Whereas in today's climate, where, as we discussed earlier, success is often seen by the pushing through and prioritising productivity over wellbeing, many of us, without realising are in this chronic state of stress. Which over time, as well as impacting our businesses, & relationships negatively, it also impacts our wellbeing, leading to physical, mental & emotional decline.

This is exactly why it is so key to raising our awareness about our nervous system & the tools we have available to support regulation. It, in my opinion, is the most important consideration when creating a realistic pathway to whatever "success" actually is , to you.

When we can raise our self-awareness, and take control to regulate our nervous system, there is an incredible super power to enable a life in which you thrive. And the best news is, that it can be really simple to do once you know how.

Breathwork is the easiest & fastest way to take control of your nervous system in a very short time. Just 2 minutes of conscious breathing can reduce stress & return you to a regulated state.

Quite honestly, during my training, when I learned of the power we have within us, through our breath alone, I was outraged that this information wasn't more freely available. Why wasn't I/we taught this in school? It was there, in that moment, that I found my mission.

As well as breathwork we can support our nervous system by the simple daily things we often neglect like getting enough sleep (breathwork can really support this), eating well, drinking enough water, spending time outside in nature & many other things, however breathwork is such a simple tool that will always be with you, & accessible no matter where you go.

When our nervous system is regulated, we can lead from a place of love, we can respond instead of react, we can hold more clients, attention, revenue, joy, responsibility & presence & authenticity.

Think of someone you admire, imagine them walking into the room, holding space, holding an energy that screams confidence, compassion, safety & trust. This person you see now before you, I can promise you is held in a regulated space. That is all available to you too.

When you feel stuck, overwhelmed, or are procrastinating, pleasing, all of these behaviours are signs that you are in need of regulation. The easiest & quickest tool to restore a regulated state is taking some conscious, deep, slow breaths.

3. Know your Strengths & Values – what makes you uniquely powerful? It's easy to reel off what you aren't so good at, but what if you could realise your powers & create more ease & flow by utilising them? Breathwork has been a tool that aids me & my clients to reconnect to an inner peace that allows access to clarity, increased self awareness and deep connection. Could you find ways to identify areas that are really important to you?

4. Permission to pause... Create from alignment not hustle – working with your energy, not against it. Intuition, capacity and cycles – energy matters. Remember you don't need to choose between success and wellbeing, you get to have both, so include practical pause practices reintroduce cyclic living feminine wisdom as leadership powers in contrast to the linear, hustle driven patriarchal model.

5. Reclaiming time & energy. Build systems that support you. Include boundaries, acts of self respect not restriction from scarcity to energy mastery, self leadership, strategies 7 tools to support this. Identify as the CEO.

6. The identity trap – how burnout is entangled with identity, particularly with high-achievers, mothers, carers. An invitation Tools, support & guidance to meet their true selves beyond roles.

7. Create spaciousness – rest, play & spaciousness are not luxuries, they are an important part of your strategy.

8. Emotional Alchemy – safety in releasing stored emotions, how the breath can support emotional regulation & activate inner healing. Safety is key to embracing a new path to success on your terms.

9. The power of Presence. Mindfulness breath and nervous system work can bring you back into the now. Success becomes sustainable in the present, not in the future, its part of the process not just an end goal.

10. Rewiring beliefs around success. Identify unconscious beliefs driving your performance in overworking & self-abandonment. Support to help you rewrite your inner definition of what success means, feels like & is to you. Cultivate Self-belief – again, breath will support you to reconnect to that confidence you were born with, believing in you makes you magnetic to attract what you desire more of.

11. The Joy Frequency. Make Joy a serious strategy! Its an important part of life, therefore an important part of this conversation. It has a key role in supporting regulation. Creativity & flow. Lets explore how you can embrace & step into joy daily. As a strategy for success.

12. Sisterhood 7 Support. Burnout & business can go hand in hand. We tend to withdraw more & more from the world if we are constantly 'on' or busy. The deeper we spiral into loops of constant burnout, the more isolated we can feel. Having a community, a regulated & supportive space (mention a membership) to accelerate healing, deep connections & others who understand can make all the difference.

13. Make it a real focus. It is so easy to read a chapter like this and be moved to change but then not action it. Why not take a moment to set a reminder, to create a system or to give real time and attention to these practises to they can best support you.

It isn't always easy to become the leader of your life. Stepping into empowered choice, exploring these options to support your journey will take commitment. The ripple effect from shifting the narrative for you and your family, your business and beyond is huge.

Lead with vulnerability – it's OK to not have your shizzle together 24/7.

The secret nobody is telling you is that nobody has it all together all of the time! This path of sustainable success isn't linear, but you get to experience joy, to lead yourself & others while being held & supported yourself as you transition into your new era.

Starting from within, breath by breath, you have the autonomy to shift everything. And the power is, you don't need to do it all alone. You have stepped into a space where you are breaking cycles, changing narratives & living & breathing your very own version of success, your own way. Breathe friend... it is the most simple and yet most powerful thing you can do.

Dee Airey

Clarity & Confidence Strategist, Personal Brand & Studio Photographer, Management & Leadership Coach, Talent Acquisition & Retention Strategist

How to Survive & Thrive with Increased Competition & Market Saturation

I dedicate this piece to Peter, Niall and Becca for standing by me, behind me and ahead of me, for their love and support while I figured it all out. All roads have led to here and I love you for just being. You are the pillars of my big 'why' in life.

FB - @deeairey IG - @deeaireycoaching

INCREASED COMPETITION
& MARKET SATURATION

Introduction

I'm Dee Airey, a personal brand photographer and Clarity & Confidence Strategist. I wear my business strategy hat most of the time, and I've owned and co-owned businesses for over 20 years. That means I've bumped into stifling competition and so-called market saturation more times than I can count, and I've had to find ways to navigate the challenges and push through.

Photography and online business strategy are possibly two of the most saturated industries out there. So for me, dealing with competition isn't a one-off, it's a constant. And while I absolutely want my businesses to survive, more than anything, I want to *genuinely and sincerely serve* the people I work with. The most powerful tools I've discovered - what I now consider my *weapons of mass destruction against competition and saturation* - are being crystal clear on my brand identity and knowing my ideal client inside out.

Photography and online business strategy are possibly two of the most saturated industries out there. So for me, dealing with competition isn't a one-off, it's a constant. And while I absolutely want my businesses to survive, more than anything, I want to genuinely and sincerely serve the people I work with. The most powerful tools I've discovered - what I now consider my weapons of mass destruction against competition and saturation - are being crystal clear on my brand identity and knowing my ideal client inside out.

Yes, competition is real. Yes, saturation is a thing. But much of that noise exists at a very average, middle-of-the-road level. That's where the crowds are. That's where the panic and the price-slashing live. That's where people are floundering, shouting into the void, hoping someone hears them.

I'm not here for that. I'm here to help you rise above it. Because when you know exactly who you're here to serve, and you build a brand and message that speaks directly to *them*, everything changes. You move from survival to service. And that, in my experience, is a win-win every time.

We hear it all the time: *"The market is saturated." "There's too much competition." "There's no room left."* I heard it all the time: *"There are too many photographers out there, you'll never get work!"*. But the truth is, this narrative is more perception than reality.

Yes, there may be many people offering what looks like the same product or service on the surface. But here's the thing: no two business owners are the same. And no two clients are looking for exactly the same thing.

I have my studio on a small high street in the market town of Tunbridge Wells, Kent, UK and there are two Indian restaurants next door to each other. One is owned by a well- known celebrity chef. It's beautifully designed, the inside is spacious and airy and you get an idea of how much you're going to spend as soon as you walk inside. It has a romantic mezzanine level gallery with a table set just for two, and a long bar that can hold its own against any pub. Next door is your typical cosy and snug Indian restaurant, reminding me of my younger Friday nights of drinking and dancing, followed by a curry with my friends, before falling into a cab to get home. And you could fill the table with as much as you like, all at an affordable price. Both restaurants are busy. Why? Because they are very different and their clientele doesn't want the same thing. Some want high end pricey small dishes, and others want a great feed on a budget. The brand identity of these restaurants is very clear and strong, and this is an indicator, to me, that it's possible to survive and thrive when competition is right on top of you.

For many businesses, what's often missing is *clarity* - not just in how we position ourselves, but in how we understand the market we're in.
Market research isn't something you do at the beginning and tick off the list. It's an ongoing, evolving part of building a business that lasts. You need to know where your competitors are at, what they're offering, how they're marketing, and more importantly, what they *aren't* doing. That's where your opportunities lie.

Competition isn't the enemy. Complacency is.

I've seen this in my own businesses - particularly my photography business. Photography is *infamous* for being saturated. Yet, I continue to grow and thrive because I'm constantly scanning the market. I look at what others are doing, and ask myself, "What am I doing differently? What do I know I'm doing better?" I stay in my lane and focus on where I add real value.

One thing I won't do? I won't drop my prices. (Full disclosure - I used to do that before I understood my ideal client and before I had any identity that I could call my brand). And that's a big one. Because when the market gets noisy, many entrepreneurs panic and start slashing their fees. It's a knee-jerk reaction, but what it really does is pull you into the murky middle - a place I call the *land of mediocrity*. And once you're there, it's hard to climb back out.

Lowering your prices to 'compete' might feel like survival, but it's often occupational suicide. You're not here to win the race to the bottom, you're here to show up at the top of your game for the people who are looking specifically for what you offer.

There are clients out there who care deeply about what you can do for them. Not how cheap you are. And when the pressure's on, that's your golden opportunity to step up and show where the value lies in your service. That's your chance to rise.

And that brings me to another vital piece: messaging. When the market feels full, and competition is fierce, what most people do is shout louder: *"Look at me!" "I'm the best!" "Pick me!"* It's the equivalent of waving your arms around in a noisy crowd and hoping someone sees you.
But shouting into the void doesn't build trust or connection. What cuts through the noise is intentional, clear, *relatable* messaging - words that speak directly to your people. Not everyone. Just the right ones.

So instead of yelling about how brilliant you are, speak to your ideal client like you already know them. Because when you do that, the right people lean in. They recognise themselves in your words. They know you're talking to *them*, not the masses. And that creates something far more powerful than hype - it creates resonance.

The truth is, when competition heats up, it's not a time to panic. It's a chance to level up. While everyone else runs for the hills in a bid to survive, you go the other way and thrive. You rise above the noise. That's how you stand out - not by being louder, but by being clearer, more intentional, and more aligned.

Here are 3 ways to navigate your way through Increased Competition & Market Saturation

Nail Your Niche & Know Your Client

Now is the time to take a really honest look at your marketing, your content strategy, and your messaging. Not just what you're putting out there, but *how* you're doing it.

Are you busy shouting about how wonderful your service is? Going into the mechanics of how it works? Talking about how hard you've worked or how qualified you are? Maybe you're sharing your list of accolades, hoping people will feel reassured that you know your stuff. And listen, I get it. It's human. You're proud of what you've built, and you *should* be. But here's the thing. That's not what gets people to buy.

Let me take you back to when I first started out. I honestly thought the name of the game was to grab as much work as possible from anyone who showed the slightest bit of interest. This whole 'niche and ideal client' thing? It meant absolutely nothing to me. I just wanted to get on and do my job. I didn't want to get bogged down in all this business strategy stuff. Plus, I truly believed that niching down was *limiting*, that it would stop me from getting clients. I couldn't have been more wrong.

For as long as I've been shooting, photography has always been labelled as a saturated market. And do you know what? *It is saturated.* But it's saturated in the middle pool - the place where everyone's just "having a go," shooting for anybody and everybody, scrabbling for gigs, slashing prices, and hoping something sticks. It's cheap, it's messy, and it's exhausting.

Once I finally took the time to sit down, do the work, and figure out *who* I really wanted to serve, everything changed. It was like the fog lifted. Suddenly, marketing felt easier. Attracting and keeping clients became easier. My whole business started to feel more aligned. I was no longer trying to appeal to everyone - I was talking directly to the people I actually wanted to work with. And they started to respond.

Let's go back to something simple. Coffee. You pick up the Rich Italian Blend Coffee Bags - not the smooth, creamy Americano. Why? Because you love a strong, full- bodied brew that makes you feel like you've just pulled into a roadside café in the Tuscan hills. You're not here for mellow. You're here for bold. For flavour. For impact.

Do you care about how it's made? Do you read the label to see who roasted it or what machines they used? Nope. You care about how it makes *you* feel. And that's what clients are looking for too. They want what speaks to them. Not what impresses you. So, who is your product or service talking to right now? If your answer is "everyone" or "anyone who'll buy," then you're in that noisy, messy middle. That's what market saturation really is - a whole lot of shouting with very little meaning.

But when you nail your niche, you step out of the noise. You stop surviving and start thriving by building something solid. You shift your focus away from *you* and onto the client, and trust me, that's where the magic happens.

People in that saturation pool are often just trying to survive. But when you're focused on your ideal client, you're not in survival mode anymore. You're creating connection. You're delivering clarity. You're showing up with something they want, and that's what sets you apart.

How to Get Specific (and Confident) About Your Ideal Client

So how do you actually nail your niche and identify your ideal client in a way that changes your business?

Here's a simple process:

Start with who lights you up
Think about the people you've worked with in the past - who did you love working with? Who made your job feel easy and energising? Who paid on time, respected your boundaries, and raved about the result? That's your starting point.

Get into the nitty gritty
Don't stop at age and gender. Ask: What do they value? What are they struggling with right now? What frustrates them? What do they dream of? The more specific you get, the more powerful your messaging becomes. For me, it's people who are camera-shy. That's a huge clue - it tells me what they're *afraid* of, and what they need from me. I build everything around that.

Write your Ideal Client Profile
Yes, literally write it. Give them a name. Describe what a day in their life looks like. What they want. What they fear. What they're Googling at midnight. You're not making this up; you're just pulling together all the client clues you already have.

Curate your messaging around them
Review your website, your content, your captions. Are you *talking about yourself*, or are you talking *to them*? Make sure everything you say connects with your ideal client's wants, needs, and emotions.

Build a Brand That Connects, Not Just Sells

I'll be honest - when I started out, I had zero appetite for brand building. None. As far as I was concerned, I was a photographer. Just me and my camera. That was the business. Done.

I even dragged a quick image off the internet and called it my logo. That was my "brand work." Tick! Move on. I honestly thought branding was for the big guns, or for people with way too much time on their hands.

But just like with niching, I couldn't have been more wrong.
Your brand isn't just a logo, a colour palette, or a half-decent website. It's so much more than that. Your brand is the *relationship* you build with your ideal client. It's the voice, the vibe, the feeling someone gets when they experience your business. It's the look, the tone, the energy, and yes - the attitude of everything you put out into the world.

Your brand has a heartbeat. And if you're an entrepreneur - spoiler alert - you are your brand. Your energy, your values, your personality... they all feed directly into how your business shows up. You are the walking, talking, living version of what your brand stands for.

When you're running a personal brand (and let's face it, most small businesses are), people aren't just buying your product or service - they're buying you. They want to know what you care about. What makes you tick. What matters to you.

Because here's the truth: connection breeds trust. And trust lurks in the shadows of genuine, human connection.

Especially in a competitive or "saturated" market, where everyone's flinging their offers around and shouting to be seen, your brand is the anchor that holds it all together. It's what gives people a reason to choose *you* over someone else.

This is your time to get creative. If you haven't already, take a proper look at your brand identity. Is it really aligned with who you are and who you serve? Are you showing up consistently as *you*? Or are you trying to look "professional" and blend in with the crowd?

Show up for your ideal client. Not just once. *Consistently.* Let them feel like they know you. Let the connection build over time.

Your messaging plays a big role here too. What do you stand for? What lights you up? If you're passionate about the environment, talk about it. If you're an animal lover, share that side of you. If you're all about lifting other women up, say it loud and say it often.

Because your ideal client isn't just connecting with your offer. They're connecting with *you*. They're far more likely to resonate with your values, your personality, and your story than with a polished list of qualifications or a fancy sales pitch. You're not just here to sell. You're here to connect. And when your brand is aligned, your messaging is real, and your presence is consistent, that connection becomes magnetic.

How to Build a Brand Strategy That Feels (and Looks) Like You

Let's talk branding, not just visuals, but real brand *identity*. Here's how to create something that connects:

Define your brand personality
Your brand is what people would say about the business (as if it were a person) when you're not in the room. So, if your brand

really was a person, how would they behave? Are they calm and nurturing, bold and punchy, warm and relatable? Choose 3 personality traits. These will guide your visuals, your tone of voice, and even your client experience.

Clarify your values and beliefs
What do you stand for? What don't you stand for? These are the things that create emotional connection.

I share openly that I'm anti-posing in photography. That's my line in the sand, and it's one my ideal clients gravitate to.

Build your Brand Strategy Foundations

Write down:
Your Why: Why you do what you do
Your Vision: Where your business is headed
Your Mission: How you help people
Your Brand Words: A few keywords that define your style/energy
Your Ideal Client: Who they are, what they want, how they think

Map out the Client Experience
Every interaction a client has with you: the tone you use in emails, your onboarding process, even down to the process your client goes through to pay you. How easy is the communication process with you before, during and after the service? It's all part of your brand. Design it intentionally.

Make yourself recognisable
You don't need a viral logo, you need a clear message. Something you're known for. *I'm known as the non-posing people photographer for camera-shy people. I'm known for helping driven and entrepreneurial women over 40.* That sticks. That's brand clarity.

Hold Your Value & Raise Your Standards

Let me be really clear: you *do not* need to play the discount game. When competition ramps up or the economy takes a hit, the knee-jerk reaction for most small business owners is to panic and drop their prices. *"I'll just make myself more affordable." "I'll offer a few juicy discounts."* I've heard it, I've done it, and I've regretted it.

Here's the truth: there is still a lot of money out there, and people are still spending. Just not with everyone.

So, instead of rushing to slash your prices, *pause.* Breathe. Do the opposite of what panic is telling you. This is the moment to refine your offer, *not reduce it.* This is your cue to elevate your client experience so that working with you feels like *something special.* It's time to double down on *value*, not price.

You might even consider raising your prices.
Yes, I said it. I know it's scary. I know it can feel counterintuitive when the world around you is tightening its belt. But sometimes, fewer enquiries at a higher price point is exactly what you need to maintain your income and your sanity. What you're doing here is shifting your ideal client - from bargain hunters to people who genuinely value what you do. People who aren't just looking for 'cheap', but for *good*. For trust. For consistency. *For you.*

Because here's the thing: when times get tough, prices often go up. Established brands hold their place in the market. They don't suddenly become cheap. They increase the value of what they offer. And you know what? Clients trust that. Clients want that.

Let me paint you a picture.

You've got a favourite restaurant. Let's say they do the best surf 'n' turf - a juicy 8oz sirloin steak with huge, buttery prawns. It's your go-to treat spot, and that dish sets you back £49. You don't go every week, but when you do, you know it's going to be good. You trust it. You've had bad steaks before, so when you find a place that gets it right, you stick with it.

Now imagine walking past another restaurant down the road. They've got a big sign in the window: "Steak & Prawns – Only £3.99!" What's your gut reaction? You don't think *"bargain!"*, you think what's wrong with it? You question the quality. You imagine tough chewy meat, little frozen prawns, and quite possibly food poisoning for dessert. It's off- putting.

That's how your potential clients feel when they see your prices plummet. Instead of attracting more people, you risk repelling the right ones. And let's say you do get someone in at that rock-bottom price. What happens then? More often than not, they'll expect a Rolls Royce experience on a Ford Fiesta budget. You'll bend over backwards for very little return, and it'll leave you burnt out, bitter, and even more skint than when you started.

So no, I won't play the discount game. And I strongly advise you don't either.

Competition is healthy - it forces you to step up. It weeds out the average and rewards the intentional. And the more intentional you are with your standards, your pricing, and your client experience, the more you'll attract people who are looking for *exactly what you do*, and are happy to pay for it.

This is how you not only *survive and thrive* amidst the panic, chaos and noise - you rise above it.

How to Raise Your Prices and Still Attract Clients (Without the Panic)

Here's how to hold your value and raise your standards without losing your mind, or your clients.

Get clear on what you're no longer available for
Say it out loud. Write it down. I'm no longer available for time wasters and ghosters, slow payers, or last-minute panic clients. This isn't about being picky, it's about protecting your time, energy, and of course your confidence.

Evaluate your service or product offering
What do you currently do brilliantly? What do clients love most? Elevate that. You don't need to do more, or give anything away, you just need to make the value more prominent.

Refine for your dream client
This is about quality over quantity. Design your offer for the people who value you most. You might even create different tiers or packages that reflect different levels of involvement or transformation. This will help you to attract a better quality client, and steer you away from the intensity of your competitors and the market.

Price based on value, not fear
Don't price from a place of *"what if they say no?"* Price from *"what would feel fair and worthwhile for the service I'm delivering?"* Then commit to it. Breathe through the wobble.

Say "no" with confidence
If someone pushes for a discount, practise saying: "That's not something I'm offering right now, but I'd be happy to refer you to someone else." It's a game-changer. And you'll feel good.

Be clear in communicating your worth
Update your website, your social media content, your enquiry responses. Speak confidently about the transformation or experience you provide. Make your value obvious and captivating before they even ask *"how much?"*.

My Experience

The First Time I Refused to Drop My Prices

In the early days, I used to tinker with my photography prices almost daily. I'd browse other photographers' websites, not for inspiration or proper market research, but to copy. I had no confidence in my pricing, so I'd raise or lower it depending on what I saw others doing. It was chaotic, and looking back, I can see how much it chipped away at my confidence in such a competitive and busy market.

Money is a difficult subject for so many entrepreneurs. It makes us nervous. I remember the moment I decided to bite the bullet and set my prices properly. I asked myself, *"What would I pay for this service?"* It meant raising my rates, and committing to them. It was terrifying.

I was working with a coach at the time who gave me one of the best pieces of advice I've ever received. She said, *"Dee, your photography is great, but go back through your work and get even better images on your website. Raise the quality to match the pricing."* So I did. I re-edited some of my favourite work and curated it with more intention. I tightened up my visual style and made everything feel more consistent.

And here's what happened: yes, I got fewer enquiries, but they were better quality. I was getting people asking what they'd get, not just *"how much?"* I stuck to my guns, even through some awkward conversations. If someone asked for a discount, my heart would pound, but I held the line. Sometimes I'd offer a small bonus - an extra handful of images that cost me nothing to deliver - but never a discount.

And when someone said, *"That's too expensive"*? I would smile and recommended someone else. It felt risky, but it was also powerful. I was finally in control. And in the long term it's paid off.

When the Client Wasn't the Right Fit

I learned the power of niching the hard way, and it started with a golf course.

Back when I was still saying yes to anything that resembled paid work, I was asked to photograph a golf club. It was a "good opportunity" someone said. But here's the truth: I hated every minute of it. I don't even play golf. I know there are 9 holes... or is it 18? That's the extent of my knowledge. I felt completely disconnected. There was no creativity, no connection, no buzz; and I knew, deep down, the photos just weren't good enough.

Looking back, the whole experience taught me something powerful: just because someone's willing to pay you doesn't mean it's the right job. I was out of alignment. The energy wasn't there. I wasn't doing my best work because I wasn't *interested*. I wasn't *invested*. And I definitely wasn't serving anyone - not them, and not me.

Needless to say, those images were never used. I cringe now thinking about what they must have said after receiving them. And I don't blame them. I wasn't the right person for that job, and it showed. And they definitely weren't the right client for me.

That experience was a turning point for me. I realised I'm at my best when I work with people, not places. I'm a people photographer, through and through. Give me a real person with real emotions over a manicured lawn and clubhouse interior any day.

From that point on, I got ruthless with my boundaries and brave about my niche. I stopped trying to be all things to all people, and I started to focus on the work I *actually* love doing. And do you know what happened? The quality of my clients work lifted, and so did my confidence.

I learned to say "no" and feel good about it.

Letting My Clients Shape My Brand

Because I'd taken the time to do the work: identify my niche, understand my ideal client, and price intentionally, my brand started to evolve naturally. It started to speak. And not just to anyone, but to the right people.

I paid close attention to what my clients were saying in their reviews and messages. A theme started to emerge. Time and time again, they mentioned how at ease they felt, how relaxed the experience was, how they didn't feel awkward or forced in front of the camera. And most importantly? They all said some version of *"I usually hate having my photo taken."*

That's when I realised: *this is what I'm known for.* This is my superpower. And so I wove it into my brand message intentionally.

Photography is a crowded industry. But a lot of it is stiff, overly posed, or trying too hard to be cool or trendy. I went the other way. I leaned in to being real. I started saying it out loud *"I work with people who don't love the camera."* That sentence alone helped my ideal clients find me.

Now, when people come to me, they already know what kind of experience they'll get. And that alignment makes all the difference. We're on the same page before we even begin.

But here's the thing, if I hadn't done the work on my brand and niche, if I was still a jack- of-all-trades, that feedback could've gone unnoticed. Worse, I could've been building a brand that didn't reflect what people actually valued about me.

Your clients will often tell you what your brand already is. You just need to listen and then make sure your business reflects it.

What NOT to Do in a Crowded Market

There's a lot of noise in saturated markets, and much of it is being created by business owners making the same mistakes over and over. I've made a few of them myself, so what I'm sharing here isn't just theory, it's a hard-earned experience.

Don't Ignore Your Authenticity

Your authenticity is your brand's secret sauce. It's the most powerful thing you have, and yet it's often the first thing entrepreneurs dilute or discard. Why? Because being fully yourself feels risky. What if it's not "professional"? What if it puts people off?

Here's what I've learned: even the parts of you that you've judged or wanted to hide, those things are often your *superpowers*.

I found my voice in my Clarity & Confidence Strategy work when I allowed myself to speak from a more honest, vulnerable place. I talked about things I once thought I should hide: my age, my weight, the fact that I've been married twice (yes, even as a wedding photographer!). But the moment I shared those things, people leaned in. Why? Because they saw a real human. They saw *themselves*.

You can be similar to others in your field - but you are still entirely and uniquely you. That's what your ideal client connects to. Don't water that down.

Don't Copy Someone Else's Identity

Please, please don't make the mistake I made early on, basing your brand, pricing, or messaging on what someone else is doing. You can't take on someone else's voice and expect it to land. They have their values, you have yours. They're on their journey, you're on yours.

It's fine to be inspired by others. But straight-up copying someone else because it looks like it's working for them? That's a dead-end. You'll never feel fully confident or in control of your business if you're borrowing someone else's voice.

Instead, focus on finding *your* voice. One that reflects *your* personality, values, quirks, and story. That's what makes you magnetic.

Don't Ignore Marketing (Seriously, Don't)

This one's a big one: *never sidestep marketing.* You *must* market your business.

So many entrepreneurs fall into the trap of thinking: "*If I do a good job, word will spread.*" And yes, referrals are lovely. But relying solely on them is like trying to win a race without putting your trainers on. There's a reason the big brands dominate: marketing. Strategic, intentional, consistent marketing. They don't leave visibility to chance. And neither should you.

You don't have to be everywhere, but you do need to show up. Whether it's email, social, networking, or something else, get your voice and your message out there.

Don't Make Your Content All About You

This one trips up a lot of personal brands. We get so caught up in 'sharing our story' that we forget the golden rule of great messaging: Your content should talk to your client, about your client. Yes, your experiences matter. Yes, it's important to be visible and personal. But your messaging should always circle back to the person reading it. What do *they* need? What do *they* want to feel, do, or believe? How are you helping *them*? It's a conversation, not a monologue.

When you stop treating your content like a performance, and instead treat it like a connection, everything shifts. You don't have to shout about how brilliant you are. Just show up and speak directly to your ideal client's heart, mind, and pain points. That's what converts.

In Summary

At a time when competition seems intense and your market is saturated, trying to be someone else, hiding who you are, avoiding marketing, or shouting into the void without really connecting - these are the things that will keep you stuck. Instead, own your story, market with intention, speak with purpose, and never forget who you're here for.

You'll confidently rise above the noise. Not because you're louder, but because you're *clearer*.

Conclusion: Rise Above the Noise

In summary, yes, these are challenging times. Whether your competition right on your doorstep, or if the market becomes flooded with people doing what you do. This can make the financial climate feel shaky and uncertain for you. But here's what I want you to know: there is a lot of money out there. There are still clients looking for exactly what you offer. People are will spend with you, but they just need to find you. They need to know you're there. They don't want the chaos and noise any more than you do. And that's where you come in.

When you act from at place of panicking, dropping prices, blending into the crowd, you start to shrink. There is no safety in numbers in business. Huddling with the masses won't help you through. It just keeps you stuck in the noise. You'll blend into the competition, and that's not where you want to be.

Challenging times call for courage.

When the market is tough and competition is closing in, this is your moment to take up the challenge. Review your business with fresh eyes. Do your market research - not to copy, but to identify the gaps and opportunities. Raise the value of your offer so that it genuinely stands apart. Speak directly to your ideal client, because chances are, they're struggling to navigate the saturated market. They're looking for someone who understands their needs and has the confidence to serve them well.

Curate a brand with strength, clear messaging, and tenacity. Let it reflect your story and your standards. Lead with service, not scarcity. This whole journey has terrified me many times, but it's also what's kept me going. It's what's helped me not just survive but thrive in tough markets.

The truth is you don't need to be louder. You just need to be more aligned. And when you are, your people will hear you.

Heidi Williams

An audaciously brilliant launch copy-writer and strategist that LOVES to use my talent with words to empower thought leaders like you to connect with and inspire your people.

One Post, £2000. The Buyer Journey That Changed Everything.

"People love to buy..."

Facebook - Heidi Williams

ONE POST, £2000. THE BUYER JOURNEY THAT CHANGED EVERYTHING.

(About that time I gave someone £2K after knowing them for just 24 hours, no regrets)

"People don't like being sold, but they love to buy." Jeffrey Gitomer

I hit the Buy Now button and felt that surge of excitement, that dopamine-hit of expectation. I could feel the stir of possibility - of what lay the other side of nailing this piece that had been eluding me, for so long.

How it would finally feel to bring all the pieces of work I'd been doing together.

How it would help me to create a way of positioning my offers to the further along clients that were perfect for my work.

How THAT was the missing piece that would unlock alllll the possibilities.

My tummy fizzed with excitement, and as I put my card away, bathing in the happy glow of someone Whose. Life. Is. Going. To. Change, I suddenly realised I hadn't seen this Coach in my feed before yesterday.

I wasn't actually sure how I came to follow her; I hadn't heard of her before and I hadn't actively been looking for the solution she was offering – In fact, I'd been attached to the idea that the problem I needed to solve was THIS (other) thing and yet, within days of seeing a single post from her, I'd binged everything she put out, did a complete 360 on what it was I *thought* I actually needed to invest in – and was hitting Buy Now on a £2,000 pay-in-full offer.

Why?

That's exactly what I'm going to break down for you in this chapter - because your ability to take someone from *just seeing you* to *buying from you fast*, is directly tied to how much money you make online, particularly in today's saturated and highly competitive market.

Making that snap £2k purchase opened my eyes: not just to the offer - but to the *way* it was *marketed*.

I became obsessed with what makes that happen: what's the buyer psychology behind content that pulls someone from cold to sold in under 24 hours?

What's the secret sauce that makes your audience stop scrolling, skip the "maybe," and move straight to "I'm in" - when so much other content just passed them by?

In this chapter, I'm going to show you the three key things that coaches, consultants, therapists and experts who sell fast (and consistently) from their content are doing differently.

And I'll show you the shifts you can make to the way you articulate your work - so your message lands deeper, faster, and turns lurkers into clients who sell *themselves* on working with you

Because those who thrive don't make more sales because they're more skilled - they sell more because their messaging does the heavy lifting of having their ideal clients sell themselves on working with them, before they even make the pitch.

What makes us buy from one coach rather than another − and what makes us buy fast?

I want to invite you to think about the last time you bought something which captivated you really, really quickly:
What sparked that initial *"down the rabbit hole"* journey?

Maybe it was a FB ad, or a reel or post?

What WAS it about that piece of content that pulled you in deeper – to the next piece and the next piece – what were the components that made you binge your way through, each step selling yourself the certainty that *this* is what you needed, and finally – what WAS it, specifically, that had you close yourself on the sale, that meant you whipped out your card because you HAD to have this thing?

And when you think about the answers your brain is already bubbling up...to what extent do you think your content is doing a good job of those things right now? If we did a quick audit – how would it score in this regard?

Perhaps you see the gap in the extent to which your own content isn't acting like a funnel, pulling your audience in deeper because – to be blunt, a lot of content is the equivalent to handing out book pages at random:

It doesn't stack together in a way that inherently intensifies that sense of demand, that builds curiosity or sparks desire - in a way that means you *have* to 'turn the page' and get the next piece.

And that's because there's a blind spot in the industry. What you've been taught about what you need your content to "do" for you doesn't match what your content ***actually*** needs to do, to make sales directly.

And that's not your fault because it USED to work differently, it used to be possible to just show up consistently, share insights and get booked out.

But across the board, I see really experienced coaches and leaders, marketing strategists and business coaches *still* teaching you to create content for "connection", "authority" and "engagement". They have you look at Answer The Public for content ideas (the worst idea ever by the way - ask me why when we jump on a call together), and they have you create "pillars" against which to "give value".

But none of this actually pulls your buyer through the buying process, fast.

Because it doesn't get their heart beating faster. It doesn't stir that spark of possibility or light up the part of them that feels hope and hunger at the same time. It doesn't create the kind of magnetic curiosity that makes them crave the next post, the next piece, the next step - until buying becomes the obvious, inevitable, *only* choice.

Traditional strategies and methodologies are based on the concept of nurturing your audience, and being visible enough that when they're ready to buy, they move toward you. And when the market was less crowded and there was less choice - before a thousand coaches taught a hundred thousand more how to coach coaches to coach coaches…that approach built some really, really big businesses.

But in today's crowded market, that doesn't stand you out anymore, it's just white noise.

Which means you create more - but that doesn't solve the problem because it was never about volume.

You start to think the problem is your strategy, or your offer, or your audience.

So you tinker and fix and tweak and fine-tune - you're highly susceptible to you're shiny object marketing, promising the "secret" you're missing, and pulled every which way by coaches with sales engines purpose-built to show you EXACTLY what the real problem, the secret-sauce is.

Maybe you've swung like a pendulum from seeing *THE* solution for you as marketing a high-ticket offer to a higher-level audience and so you learn all the strategies to make *that* possible, and when the response is lacklustre you swing back to the idea that what you REALLY need is a low-ticket offer to give them a taste of your work, first.

And all the while, the work you're doing deepens and evolves so even though you've spent time creating trainings and content to sell your work, you feel like they're quickly outdated for what you'd teach now - they're not powerful or potent enough anymore and so you create afresh and go again and feel like you're spinning your wheels.

You're so, so busy in creation and development and marketing - and alllll the ideas you have, that you're just not getting the traction your powerful work *should* be getting.

If you're nodding along, realising your content might be more "random pages" than page-turning narrative - you're not alone…

Most of my clients come to me creating high-value content that should convert consistently… but doesn't.

Not because their work isn't powerful - but because there are invisible blockers sabotaging the sale *before* the offer even lands.

So let's name them.

Because once you can see where your message is breaking down - you can rebuild it in a way that pulls in buyers faster, and with far less effort.

There are three major barriers I see over and over again that stop brilliant coaches, consultants, and creatives from selling direct from content.

Let's break them down.

Barrier 1: You're not selling what your audience wants to buy, you're selling what you WANT them to want to buy

And I used to hesitate to say this - because surely as an Expert you know what outcomes your work delivers - and yet it's the optimisations I do with my multi-six-figure clients in this specific area, that makes them the most money, EVEN when they're well established and their other offers sell like hotcakes. This is definitely not a rookie-error, and it is likely to be affecting you.

So the simple, fundamental principle here is that **we buy to solve a need that we recognise we have.**

And the operative word is recognise – but the problem is that as an Expert, you know how powerful your work is and you know it's exactly what your clients need, which means it's easy to slip into leading with what YOU know they need, leading with the work itself, instead of what they actually desire and are looking for.

For example, that might sound like…"You need to reprogram your subconscious," or "You need to automate your funnels," or "You need to increase your emotional intelligence." Or "You need to get into alignment".

These may well be the solutions they need – and some of your audience are aware and pro-actively looking for those solutions - but a bigger proportion are looking for the OUTCOME this work leads to, but they aren't necessarily joining the dots that *THIS* is the piece of work that will help them achieve that outcome, that this is what they need for that to happen, that this is their missing piece.

Let me give you an example: One of my clients ran a masterclass to help online coaches to "overcome fear" - she was using it as a lead-in to her paid work but just wasn't getting the sign-ups. Because the problem was that her ideal client for her work doesn't necessarily resonate with or relate to the idea that she is "stuck in fear" - some might, for sure, but those that do are often *so* stuck in this fear, that they're not necessarily ready to take action and move out of it.

The clients you're best suited to serve (and the ones that will pay you) are *already* in motion - they're taking action, they've tried stuff already, they're seeking solutions. But they'll only move toward your offer if they recognise it's what they want and need. If your messaging frames their situation through your expert lens - say, calling it fear - but they don't see it that way, they'll scroll past, even though your solution might be exactly what they need.

When I asked my client what the symptoms of that fear were - what it looked like in action, she rattled off half a dozen symptoms they'd absolutely relate to: writing a post but not putting it out because you're worried what people might think, re-writing your sales page for the umpteenth time because you feel like you're still not QUITE nailing it, doing another certification or saying

"When I've just…(fill in the blank) then I'll be ready to raise my prices/launch this programme".

They'd relate to these symptoms and recognise this workshop is for them, even though they may not relate to the idea they're in fear. Because what YOU think they need to hear - or what you know will fix their problem - isn't necessarily what they're actively looking for, and would pay someone in a heartbeat to solve.

Which means you could spend months putting out content, writing emails, creating trainings and not getting much traction because you're speaking to something they don't even recognise as being the problem that needs solving - whilst another coach could put out ONE post that hits the nail on the head and hard-lands and they'll immediately look for more, and move to buy.

Humans respond when they feel seen and recognised. They respond to relief, to the promise of less pain, more freedom, a clear roadmap to their goal, the specific on-the-button answer they've been looking for, their deeply held desires.

Take a look at your content - are you selling a clear, tangible, desirable outcome that your audience *know* they want – or are you selling them the modality of your work, or the thing you think they need, or the components that will help them - but which they don't fully recognise they need?

If your outcome feels intangible, ask yourself the simple question "…so that what…?" What will doing this piece of work with you make possible for them?

Clients buy to solve problems: they don't buy confidence, they buy the confidence to step into a senior leadership role, they don't buy alignment, they buy into the possibility of making

£20k months feel easy and peaceful - we want to help them envision what's possible for them, the other side of this work

For example: "I help ambitious women unlock their career potential."

Is clearer with context and tangibility: "I help high-achieving women land next-level leadership roles with a £50k+ salary jump - without working longer hours or losing their weekends."

For example: "I help you reconnect with your intuition."

Becomes: "I help you finally trust your gut in big decisions - so you stop outsourcing your power and finally build the business you actually want to run."

For example: "I help you attract aligned love."

Becomes "I help high-achieving women stop overthinking every message and wondering where they stand - and find love that feels safe, clear, and mutual."

So, back to the question: what makes us buy fast? It starts with a crystal-clear outcome - that feels instantly connected to what we deeply want, in a way we can see and feel."

Let me give you another quick example. My client was selling a £300 offer in the nutrition space, but it wasn't selling at the level it should have been, given the size of his audience. He'd had copywriters rewrite it, he'd switched ad strategists, he'd done all the things to make it sound like a really compelling offer, but it just wasn't flying.

He asked me to take a look, and while I saw a few smart shifts that could help, none of them were going to make sales suddenly pop off - because the page was already strong. I see this all the time: smart, resonant, well-written copy on beautifully designed pages that still doesn't convert - not because it's saying the wrong things, but because it's solving the wrong problem.

What really threw him was this: *"This is what my audience tell me, time and time again, that they want help with."*

There was clearly demand - yet the sales told a different story*

* (*As an aside, another mistake that gets made ALL the time here that costs wasted time and money, is relying on insights from an audience that aren't paying you to solve the problem they say they want to solve, at the level of spend you're asking for − it's the equivalent of asking people who've never bought a car what features they want in a luxury model - and then building your whole business around their wishlist − when they were never going to buy it in the first place.*)

And when I did the research, it became clear that the outcome they said they wanted - "healthy eating made simple" - wasn't something they valued enough to pay hundreds for. They were already solving that with his beautiful £20 recipe books. The stakes weren't high enough, the problem didn't feel urgent or "costly" enough and the transformation wasn't meaningful or impactful enough to compel them to spend more.

So instead, we looked at what outcome they **would** value more highly. In his 1:1 work he was getting incredible results in terms of weight-loss, reversing pre-diabetes and drastically improving metabolic health and it was clear that these results were highly important to his clients - they were life-changing, in fact. I could see an opportunity to re-frame the offer as a starting-point to his higher-ticket 1:1 work, rather than as an end point for his book purchasers, so we repositioned the offer as The Metabolic Fix, and I wrote a quiz which gave a personalised metabolic health score. He made £30k in direct sales from this offer in a month AND it led beautifully into his deeper, more personalised 1:1 support for those who wanted a more premium service.

When I help my clients design a premium-level offer, the question that often comes up is "*who* would pay for this" – and it's critical that we know the answer to that question, but we answer it best by shifting the emphasis to "who *would* pay for this" – who is the person for whom the result is high-value enough that they would pay a premium?

So, to overcome barrier 1 identify the outcome that your audience values highly enough to pay a premium for, one which they "see and agree" they need help with and which is tangible and specific - not ethereal and esoteric, fluffy and meaningless.

And sell it to the person who is READY for your work, your magic, by positioning it as the *only*, inevitable, essential next-step move - their missing piece; we're going to dig more into that next.

Barrier 2: You don't stand out as THE ONE to choose

With the rise of AI (which is rapidly commoditising everything from content creation to coaching frameworks - and coaches themselves!), a hyper-saturated market, an increasingly sceptical audience, and more noise than ever - just getting noticed, let alone chosen, is a very real challenge in today's market.

There are literally *hundreds* of people offering what you offer and promising what you promise - and you're not just up against people in your niche, you're competing with anyone offering a route to the same result.

But that purchase I made happened so fast because she positioned herself as the **only one** who could do this with me in this particular way and then she connected that to a powerful sense of possibility, by sharing the evidence of just how effective and fast this method was, by showing the results of others.

I wasn't comparing her offer - I wasn't trying to decide between two similar options which would have seen me hesitate and second-guess and need to know every little detail, build up trust and be sure this was the right choice.

It's the difference between going shoe shopping and seeing THE pair, and knowing without a doubt that these are THE ONES, they stand out a mile, you love everything about them, you don't need to see more shoes....versus traipsing around every shoe shop in town, because you like several similar ones but nothing stands out so you can't *quite* choose between them.

Competition becomes irrelevant when you create a category that only you can own - because saturation only exists when you're in the same comparison pool, saying the same things, in the same way, as everyone else.

As Seth Godin puts it: *"In a sea of sameness, be a purple cow."*

When you position yourself as the only one - the coach delivering *this outcome, in this way, through your unique lens* - and you combine that with messaging that hits the emotional bullseye *and* evidence that proves your process actually works, you're no longer trying to be chosen - you're leading.

You're the obvious choice - not because you said the right things, but because your positioning, your proof, and your resonance did the work for you.

So, part of positioning yourself as the only one is helping your audience see why you're the only one - not just through emotion or energy - but by clearly articulating the unique **way** you get results.

Most business coaches will tell you the "how" doesn't matter: "sell the destination, not the journey" is a constant refrain.

But I disagree - if you don't communicate *how* your work creates the results, how will anyone know why they should choose you, specifically?

Your "how" is a powerful asset - not as a list of steps or modalities, but as the lens that makes your method distinct, credible, and desirable - and it's also how you build excitement around the micro-outcomes your process delivers along the way.

This is especially important for more nuanced work, where *how* you work is part of the value. It's what makes the experience feel personal, potent, and different from every other option out there.

Where most messaging goes wrong is in deep-diving into the intricacies of the work from the coach's perspective, getting caught in the nitty-gritty of *exactly what you do, but not what the client gets* and what that makes possible for them - it doesn't clearly join the dots back to the bigger transformation or show how each piece connects to what your client actually wants.

It's the equivalent of asking a car engineer to write your sales copy - they'll describe the internal mechanisms in loving detail, but won't make that emotional connection back to how your buyer wants to FEEL when they sit in the car, or who they'll be. Or the practical connections to what the buyer truly values

- safety, reliability, comfort, and leading with how this car solves those needs.
Take a look at the section of your sales page where you introduce your offer and make sure that you're not overwhelming with detail around what they get and underwhelming with what that means and makes possible for them.

What's so powerful about offer positioning work is that I can have two clients who, ostensibly, offer the *same service*, but when we position it through their unique lens - their voice, their spin, their perspective, the offer messaging sounds and feels completely different.

And that's because how we position your work as the answer to the problems your client has and your unique perspective, spin, angles and emphasis in terms of what you consider to be the vital components for solving that problem, is uniquely yours.

Your points of differentiation don't come from being the loudest, the flashiest, or the most raw, they come from owning what you know, how you do it, and what that unlocks for the people ready to pay for real results.

Nobody else teaches what you teach, the way you teach it, or gets results the way you get them.

And when you own that fully, you become incomparable.

In a market flooded with vague, fluffy messaging, getting laser-sharp on your edge, owning your unique perspective and clearly articulating how your work solves your client's problems, for *whom*, and *why* your approach is different - immediately sets you apart.

Because effective positioning is the game-changer that enables you to create your own category and become incomparable.

The most successful leaders in the online space didn't dominate because they shouted the loudest, they became the go-to authority by positioning themselves as the only choice. And one of the ways they've done that is to create and name a unique methodology, solving a well-defined problem, and delivering results in a way no one else was talking about.

For example, take Mike Michalowicz, creator of the *Profit First method*. He didn't *invent* budgeting or cash flow, but by framing the Profit First method around "pay yourself first" and naming it, then creating a book which resonated deeply with the specific mistakes entrepreneurs were making the world over (in a way that had them kicking themselves with instant recognition) and how to solve them - he created a completely new category, which became a movement - and made him millions.

Let me show you some more examples:

Lisa Johnson – *One to Many*

Lisa didn't invent passive income, group programs, or evergreen funnels. But she coined the phrase *One to Many* right at the moment that a movement toward creating leveraged income through group programmes instead of 1:1 was happening AND at a point when Covid had created a surge in online course consumption, digital entrepreneurship, and scalable, work-from-home business models.

She became synonymous with recurring revenue and passive income, and firmly positioned herself as the go-to authority for coaches ready to step out of 1:1 and into a more expansive business model.

When you name and simplify a result into a repeatable methodology (like "One to Many") you build instant authority and create a new lane.

_____

Natasha Bray – *Heart Healing®*

Natasha didn't just offer emotional healing. She combined therapy, subconscious work, and energetics into a trademarked system: *Heart Healing®*.

But more powerfully, she framed internal trauma as the missing link between self worth and stuck income - especially in high-earning entrepreneurs.

That insight tapped into a silent epidemic of success-driven women carrying emotional wounds that strategy alone couldn't fix - that were actively **LOOKING** for a solution, for a reason it *"still wasn't working despite having all the right things in place"* so her work brilliantly positioned as the "missing piece", connecting healing to wealth in a way that felt deeply resonant and irresistible - and as the gateway to big money and big impact

This kind of category creation comes from *codifying* a process people feel but don't know how to name, or visualise or frame - and then delivering it with a unique approach, consistency and depth.

She isn't the only one doing this sort of work, but she's dominated the market by positioning her work in a category all of its own, by combining modalities and creating unique methodologies that get tangible, proven, powerful results.

Often, when we see this kind of work, we think they have an unfair advantage, we think they're somehow uniquely qualified to create this legacy-level work, but the reality is they've just 100% owned doing what they do, the way they do it - and the results that gets; they've just positioned powerfully.

It's only in hindsight, after it works, that the market calls it genius and it looks like the idea was there all along, for anyone to take. It's easy to label category-leading differentiation as obvious in retrospect but it's like great song lyrics, they don't exist until they do - and then everyone wishes they wrote that song.

Jessica Cunningham – *Belief Coding*®

Jessica didn't just repackage mindset work. She created a *system* which positioned to getting fast results, as an antidote to all the offers that would take you through months of healing and integration work. She tapped into a deep desire for rapid change, for just "fixing" yourself fast and created a sense of limitless possibility and rapid results that would change the game for you.

"Coding" feels scientific. It bridges mindset + neuroscience + subconscious work in a way that:

* Makes the unseen sound tangible
* Distinguishes her from generic coaches
* Creates a certifiable method others now train in

And by trademarking Belief Coding® and building a certification business around it, she moved from practitioner to *framework founder* – which builds exponential authority. Her approach positions to the idea of limitless opportunities and speaks directly to the frustrations and hopes of entrepreneurs trying to get out of their own way, in a uniquely new way. And our brains love New, we're wired for curiosity to the kind of offers that look and feel and sound like something you haven't tried before, haven't heard before - particularly when we combine those narratives with evidence of the *incredible* results others have using these methodologies.

The final barrier is one I see all the time:

Barrier 3. You're posting consistently, but your content isn't activating your audience to buy.

This is because it's missing the psychological and emotional triggers, and strategic cues that shift someone from *"This is interesting"* to *"I need this now."*

Time-was, we used to say it takes 7 touchpoints to make a sale. But research from Google suggests its 20+ in today's noisy online spaces.

Which means your content has to make people *want* to binge you. If it doesn't, they see one post, keep scrolling, and end up falling into someone else's rabbit hole. You might've sparked interest - but not enough to hook them. So they forget you, and buy from the person who pulled them in deeper, faster.

I often say to my audience: if you posted on your feed as though you were paying for it you'd be much, much more intentional about what you wrote and shared.

Because right now, a lot of content is just noise.

I audited a coach's feed this morning - her posts were smart and valuable. But none of them really *went* anywhere. They didn't spark curiosity (because they gave all the answers), they didn't build momentum. She shared insights but didn't connect into what it would truly mean to solve the problem she was speaking to, didn't join the dots and have them see the possibilities of solving that problem - and didn't position her as THE person to help them solve that.

She invited them to "book a call" - but for someone reading the post cold, that's a leap. There's too much friction.

What you *actually* want is content that grabs attention, creates intrigue, and guides the right person from browser to buyer. Content that is purposefully and intentionally mapped against the desires your ideal clients have and what stands in the way of them getting them - which positions what YOU know as the magic key that unlocks that possibility for them.

When your content shows your audience that you truly see them - and delivers a sharp, insight-rich hit of your genius, positioning you as the *only* one who can get them to what they want - that 20-touchpoint buyer journey collapses.

And you can convert from a single post starting a rabbit-hole-tumble that has them buy in 24 hours, just like I did.

So how do we create content that does that?

There's three core components of high-converting, buyer-activating content:

1. A binge-worthy conversion narrative
2. Offer positioning that bakes in sales psychology
3. A sales system embedded *directly* into your content

Unfortunately, we don't have space to cover all these things here, so we're just going to focus on embedding a sales system into your content.

Because when your content acts like a binge-able sales system, people don't just consume more - they move closer to buying. Even if they've only just found you, the right sequence can activate demand fast.

But it's not just about getting them to binge - it's about building momentum toward the sale.

Your content should be the sales engine.
My clients have said to me I want my messaging to sell people on me the way yours sold me on you.

And the *reason* they sell themselves on working with me is because I ditched ALL the content creation strategies that focused on giving value, educating, creating connection, building authority, proving, convincing, over-explaining - and instead got really intentional about creating content that mimics the sales process, to lead them to a buying decision more quickly

We do that by embedding the same sales processes you'd use to sell in a sales conversation- INTO your messaging.
So, selling follows a framework - you'll have heard I'm sure of AIDA: attention, interest, desire, action.

It's designed to pull your person through the buying process - and that's what you want your content to do.

So, first, we capture attention by landing precisely on what they desire and struggle with.

And the crucial point, as we've already discussed, is speaking to what THEY know they want, not what you know they need

We get their attention when we lead with their DESIRES and problems that create instant recognition and resonance.

And then, we move them to intrigue by sharing insights about why they're stuck and what's missing - when we get this right, they can't not hear the next piece.

This is absolutely critical to having them binge your content and reach out to buy: speaking so directly and relevantly to them, in a way that has them feel so seen, and then showing them an insight that creates that penny-drop moment, that THIS is the missing piece.

I call these *Goldilocks level insights* - just like the porridge, not too hot or cold - or in this case not too complex or too simple.

These marketing-gold "ah-ha" moments come from your sales calls or coaching sessions - they're the things which you've seen make sense to your client about what's really going on, they're the things that have them say "I'm in" on a sales call because they see that you see them. (And they're often things you don't realise need explaining because you're so close to your work you don't realise they haven't joined the dots.)

We use these "ah-hahs" to create belief-shifting content that has them feel seen and shifts their thinking around the problem and what they actually need, next.

Now the mistake that gets made here is positioning the insight as "here's the problem" and the solution as "buy my thing", but to have them sell themselves on you, we need to show them truths and insights that have them *lead themselves to wanting the answers and seeing you as the solution.* It's like when you go in for that first kiss, you incline your head, you move forward, but you want them to move toward you, too.

And this is the single biggest mistake I see being made when I audit content - because my ideal clients know to share high quality insights, but it's such a tight-rope, and it's so hard to see what you're doing wrong when you're so close to it.

So we've got attention and interest, next we create desire by showing them the exact shifts they need to make.

115

And, crucially, this is not a 5-step plan - that's just information and they can Google and ChatGPT their way to any kind of solution; information is not what's missing. Instead, we have them see the shift from the insight we've shared and we connect into what will change when they solve this problem - rather than the exact blow-by-blow steps of how to solve this problem.

Then finally, we amplify that desire and move them into action by showing what's possible through evidence of what others have achieved - through sharing results.

And this is really important because it creates a sense of possibility. And if you think back to when you bought fast I guarantee that what got your attention was that it was speaking to an outcome you wanted, or a problem you recognised and your intrigue deepened because it gave you a glimpse of why you weren't getting that outcome (in a way you'd never heard nailed quite so precisely and resonantly) and why doing it *THIS* way would change that.

Then what motivated you into that final stage of action was seeing what's possible, seeing the results when you fix this problem, or when you get this desire.

And this is vital because seeing what's possible is your most powerful buy-lever (and in almost every content audit I do, it's not being leveraged enough)

It creates a dopamine hit which primes your audience to buy, by having them see what *THEY* could create or achieve or have, or do, or be, with this thing.

And that's EXCITING. And powerful.

Sharing results compounds this because it's the *evidence* it's possible, for people like them.

We buy on emotion, for sure, but we back that up with logic - and so possibility-thinking creates a powerful sense of desire, whilst your results provide the logical back-up that this could be your reality too, and that's what tips people into buy mode.

And when you get this right, BOOM - your dream clients are activated, they see you as having *the* solution, they see you as getting results for people like them – and they buy fast.

I'm going to include some examples of this kind of content in the resources link below because embedding AIDA in my content, and my client's content, instead of following "connect-engage-authority" strategies, completely changed how quickly my people find and buy from me and my clients.

I've had clients enter my world and buy multiple offers from me within 48 hours. I've sold out 6 programmes in the last 6 months.

My clients have had their first £20k months, they've sold out events, they've filled programmes, and they've got their very first sign-ups from content.

And when you combine this with your binge-worthy conversion narrative AND bake high-converting sales psychology into your offer positioning, your clients can't not buy.

If you've enjoyed what we've covered here and want my help to install this in your business - and if you'd like to see some more examples and detail of the methodologies I'm sharing here, you can head over to www.imheidiwilliams.com/bookchapter and get additional resources.

Hayley Baxter

Founder of Corbar Accounting Ltd. The off-grid Accountant.

It started with a dream.

For every business owner staring at the ceiling at 3am, wondering if there's enough to pay the tax bill - this is for you.

Instagram - @theoffgridaccountant

IT STARTED WITH A DREAM AND NOW YOU'RE FEELING PRESSURE

You took the step in the world of entrepreneurship, working for yourself, self- employed whatever you want to call it.

Congratulations, it's fabulous to meet you here.

Whether you are on your first venture or your fiftieth venture, it's sure to be a learning curve and if it's not your first time, it will be different than the last time.

I want you to know that if you're feeling like a duck out of water or whatever the saying is, however seasoned you are, however much experience you have, we're all on a journey and no one knows or holds a magic key.

I get it, you started with a dream, and you thought the hardest step would be taking the first one and now you find yourself drowning in compliance, legalities, deadlines, cash worries and that never fading feeling of am I doing this right?

And then just as you think "I've cracked this". Wham! Along comes a raft of changes.

Most likely you did a bit of research, but did you really realise how challenging it would be at times, with all the many different hats you would need to wear?

The rules you never signed up for

When did starting a business translate into becoming a tax expert?

Of all the things I didn't realise about becoming a business owner is that I would need to become an expert in many different taxes along with various elements of legal red tape and I'm an accountant!

Because let's be honest it's not just tax it's Insurance, GDPR, Employment law, Cyber Security the list could go on and on, but I don't want to bore you before we really get to the good stuff.

The fact is, like it or not, compliance, red tape whatever you want to call it, in today's world there's no hiding from it as a business owner.

You could even be fooled into thinking running a business is just compliance role.

It's enough to put you off, I really do get it. It's the things business owners never talk about.

Question though, if they did, would it have stopped you from embarking on this journey?

And you are truly not alone, every single business faces these things, even if some have more help than others. It is always comforting to know you are not alone.

And of course, you have totally got this – it's all totally manageable. Organisation and determination go a long way.

What we get wrong about compliance

There's a misconception out in the world of business that tax, particularly, is a once a year or once a quarter thing. We are reactive to it.

Making it part of your daily / weekly business rhythm will serve you so much more as a business owner. Be proactive.

Think about it, instead of it being this fearful, procrastination, humming constantly in your mind, if you just embrace it head on and make it part of the everyday, you take all that away.

I'm sure you will have heard in some form or other Benjamin Franklin's well know quote "Nothing is certain in this life, except death and taxes", never a truer word spoken in my opinion.

There is not much I feel I can help you with on the death front, but taxes – we can totally get to grips with.

Now, unless you are the person that loves compliance, most of us see it as a must do, tick box task. Leaving it until the last minute, so on and so forth.

In business it's wise to get a bit savvier about these things.

I'm sure you know by now a big part of being a business owner is making decision after decision. And of course, for every big decision you make there is a regulatory ripple effect, and so without being savvy in this area you may trip yourself up. And just to be clear I'm not talking about being an expert in everything – my aim of this chapter is not to overwhelm you more! But for you to have enough of the ingredients in your mind (or in this reference book), which means you ask the questions or have the thought process rather than just running blind by the seat of your pants, (which every business owner everywhere will have done at some point, believe me!).

Let's just consider it for a second. Using hiring a new team member as an example. Ripple effects:

- Without understanding some of the changes coming about in employment law
- Without understanding of the PAYE changes for employers
- Without understanding of the true cost – not just the salary you pay them, but their equipment, their training, their benefits

You can quite easily end up in a pickle and that's just with the new team member costing you more than expected, and not even getting started on any other compliance angle, of which there are many.

So, by now hopefully you can see that burying your head doesn't make any of these things different, they are all happening and will affect you regardless, however meeting them head on, means you will be wiser to the impacts, with more of an understanding of what they might be.

And don't get me wrong, it's impossible to know everything about everything, this is about raising your awareness to become a more rounded business owner rather than being caught up in worry.

"The first step toward change is awareness. The second step is acceptance."
- Nathaniel Branden

Why is your accountant only talking to you once a year?

Sometimes when I talk to business owners about their business finances, after a bit of delving we end up at a very typical response of "My accountant only asks for things once a year – if it's good enough for them, that's good enough for me".

I'm sorry but for the most part this isn't helpful for most businesses.

Part of my mission as a business owner of an accountancy practice, along with a growing number of other accountants and bookkeepers, is to try and bring about a change to this.

As a minimum, talking to your accountant around month 9 of your financial year is crucial for good tax planning. You can't influence the tax you pay after your year has ended. You can't have an idea of how much tax you might have to pay if you are not looking at your numbers. Ideally, I try to check in with my clients (over a hot beverage of choice, of course) at least quarterly.

And it's even more than just about the tax angle – you started your business with a dream of what it would be and how your life would be and part of that would have had a financial element to it. If you've not had that conversation or thought about what you are trying to achieve, then it's almost impossible for your business finances to really be working for you in the best way to support this dream, let alone be running things in the most tax efficient way.

In my opinion, even if just at a basic level this is where your accountant can really help you, please raise this conversation with them.

If you are a business owner who is doing their own tax returns. I still would urge you to consider some of these things. Otherwise, you end up running a business you don't enjoy and you're not getting out of it what you need, which was the whole point in the first place.

Now don't get me wrong I'm not saying knowing all this makes the practicality of doing the doing and getting to "live the dream "as it were, easier, it absolutely doesn't, but it does mean that when you arrive it will be where you want to be.

The snowball effect – how it can tumble out of control

OK so before you begin to think I'm Mary Poppins, practically perfect in every way, let me share a little story with you. Let's call it…..

The wakeup call

It's 3am and I've been tossing and turning for at least the last 2 hours, my minds in overdrive. The VAT bill is due in a few days' time, my bank balance is close to £0 and the VAT bill is close to £6k. Thoughts running through my mind:

- How am I going to pay it?
- Who owes me money, that I can get to pay immediately?
- Perhaps I could loan it?

And not forgetting the - How can I support other businesses financially if I can't manage my own? I have no excuse.

The real problem - I wasn't in control of my numbers.

I wasn't in sync with my money.

It wasn't that I didn't have a profitable business.

It was that my bookkeeping wasn't up to date, I didn't have a budget, I didn't have cash flow.

I was 'shock' my own worst client.

There I've said it.

It was a huge wake up call.

And of course, you and I both know it didn't have to be this way.

Now I know, I hear you…. but it's easy for you, you're an accountant, you can easily get on top on things.

Tough love – so can you. And you know what else - it is your job.

It's not your accountant's or your bookkeeper's job. It's yours, as the CEO of your business and your life – you are responsible for being in sync with your money.

Now I truly believe numbers are your friend, and any business owner who says they don't look at their business numbers is riding a wave of luck that one day will come crashing down.

And before you say anything else it is totally doable.

You just need a little guidance (that's why I'm here) and a little determination (which I know you have).

The weekly date that will set you free

So many business owners I speak with are fearful of numbers.

Some are burying their heads, others feel fine so long as there is cash in the bank, some want to know more but are afraid they will look silly asking, some sort of know but never fully feel like they really know. Any which way the result is the same, they are not getting to grips with their business finances.

I do get it, why you're scared of numbers. Let's face it the unknown is a little scary.

But the gift and there really is a gift which can be superbly summed up in the quote attributed to Sir Francis Bacon "Knowledge is power".

You are an amazing expert at what you do. I know that even if you don't.

You are also human and, on a journey, just like millions of others on this planet, some may have trodden more steps than you but that doesn't mean they don't face similar challenges.

And this is where using the information you have available to you and really getting to grips with your business finances unlocks so many blocks for every business owner. Yes, read that again, every business owner. It makes no difference if you are starting out or running a 7 figure (or whatever sized) business.

Staying in sync with your money, makes a difference.

So, what do I actually mean by this.
Well, I want you to take a deep breath before you read on – especially if you are one to be seen running in the opposite direction when we start talking numbers.

Tough love – you must get clear on what's actually going on.

The first steps you take in doing this will be the hardest but like most hard steps, the outcome is worth it.

Phase 1 is Reset and Let's get visible, to be clear not the kind where you have to bare your soul or do a jig on social media.

To really own your numbers, you need to have visibility of them.

If you're not using accounting software (Xero, QuickBooks, Sage, Free Agent etc.), where have you been? It's so accessible nowadays – I'm sorry there's just no excuse. And in case you think there is, I've called out and put to bed, some common excuses next.

Excuse number 1 - I'm not big enough I can manage it on a spreadsheet – no you can't, well you can but it won't end well. Getting to grips with software whilst you are small is a great advantage – you'll already have the systems and processes in place ready for when you grow – a huge win.

Excuse number 2 – Accounting software is too expensive – sorry it's not – there's so much choice, so many different price points there really is one that's just for you (there are even free options with certain bank accounts).

Excuse number 3 - I wasn't good at maths – totally not relevant

Excuse number 4 – I don't know how to use it and don't have time to learn. Good news! Today's accounting software is designed for you – the end user. It is not designed for accountants and bookkeepers. Which means its relatively easy to get to grips with and there are lots of free online training from the software providers and on YouTube.

As a growing business owner – accounting software is your best friend.

As any business owner – accounting software is your best friend.

Now is the doing part, the action - rip the plaster off - get your bookkeeping up to date.

If you DIY your own bookkeeping go ahead and get stuck right in, if you work with a bookkeeper make sure they have all they need from you to get everything up to date.

There it is step 1 – get your day to day bookkeeping up to date using accounting software. And before you go down the hole of blah blah another accountant telling me to get my bookkeeping up to date think on this:

No business in the world however big or small, however established can have a grip on their true business performance if they don't have a start point of up-to-date bookkeeping.

As I've been busting up excuses - it feels an appropriate point to call truth on a common false belief:

One that I think is possibly the cruellest joke of all, on business owners.
Cash = Profit – it's a lie.

Cash does not equal profit, and profit does not equal cash.
So many things affect this relationship. That's why a little understanding around this area can go a long way.

So why is it different. Being simple about it, partly because of timing and partly because not all items are recorded in you profit and loss account, some will be on your balance sheet.

An easy example of something that might cause a difference is - if you raise a sales invoice to your client. Your profit for that month will usually include those sales, however it does not mean you physically have that money in the bank yet and in this given month your cash and profit will differ.

So, if you're the business owner looking at your bank balance every month, thinking well it's still positive, I don't need to do more than this, please think again.

Now own it

By now even if I have only done half a job - you must be on the bandwagon of being in sync with your business.

Yet many business owners go month to month, quarter to quarter, year to year without really knowing what their business finances really mean.

Its time right now to break this cycle.

The monthly finance review is if nothing else, an appointment with yourself to look at your money.

Back to excuse busting:

Excuse number 1 - I'm only small, there's only me, I don't need a monthly finance review – I'm sorry you do – you owe it to your business and yourself.
Excuse number 2 - I look at my cash balance every week – sorry not enough – its only telling you one piece of a bigger puzzle
Excuse number 3 - I don't understand it all anyway – and you're never going to if you don't start.

You don't need to become a finance expert superhero on day 1 – what you do need to do, is to start to get to grips with your business finances.

Other than getting your bookkeeping up to date, how else can you manage this?

When I wanted to go from my worst client to my best client, I introduced Finance Fridays. OK not very original but I'm not trying to be, I'm trying to make a huge success of my business and part of this is - you know it – getting in sync with my money.

So, every Friday there is time on my task list to do something on finance. If you do nothing else introducing this one thing means you are already ahead of so many other businesses (yes even big businesses).

It doesn't have to be a long time, it doesn't have to be the same amount of time every week, but every week includes some time.

And ideally a longer time slot towards the start of the month – this is the chance to finish off the month before and then have time to sit and look at it.

Yes, I'll say it again - time to sit and look at it – this is your monthly finance review.

This is where the magic happens.
If you work with a bookkeeper, this is still advisable, as you are the owner, part of your responsibility is the finances, even if someone else if preparing the data for you, you need an awareness of what's going on.

This means you become the person who is looking at numbers at least 52 times a year, instead of let's be honest – 12 times a year if you were lucky, more likely 4 times a year or don't be ashamed to say, we're friends now after all, 1 time a year.

Top tip before I hear another excuse "I don't work Fridays!" It really doesn't have to be a Friday.

The power of knowing your numbers

There are some key numbers every business owner needs to know, opinions may differ and there are some good reasons why using different numbers at different times is best, however let's just stick with the task of moving the needle.

1. Net Profit – before and after tax

2. Gross Profit
3. Cash flow
4. Break even

Let's take them in turn:

Net Profit before tax (and after tax)

What is it? This is the number that is remaining from your sales (excluding VAT) after all costs (excluding VAT) are taken off. And the after-tax version is with the tax taken off.

Why it matters? The before tax version is the number that helps you forecast your tax bill throughout the year. And if indeed it is not a profit and in fact it is a loss, you know what the gap is you need to plug. The after-tax version is probably a big part of why you do it.

Many focus on sales and yes of course the sales side of the fence is important, but what the point is if you are not making profit – the profit is the bit where you can take a slice for yourself.

Gross profit

What is it? This is your sales less any costs directly associated with the generation of those sales. If you are a supermarket and you sell beans for £1, and the beans cost you 60p to buy: £1 is your sales value, 60p is your cost of sales and 40p would be your gross profit once you sell them.

Why it matters? This is the start of the chain. The Gross profit is what everything else must be taken out of. It's always worth knowing and measuring as a reduction in this can have a direct knock-on effect to everything else. It's a warning sign.

Cashflow

What is it? This an estimate over a period, of all your expected cash inflows and out flows.

You basically start with your bank balance as at today, and you add on any sales or monies in, you believe you will get, and you take off any costs or things you are expecting to pay for. You try to forecast this as specifically as you can i.e. over a few weeks, day by day or a few months, month by month. How you do this will depend on how tight things are. If they are very tight go day by day.

Why it matters? It gives you peace of mind knowing that you have enough cash to pay for everything. Or it shows you where you're going to run into trouble and you need to find a way to bridge the cash gap to keep going.

Believe it or not many businesses fail because they run out of cash rather than because they don't have a profitable business. I know this may seem an odd thing to say but it's true. Remember earlier when I busted the myth that cash does not equal profit and profit does not equal cash.

A simple scenario to bring it to life. Say you make a sale to a client. They are going to pay you in 30 days. To fulfil this sale, you need to pay for software and various training materials, which you need to pay out immediately. So, you are letting go of cash before you are getting cash in. Even if you make a good profit on the sale there is a timing difference between the incoming and outgoing. You must have enough in the "pot" to fund this or you are going to run into trouble. And before you know it you won't have a business.

Managing cashflow is not just for businesses with limitations on cash. It's about managing your cash funds most effectively. And it's all part of becoming that grown up business owner.

Breakeven

What is it? This is the point at which your sales exactly cover your costs. At this point your profit will be £0.

Why it matters? It's about peace of mind. If you know your monthly break-even point is £5k – you become really focussed to deliver £5k of sales in that month and you also know if you deliver more, you are profit making. It's a great way to focus the mind and shut out the noise.

Become in sync

The biggest fear I hear from speaking to business owners when it comes to all this is the fear they are unknowingly doing something incorrectly or that they forget something or miss a deadline.

It can be hugely worrisome for business owners, wherever they are on their journey.

Some of the things I hear are:

- I never felt up to date or on top of business numbers.
- Have I missed a deadline for something without realising it?
- That tax bill was a huge surprise, and I didn't even know I'd missed the filing deadline – what kind of a business owner does that make me?

I've said it before, and I'll say it again - you are not alone – I've probably heard every story possible about why a deadline was missed – life is busy – business is busy – stuff happens that takes your mind away from remembering the thing that you need to remember.

I know business owners from all walks of life that have missed deadlines and incurred fines and yes confession time, even me – remember when I told I was my worst client for a while!

Apart from feeling like I had egg on my face / worrying about how I can help clients with this if I can't even do it for myself and the fact I said goodbye to £150 – Did the world end? No. Did my business carry on? Yes. Did it make me more determined to do things differently? Absolutely.

So, we take it step by step.

That old chestnut, Confidence

I just wanted to say something about confidence, as I feel it really does feature hugely in, well, I suppose the journey of life, but for now let's just stick to the journey of business.

Confidence or rather lack of confidence is one of the biggest things that has held me back in my life. People think I'm confidant but really that's just a determination in me to not let a lack of confidence stop me.

And the truth is, being in sync with your money or on top of your business finances, when you strip it all back, confidence plays a big part in it.

You really can get to grips with your business finances.

You don't need to be an expert.

You don't need to know the jargon.

You do need to know where you are and what this means. And you totally can.

A short outline of main UK business taxes as at May 2025

Now let's get to grips with the taxes – what you need to know.

Please note tax law can and does change and so it is worth checking up to date regulations.

So, the key taxes every business owner needs an awareness of (note I said awareness not to be an expert):

- Corporation Tax
- VAT
- Income Tax
- PAYE/NIC

Corporation tax

This is the tax a Limited Company pays on its profits.
It's always helpful to think of a limited company as its own person – in legal terms that's exactly what it is – every individual person has an obligation to pay its taxes and that tax for the Limited Company is Corporation Tax.

For profits under 1.5 million
- It's expected to be paid 9 months and 1 day after its financial year end.

The financial year for a company, typically starts on the day they start trading. It does not have to be the fiscal year which we know as April – March.

A Corporation tax return is required to be submitted to HMRC. This is usually done off the back of your Limited Company accounts being prepared and submitted to Companies House.

VAT (Value Added Tax)

This is a sales tax, ultimately paid by an end consumer.

If you are a VAT registered company, you will need to charge VAT on the sales you make and keep a record of it.

As a VAT registered company you can also, recover any VAT that is charged to you by your suppliers.

As a VAT registered business, think of yourself as a VAT administrator.
You can be a VAT registered business regardless of your business set up. (i.e. you could be VAT registered as a Sole Trader or Limited Company).
The good news is modern accounting software (e.g. Xero, Sage, QuickBooks, Free Agent etc.) does all the heavy lifting for you. And by that, I mean once you tell the software you are a VAT registered business, it will charge the VAT on sales for you and split out the VAT you can recover on purchases.

The bit you need to ensure is that you are only recovering VAT on items you are permitted to recover it on. For a starter you can find some useful information on the HMRC website.

VAT returns are typically submitted quarterly. The VAT return is where you send information to HMRC advising them of a number of things, like, your Vatable sales total, how much VAT you have charged on your sales and the same for purchases, and ultimately this shows how much VAT you need to pay to HMRC (or how much they might need to pay back to you).

The payment is required around 5 weeks after the quarter ends by the 7th of the month.

PAYE Tax (Paye As You Earn)

This is an area business owners can get a bit muddled.

PAYE tax is tax that you are paying on behalf of your employees.

The PAYE system is a reporting and collecting process, that is designed so individual people that are employed don't need to administer their own taxes, you as an employer do it on their behalf. You act as an administrator for HMRC and deduct the tax from an individual's pay and pay it to HMRC on their behalf.

It can sometimes feel like it's an extra cost to you but really you are just administering it.

Let's bring this to life - when you say you will pay an employee a monthly salary of £2,500, this is usually a gross figure or a figure before tax. What you pay that person in cash terms (i.e. the money you transfer from your business bank account to theirs) will be maybe £2100 – the other £400 you will pay to HMRC on their behalf. So, it's still costing you the £2500 you expected, it's just that you are paying it to two separate places.

The PAYE process, calculations and submissions are typically managed through Payroll software.

NIC (National Insurance Contributions)

There are two types – Employees NIC's and Employers NIC's. Employees NIC works in the same way as PAYE – it's a tax on the individual employee and you are just being HMRC's administrator by paying it to them on your employees' behalf.

Employers NIC is a tax on you as an employer.

The tax pay period always runs from 6th of one month to 5th of the next. You choose a date within that period to pay your employees. The PAYE and NIC for that period is due for payment with HMRC by 22nd of the month – HMRC require it paid to them by 19th of month, so they have it in their bank by 22nd.

Income tax

This is the tax on an individual person. Typically, a person pays their income tax in one of two ways, their employer pays it for them – see PAYE as described above. Or they complete a Self-Assessment Tax Return (SATR) and pay it themselves.

If you're a business owner the likelihood, is you file a SATR – regardless of if your business is a Limited Company, Sole Trader or Partnership.
I'm going to take each on in turn.

Sole Trader

So as a Sole Trader you will pay tax on your business profits. This is your sales less allowable business costs.

Note the word allowable – it can get tricky, but we got this – organisation and determination remember – HMRC's guides are useful to help you with this, and many accountants and bookkeepers offer free resources to help guide you.

For expenditure to be "allowable", HMRC typically come back to the words "the costs need to be incurred, Wholly and Exclusively for the purpose business" It's good to know this as a business owner and to it bear in mind when considering costs that can be charged to your business. However as always, there are some things that have specific rules and so always worth checking.

As a Limited Company business owner, typically the most common way to pay yourself is a mix of low salary and dividends.

And this is what goes onto your SATR – along with details of any other income.

The tax year basis for SATR is very technically 6th April – 5th April but can elect to run 1st April – 31st March. The submission of the return is the next 31st January (or October if you are not filing online).

HMRC like the tax to be paid in advance, and so if your tax bill is over £1,000, they typically require something called a payment on account. And this is what trips many people up.

Let's take the year 1st April 2024 – 31st March 2025.

The payments for this period are required as:
- 50% of the estimate on 31st January 2025
- 50% of the estimate on 31st July 2025
- With the true up due 31st January 2026 (along with a 50% of the estimate for the year ending March 2026).
-

A few commonly asked questions.

When is the right time to register for VAT?

As at today (May 25) the VAT threshold in the UK is £90,000 of sales in any rolling 12-month period. Please note the word "rolling" here. It is not just your financial year it is across an ongoing period of 12 months. E.g. April 24 – March 25, then May 24 – April 25, then June 24 – July 25 etc.

Once you hit the threshold or once you get to a point you believe you will hit the threshold in the next 30 days – it is mandatory to register, and you will need to start recording VAT as described in the VAT section above on your sales and purchases.

If you have not yet reached the threshold, it is worth tracking your monthly sales as a rolling 12-month figure, so there are no surprises, and you don't miss the point at which you should have registered and run into trouble before you start.

Some businesses do opt to register for VAT before they hit the threshold. The reasons for this vary. They can include things like; if you know you're going to be working with VAT registered businesses, who can recover the VAT and you have to buy a lot of Vatable products for which you could recover the VAT, it can make sense to be VAT registered regardless of if you are at the mandatory threshold or not. Sometimes people believe being VAT registered makes them look like a bigger business which can help to attract the right clients, especially when you are starting out. Sometimes it can be because you have invested heavily in equipment and want to recover the VAT you have paid on these items.

It's worth a mention here that there are different VAT schemes, some of which, as a smaller business can be worth looking into.

When is the right time to become a Limited Company?

The answer to this used to be much more straight forward than it is today, because of the change in UK Corporation Tax rates in April 2023.

There isn't a blanket approach, and it can depend on individual circumstances.
Businesses become Limited Companies for several reasons:

1. To limit the liability of the owners
2. To look like a more established business to attract the clients they are trying to
3. To save tax

Point 1 is relevant at any size of business. As a Limited Company is deemed to be a totally separate person from its owners, in principal if it runs into difficultly, it is ringfenced to itself. Whereas if you are a Sole Trader who runs into difficulties, as you and your business are one and the same your personal assets can be at risk.

Point 2, again, is relevant to any size of business. If you are looking to work business to business with larger corporations, it most likely will be a good call to set up in this way from the start.

Point 3 as a shareholder of a business you can take dividends, which are taxed on you personally, at a lower rate than if you paid yourself a salary through PAYE or if you remain as a Sole Trader (because dividends are paid out of after tax profits and so they have already had some tax taken off them). And tax savings are only realised after a certain level of **profit** (not sales) is achieved.

The bit that is often overlooked here, is that setting up and running a Limited Company has added complexities that don't exist with Sole Traders. The running costs of a Limited Company are generally higher and you as a shareholder and director have legal obligations you must fulfil. Which hugely differs from a sole trader -so more red tape and compliance.

So that's a summary of the tax bits. Please note I emphasise summary!

Part of the complexities of Tax are that the laws, values and rates around them often change, it's worth finding a good reliable source that can keep your awareness in tune. Many accountancy firms, and bookkeeping firms have newsletters you can sign up to that keep all this information on your radar and of course, HMRC.

Which accountancy software is the best?

None of them and all of them!

They all do the same thing.

They have varying price points. They all offer a free trial.

Pick a day, sign up for the free versions, give yourself a set time on each and pick the one you get along with most.

It doesn't need any more thought than this.

Back to the Weekly Process - The first 90 days

So how do you start with these Finance Fridays – well in any 90-day period there's 12 Fridays so here's how to get grips in the first 90 days.

1. Get your software up to date.
a. Process all cost invoices every single one.
b. Make sure all your sales are recorded.
c. Match your postings in the software to the ones in your bank account (this is called a bank reconciliation).

2. Ensure the bank account is reconciled – ensuring there are no mis alignments in your bank reconciliation.
3. Review your costs – look back over the last 3 – 6 months.

a. Consider, are you really using what you are paying for? (We live in the subscription world and it's easy to continue to pay for things we are no longer or have never used – fear not we are all guilty of this).
b. Is there any that you could reduce, by renegotiating or changing supplier?

4. Make sure that all the categories are correct in your bookkeeping.
a. Take some time to review this and ensure everything is categorised consistently and appropriately as this means when you're reviewing you will be looking at more accurate information and it is easier to spot trends.

5. Get clear on what your fixed costs are – this is what you are committed to pay out regardless of if you make any sales or not.

6. Understand what your breakeven point is.

7. Try and create a simple cash flow.

8. Take a deeper dive into what products and services are really driving your profit. This can be a complex area but start simple, think about these three areas as it will give you a good start:
a. How much time does it take?
b. Can you put a cost on that based on how much money you'd like to earn?
c. What resources are involved and how much do they cost

9. Review your pricing strategy.

10. Set some financial goals.

11. Make a proper date to review your finances monthly.

12. Go back to step 1 and make sure you utilise the finance Friday concept to keep things in check.

Even if you only manage steps 1-4 and do them on repeat for a time, you are beginning to tackle your business finances. If you work with an accountant or bookkeeper share it with them and you can focus more on the analysis and asking; What's it telling me? Or how can I improve it? Which is the most exciting bit in my opinion.

I've also popped here for you a monthly process – again you can either aim to follow this yourself if you are doing your own bookkeeping and if not, you can check in with whoever does your bookkeeping so that you know what is and isn't being done monthly and pick up the reviewing bit again.

The 7-step monthly process you can follow to help you keep in sync with your business finances:

1. Get your bookkeeping up to date
- Process all sales
- Process all costs
- Process payroll and post it into your software

2. Reconcile your bank

3. Review Debtors – people who owe you money
- Are they correct?
- Chase them up.

4. Review Creditors – people who you owe money too
- Are they correct?
- Remember to consider them for cashflow if you need to make the payment
5. Review your P&L

This point is to see if everything looks to be in place – is there a bill missing? Is there anything obvious that doesn't look, correct?

6. Review your balance sheet
- This is the most difficult bit to understand. So, for now have a look through and see if you recognise what is showing on there.

7. Track KPI's / Metrics

My final few thoughts

People think there's a black art to mastering your finances but when you peel back all the noise, the truth is, you either need to get more money in or less needs to go out. If you keep this in mind it will help to "ground" you.

However, you manage your diary – on paper or in Outlook or Google, spend an hour putting in all the tax deadlines and payment dates. The reality is whilst things can change, the deadlines and payment dates haven't done so for a while and so this is an easy win in your quest for being on top of it.

Sometimes, I meet business owners who are almost afraid of their accountants. And so, I thought, it worth just saying here, - If you do work with an accountant or bookkeeper or when you are ready to take that step, make sure you are working with someone you feel comfortable with. And if you don't, please consider a change. I always feel it's a real shame when I hear this and let's face it there's enough of us out there for you to find one you gel with.

How can you really be getting the help and support you deserve if you don't feel quite right asking those questions or hearing what they have to say.

Don't forget there is so much free support out there. Even **HMRC** will be super helpful to you (if you can get hold of them!).

Most of all don't forget, you're doing this to live the life you dream of.
Be organised. Be determined.

Enjoy the ride.

Sandra Ten-Hoope

Sandra is the host of Stop Waffling, Start Selling - the weekly podcast in which we dive deep into the world of persuasive storytelling, effective sales techniques, and practical strategies to help you grow your business.

From Story to Sold

"The secret of getting ahead is getting started." Agatha Christie

Linkedin - sandratenhoope

FROM STORY TO SOLD

Once upon a time, there was this woman who wrote a book about three toxic relationships that she had endured and, luckily, survived. Upon publishing the book, she was approached by several entrepreneurs, who asked her if their business could benefit from them sharing their personal stories. And if so, how much would they need to tell? The author, who had been toying with switching careers for a while, saw a business opportunity. How can you best get the "Weave Your Story into Your Business to Make Impact and Sales" message across? A podcast, naturally! Episodes were recorded, edited by a wonderful agency, and broadcast. Wow, that sounds like quite the unshakeable success story. Doesn't it just?

BUT this woman did not dare to tell the world why she never properly promoted the book. Nor the podcast... This woman, the seemingly daring author and podcast host, was actually very shaken. And stirred. By a harsh reality, both in the personal and business realm, that kept her from speaking up. Kept her from... selling. Kept her from making an impact. And... kept her from writing. She had once written without anxiety, words flowing easily, never doubting what anyone would say once she posted about her life.

Yet, ever since the book's publication, words scared her. She thought that when approached to contribute to this book about Unshakeable Entrepreneurs, she could finally realign with her inner writer. Well... weeks of "maybe tomorrow" turned into months. Staring at a blank page, wondering if she'd ever be able to come up with anything half decent, she noticed her anxiety, guilt and shame growing. The deadline loomed. Old content was looked at and deemed not relevant anymore. A "sort of" paragraph outline emerged. Yet to colour it in, she lacked courage.

Then, just as she thought about giving up, she realised: how about if I tell the truth? Share my doubts? Dare to communicate that this chapter did not come about without a lot of shaking (and stirring up emotions and fears)?

Expose how even certified storytellers, strategists, and accomplished authors sometimes stumble and fall? Explain that unshakeable does not mean being set in stone - it means trusting that whatever happens, you will be able to rebalance. Once I, for you have already guessed, that woman, she is me, dared to start with the truth, all other parts fell into place. This is why, dear reader, I am here to show you how your story can genuinely aid your business. At times, being in business feels like surfing on a restless ocean. In the words of Grandmaster Flash: it makes me wonder how I keep from going under. But trust me, you are equipped with all you need to ride those waves - your story, truth, and voice. These will help you rebalance once you feel shaken, as they helped me write this chapter. Now, let's get started and bring you From Story to Sold!

Stories - a Sale as old as time

Without any introduction, I could have started this chapter with the outline I composed soon after receiving the invitation to participate in this project. The outline was fine: clear and concise steps to bring you From Story to Sold. However, would a general "how to" without a "why" have captured your attention, as I hope the introduction did? Would any "1-2-3" step plan have made a more substantial impact than the description of my challenges (the lack of promotion of my book and my podcast), my emotions (shame and guilt) and my light bulb moment: show the reader how, despite many hiccups, there is a way to get a story across? Ultimately, power is in the hiccups. Or better said, in the transformation!

We all encounter challenges in life and business. Some great, some small. Some joyous, some sad. And sometimes, even traumatic. When I finished my book (in which I was very open about three toxic relationships that, yes, left me with trauma), I was asked: Should we all be this open? Do we have to weave all our private stories into your business messaging? Is a Full Monty necessary to get a (business) message across? Because that may well be too big an ask...

Let me answer this quickly and clearly: NO. I want to let you know that there is never a need to show, aka tell all. If anybody knows the emotional price of sharing, it is me. Remember that your audience seeks a Tale of Transformation - a sense of recognition. Human beings have been telling each other stories since before history was recorded. To educate and to entertain.

To create a connection or bring each other comfort. But also to persuade and sell. Stories are like glue - the good ones stick. Evoke an emotion. Cut through noise, generate trust and "humanise" your offer. What every (potential) client wants to feel is: "She gets me". And how do they know? Because when you show your before and not just their after, they tap into your honesty. Which builds lasting relationships. All the "get rich within a week" bro-marketing, yes, that does get attention. But it will not take folks long to realise that the solution presented is not sustainable (if at all legitimate).

When packed up carefully, honesty does all the heavy (marketing) lifting for you! And, as I can imagine, you are now going through many memories in your mind that you are not ready to share, so take a breather! What you decide to share about your past, challenges, and transition must be honest. It still does not mean telling ALL - there is a difference! Lets break it down.

USP - YOU are the *magic sauce*

You will undoubtedly have worked with a coach or mentor who has helped you develop your "USP," your Unique Selling Point. Your USP is usually seen as a combination of all the skills and expertise you bring to the business table and your service's or product's magical features, which is not a wrong approach. Yet, from my experience and those I had the pleasure of aiding with weaving their personal story into their business, it all starts with the U, spelt as "YOU." Whatever your service or product is, others will also offer it. Nobody is cooking up the magic sauce that only you can bring to your offer(s). What makes you irresistible to your clients is often hidden in plain sight: your life experiences, worldview, and quirks. None of which seemed of value to you, but trust me, these bring the flavour that makes your clients' mouths water and ask for extras. Yes, also those ingredients from your life-pantry that you deem too spicy! If you wonder what those are, do this mini-exercise: write down three things you thought you had to hide in business. Now, flip them and add them to your spice cabinet.

Could you allow me to start?

1. Within days after finishing my book, Do not Try Him at Home, I realised that my then-partner was as much a toxic HIM as the three featured in the book. I instantly stopped promoting my book, as I was ashamed of the fake "happy ending" After a wee few years of healing, I now utilise the tale of the additional HIM, who had me captured through my son who loved him so much, as an extra "red flag" that may help others.

2. Even though I have been around in the online world for ages, I have not fully transitioned from working in corporate to an online business. Oh dear, with a podcast named Stop Waffling Start Selling, did I sufficiently "walk the sales-walk? Well, yes. I may not be a full-time podcast host, but I have a full commitment to help others transition from being anxious about sharing their stories to seeing them blossom and easily make sales.

3. I come across as an extrovert. I record podcasts and have appeared in many Facebook Lives and internet shows. Easy peasy, right? Wrong. In reality, I am an ambivert. As a young girl, I was extremely shy. Introvert was my middle name. I never sought the limelight. Loved staying indoors and reading books. And that little girl is still with me. Before every "outgoing", I feel like "no, I cannot do it" - this book being an example! Realising that I am an "ambivert, " once a challenge arises, I now take a few deep breaths, call a friend and remember all I have already overcome. That makes that Insta post, interview, video, etc., much less scary.

Back to that magic USP sauce. Now that you have identified your "flips," how much should you add to "who is the chef"? Like with any good spicy dish, start slowly. Start with one flip, one story, one spice. Add more once you feel comfortable doing so. Like with real-life cooking, it takes practice. You will sometimes feel like the flavour is a bit off. Then, take a spice, aka step back or forward. Always remember: you are the chef. You decide!

A Love Letter to your clients

That magic sauce is served over a magnificent offer, the one in which you take your clients from their challenge to the solution, and beyond!

You could simply state, "Buy my product, which will change your life." And no doubt, it will. But clients crave for you to show them the journey. Show them how working with you will make them feel. How would they benefit from it, in ways they could not imagine?

Essentially, your messaging is a Love Letter to your clients. If you were to write to your lover, would you just tell him/her about his/her features (looks, character, behaviour, etc.)? Or would you go on and on about how they make you feel? How much has your life changed since you met them, like you never thought possible? Exactly!

In the Love Letter (a social media post, a video, a sales page, copy for your website or all of the above!), you show them you have been on a similar journey. That you, too, have faced the challenge that you now help them with. They will appreciate you taking them by the hand and guiding them through your story. The turning point (i.e. breakdown, breakthrough, bold move) that directed you towards the solution you are now offering. The hurdles you faced. Which could be people, situations, and limited beliefs - is that our old foe, "I am not good enough," knocking on the door? The joy when you chose you, stopped being silent, and started sharing your magic with the world. The ripple effect that it caused - you are NOW helping them! In a language that they can relate to. Write as you speak, and keep your energy up. The audience is starting to identify and trust that YOU will offer them the solution.

Benefits with ... Benefits!

You may have heard of "sell them what they want, give them what they need". But how? Well, could you be specific about what they will REALLY gain from working with you? What is the "benefit behind the benefit" that they will achieve? Uh, what is this behind, then, San? Let me show you!

Let's say you are a business strategist who offers advice on automated processes. What you know for sure is that clients who work with you will gain more time. You could just say it as is. But what does that mean? Time is an elusive concept. Does it mean finally being able to pick up the kids in time from school and go on fun outings? More time to spend working in (and not on) their business, with their clients, offering results? Now, those are ripple effects that speak to the imagination! So, be as clear as high-quality mineral water about what you are trying to help them with.

Be consistent in your messaging - once our lover starts to use a different tone, sounds weird on the phone, does not show up regularly, we begin to doubt them. The same applies to your audience. You decide the frequency, but make that once they tune in (daily, weekly, biweekly, monthly), you are there. And, in all you say and do, focus on the connection.

Make them feel seen and valued. It will make them value you and your offers in return!

Future-proofing through storytelling

If you have been navigating the world of online marketing and sales for a while, you will have seen trends, systems, and social media platforms come and go. We navigated all that to the best of our ability. No, I am still not on TikTok. I lack basic social media creation skills (Reels? Is that a new chocolate treat?). Have not looked at even one of my many websites for too long. But I do know about storytelling, in many shapes and forms. And, I have become comfortable sharing many aspects (yet, never all) of my personal story. Which, in essence, makes my business future-proof.

My story, your story, our stories, make us unshakable. They evolve, as we do. We add spices to our magic sauce - everybody knows that flavours intensify over time. If all the social media platforms and/or economic systems ever fail us, we can still speak to each other. Connections can be made everywhere - online and offline. We will always be able to come together, tell our tales, share our stories, build trust in each other and offer our services.

Stories remain the glue that sticks us all together for better and worse. Trust in your story. Dare to share, as much or as little as you feel comfortable with. Your story is never a detour from your business.

It IS your business. *And you too shall go from Story to Sold!*

Anna Payne

Sales Strategy, Psychology Of Sales, Business Growth

How To Be The Best Seller In Your Industry: The Psychology Of Sales & Success In An Increasingly Sophisticated And Competitive Market

To every entrepreneur who has had the courage to start, been brave enough to take that leap into the unknown, and get out there and try to make the world a better place through their work. I want you to succeed, beyond your wildest dreams. This is for you...

Instagram - @annapaynesales

HOW TO BE THE BEST SELLER IN YOUR INDUSTRY

Welcome to the Sales Revolution

Today's buyers are more discerning than ever. They have more choice, shorter attention spans, and they require more trust, value, nurturing and risk reversal than ever before. They are also more informed, more selective, and more value-driven than ever. They do their research. They compare. They take their time, with longer buying cycles than ever before.

Buyers today:

* Take longer to make purchasing decisions and need multiple trust touchpoints before committing.
* Want specificity, expertise, and tailored solutions and tend to be more sceptical of generic offers.
* Invest in results and need to see the value clearly before buying.
* Buy from people they trust.

They may hate being 'sold' to, but when the conditions are right, they do still love to buy. Our job as business owners, entrepreneurs and leaders is to evolve, to meet these needs. Sales isn't necessarily harder, it's just different. But for those who haven't adapted yet, it can feel harder than ever.

Successful selling today is about understanding the psychology of why people buy (or don't), and creating an offer so compelling, and a sales experience so customer-centric that they genuinely want to become clients.

It's about helping people feel seen, understood, supported and connected. That's what today's buyer wants. That's what they're waiting for. And that's where your opportunity lies.

This is the sales revolution.

It's a shift from focusing on fast conversions to long-term connections. From the energy of trying to convince people to recognising their natural buying process and aligning with it. From chasing sales to instead becoming someone your dream clients seek out, trust, and want to buy from.

The Sales Revolution is here. Are you ready?

Let's get started…

Introduction

Sales can often feel like one of the most daunting parts of running a business. Too many entrepreneurs worry about coming across as pushy or feel awkward talking about money. They tell me they are no good at sales. In fact they find sales embarrassing or distasteful; Something to be ashamed of.

* *What if people don't like them?*
* *What if people think they're pushy?*
* *What if no one wants to buy what they're offering?*
* *What if, what if, what if…*

The main function of a business is to sell and deliver its products or services. Your very survival as a business depends on your ability to do this, so this distaste for sales and this getting hung up in the 'what ifs', even at a subconscious level can be a little… challenging, to say the least.

Fear around sales holds so many people back in business and in life. It limits their income, impact, and potential. And it means the people who need their help may never find them.

Please know that making sales doesn't have to feel awkward or pushy. It should actually feel incredible, exciting and empowering, for you AND your clients. Making sales is all about helping people, and being able to articulate how you do that in such a way that the right people can make an easy, confident decision that they want to buy what you are offering.

- Sales should be about attracting clients; becoming magnetic to them, not learning how to push, persuade or force them.
- It's about creating offers that are compelling because they truly answer the wants and needs of your target clients. And positioning them in such a way that they become irresistible
- Then delivering such value, with integrity and excellence that your clients will buy time and time again, and they will also refer others to you and give you fabulous reviews to leverage in your marketing.

I wrote a book *Everything You've been Taught About Sales Is Wrong (*Probably)* to debunk some of the dated, off-putting and downright sleazy sales methods that are out there and that fill most normal entrepreneurs with horror. In that book I teach my simple five step VALUE framework to help entrepreneurs with exactly what to do, in what order to help them make more sales in a way that feels really good for them, and for their clients. If you haven't read that book, go and grab a copy on Amazon, it covers the foundation of sales. Here, in this wonderful collaboration book, I'm building on those sales foundations, with deeper exploration of the psychology of sales and success, a subject that endlessly fascinates me.

When you understand the psychology behind why people buy, (or why they don't!) and you use this to build the right sales strategy, and take consistent action, you will thrive. This is when business feels easy, exciting and everything is infinitely possible.

We'll explore the psychology of becoming a best-selling business in today's market, and I'll walk you through key principles that help you understand what drives buying decisions. We'll talk about trust and connection. About long-term client relationships and client lifetime value. About creating sales systems that feel good for everyone involved.

And most importantly, I'll show you how to sell in a way that feels natural, aligned, and powerful, because when you do that, sales becomes easier, more enjoyable, and far more effective. Business gets easy. Success feels like it's inevitably yours.

It's necessary to know the psychology of your clients, but I believe it's equally important to understand your own psychology and how that impacts your success as an entrepreneur. What drives you? What are you great at? How do you leverage your strengths? What do you really want? Where do you hold back or limit yourself? And how do you show up with consistency, positivity, resilience and the commitment to do the hard things?

If you're ready for a better way to sell, a way that's rooted in trust, integrity, and human behaviour. That's exactly what this chapter is about. I hope you love reading this chapter as much as I've enjoyed writing it, and I hope you feel both inspired and empowered to go out and try new things.

Section 1: The Foundation of Trust

Why People Buy

Sales is really about solving problems. People buy because they want to overcome a challenge, achieve a goal, or meet a need, and they believe your offer might help them do it. To buy, your audience needs two things:

1. To connect your offer with their need or desire.
2. To trust that you can deliver the result you promise.

People need to know you exist, like you enough to pay attention and trust you to deliver on your promises. Trust is created through consistent actions, clear communication, authenticity and unshakable alignment between your actions, values, and promises.

Here's how you strengthen trust with your audience:

- **Be consistent:** Show up regularly in your marketing and stay consistent with your message about who you are, what you do, and how you help people. Trust builds when you're genuine, reliable and familiar.

- **Be good:** Deliver what you promise. Every time. In fact, aim to under-promise and over-deliver. When you get it wrong, hold your hands up, take responsibility and try to make it right.

- **Be human:** Share your story, share your values, show your personality and your quirks. Let the essence of who you truly are shine through in your content and conversations. People connect with people, not faceless businesses. And perfectly imperfect authenticity and vulnerability will always connect more than fake perfection.

To make this practical and repeatable, I developed a simple framework: The Trust Cycle. It outlines how trust builds naturally across three key stages of the buyer journey. This cycle shows how trust begins with connection, deepens through engagement and credibility, and naturally leads to conversion. When done well, it helps you make repeat sales. It supports retention, referrals, and long-term client value.

Stage 1: Connection and Engagement

This is where the relationship begins. Make that all-important first impression, then build on it consistently. Your goal at this stage is to create connection and interest.

How to create connection and engagement:

- Be clear and direct about who you help and how you help them.
- Show up where your audience is and offer value upfront (a free resource, a helpful insight, or an engaging conversation)
- Collaborate with people your audience already trusts.
- Create conversations, respond to questions, share stories, and engage with intention.
- Help them see progress or small wins quickly.

Stage 2: Credibility

Once there's connection, credibility reinforces it. This is where you become the expert they trust to deliver.

Make a Promise > Keep the Promise > Repeat.

This should be a continuous loop. Trust grows every time you show up, deliver value, and exceed expectations, whether on a micro or macro level and whether in your free content or your paid services. Each micro loop creates more trust, enabling you to earn more credibility and make easier, more aligned conversions.

How to build trust through credibility:

- Share testimonials, case studies, and client success stories. Let your results speak for themselves.
- Talk about your process, frameworks, and expertise. Show up as the confident expert and leader you are.
- Be honest about what you can and can't do. Never over-promise and under-deliver.

Stage 3: Conversion

Conversion is the natural next step once trust and credibility have been built. Make your offer clearly. Help your audience see what's included, how it works, and how it will help them achieve their goals. Ask for the sale. Acknowledge and address hesitations with empathy and clarity. Then, once the sale is made, follow through by delivering with excellence.

Trust-Building Content

Different people in your audience will be at different stages of the Trust Cycle. That's why your content on social media, in your emails, and in your conversations needs to do different jobs. Some content should connect. Some should build credibility. Some should invite conversion. Cycle through all three regularly to keep building trust with everyone in your audience. This is how you create a consistent, predictable sales system that works without relying on pushing, persuading, or pressure.

Section 2: Understanding Buying Triggers

Trust is one foundational piece of your success, but trust alone doesn't necessarily close sales and fill your inbox with payment emails. Let's go deeper. Behind every buying decision is an emotional and intellectual journey, where your prospective buyers will experience a mix of feelings and thoughts, often in quite quick succession, that either move them closer to a yes or quietly push them away.

When we understand what this looks like, we can of course optimise that journey to make sure we move them towards a positive buying decision.

Not every buyer is the same. Some will buy quickly based on emotion. Others may feel emotionally connected but need to logically justify the decision. And some just won't move unless they have a compelling reason to act now. Understanding these different decision drivers means you can speak to all types of buyers and help more of them move towards a sale.

The Role of Emotion

While most people like to think they make logical buying decisions, research shows that 95% of all purchases are driven by emotion. Logic plays a role. It typically is used to justify the decision to buy, but emotions are what capture attention, spark desire, and create the motivation to buy.

So, understand the emotional journey your clients go on and how they feel before, during and after they buy from you. Talk about it in your marketing.

Consider, what emotions do they need to feel to make a positive buying decision? Trust? Safety? Hope? Aspiration? Excitement? What less positive emotions might they also be feeling? Fear?

Distrust? Self doubt? FOMO? Referencing emotions can connect with your audience on a deeper level and make it easier for them to say "yes" to your offer.

Here are a few simple ways to use emotions practically in your messaging:

- Highlight the transformation your offer provides and how that transformation feels.
- Acknowledge pain points to show you understand their struggles. Pair this with future-pacing positive emotions and with reassurance that your solution works.
- Showcase social proof to reduce decision-making anxiety.

Emotional connection doesn't always have to come from someone else's story, often your own journey is one of your most powerful and compelling sales tools. If you've experienced the same journey, transformation, challenges, struggles, desires, or decisions your ideal clients are navigating right now, sharing that openly builds immediate trust. You become relatable, credible, and real.

I share and celebrate my wins with my audience, but I also share my challenges, my doubts and my lessons very openly. This can feel vulnerable, but I've learned that it always creates huge engagement, trust and connection. Recognising that my challenges can in fact be teachable moments for my audience, and further strengthen my relationship with them feels hugely empowering. I urge you to try the same.

The Role of Logic

Emotions drive the initial decision to buy, and emotional connection alone will create a proportion of sales conversions, from your emotionally driven buyers, who tend to buy more impulsively. But beyond these buyers, there are many more logically minded buyers, who will notice their emotional desire to buy then immediately seek clarification on the logical points (like

ROI, clear deliverables, and specific outcomes) before making their final buying decision.

For a significant proportion of buyers, the logical detail oriented part of their brain kicks in to gear, looking to 'sign-off' on the buying decision with questions like *what, who, when, how, where, is it any good, who is this person, are there reviews, is there a guarantee, will it work for me, what do I do next etc., etc.*

If this logical information isn't easily available, (on your website/sales page/reviews/FAQ's etc.) you will very quickly lose these buyers.

The Role of Urgency

Urgency is the final buying trigger. But it only works once trust and emotional connection are already in place. Urgency alone just sounds like an annoying noise that you try to ignore.
Authentic scarcity, fear of missing out (**FOMO**) and urgency are powerful motivators that leverage people's natural (and primal) desire to be included, to get ahead, to survive and thrive.

Scarcity makes your offer feel more valuable because it signals exclusivity or limited availability, while urgency encourages immediate action. Use these motivators ethically and effectively by:

- Offering time-sensitive bonuses to reward fast action. For example, "Sign up by Friday and get a free one-to-one session."
- Limiting availability. For example, "Only 10 spaces available."
- Specific cut off dates.
- Pricing urgency.

*****A Word of Caution

Scarcity and urgency can be powerful, **but they must be authentic, truthful, and used sparingly.** Overuse or fake scarcity will in a moment make your audience sceptical and erode all of your hard-earned trust, turning your marketing into meaningless noise.

Instead, focus on creating genuine reasons for urgency, like a limited cohort size, an expiring bonus, or a real deadline. And explain the reason for the urgency.

When scarcity and urgency are used ethically, they help people make decisions and take action that benefits them.

Key Takeaway 1: Use Emotion, Logic and Urgency to drive buying decisions, but use them in that order. Leading with urgency is just seen as noise. Leading with logic is boring…. Lead with emotion (that's your hook) then back it up with logic and urgency.

Key Takeaway 2: Remember, your audience isn't one-size-fits-all. Some are driven by emotion, some by logic, and some by urgency. Speak to them all.

Section 3: Principles of Persuasion

Selling well means understanding human behaviour. By learning how to ethically use and apply proven psychological principles, you can better serve your prospective clients.

Dr Robert Cialdini's six principles of persuasion, outlined in his book *Influence: The Psychology of Persuasion*, are foundational to understanding how to ethically influence others and inspire action.

Let's explore how you can use these insights to connect with your audience and build long-lasting relationships.

1. Reciprocity

People feel obligated to return favours or concessions. If someone does something for you, you naturally want to repay them in some way.

Application: Look for opportunities to give before you ask. This could be a free resource, helpful insight, or even a small favour that creates a sense of goodwill.

2. Commitment and Consistency

Once people commit to something, verbally or in writing, they are more likely to follow through with it. People strive for consistency in their commitments and beliefs.

Application: Once someone buys from you, they're more likely to buy again, as long as the experience is positive. Encourage small initial commitments which can naturally build toward a bigger yes.

3. Social Proof

People look to the behaviour and actions of others to determine their own. We are more likely to do something if we see others doing it, especially if those others are people we recognise as similar to us or are people we admire/aspire to be like.

Application: Use testimonials, reviews, case studies, and endorsements from trusted voices to show others have had a positive experience with you. If possible, highlight stories from people your audience relates to or aspires to be like.

4. Authority

People tend to respect and follow the lead of legitimate experts and authority figures.

Application: Build authority by sharing your credentials, frameworks, media features, and expert opinions. Speak confidently about your subject. Share opinions and commit to thought leadership. Publish articles, write a book, or seek out speaking opportunities that position you as a leader in your space.

5. Liking

People are more likely to be persuaded by others whom they like or have a positive association with.

Application: Build rapport and positive relationships with your audience. Highlight similarities, show your personality, be relatable and human. Make people feel good when they interact with you. People won't always remember what you said or did, but they will always remember how you made them feel.

6. Scarcity

Items and opportunities become more desirable when their availability is limited. People are motivated by the thought of losing access to something.

Application: Emphasise what's unique about your offer and why now is the right time. Use real, honest urgency like limited-time bonuses, capped enrolment, or fast-action rewards to motivate buyers without pressure.

Practical Example

These principles work most powerfully when used together. Here's what that can look like in practice:

- Imagine you're launching a new course. You've built strong relationships with your audience over time (liking). You offer a free, valuable resource beforehand (reciprocity), share testimonials from happy clients (social proof), and set a clear deadline for enrolment (scarcity).

- Now you've created an environment where potential buyers feel connected, reassured, and motivated to act. This is the power of combining psychological principles with ethical sales techniques.

Audience Benefits

These principles tap into universal human behaviours and instincts, making them effective in any sales context. They work because they help give your audience the clarity, confidence, and reassurance they need to say yes. And to feel good about it.

When you understand and apply these principles, you not only make your sales process smoother but also create a better experience for your clients. They feel more connected to you, more certain about their decision, and more excited about the transformation your offer provides.

Section 4: Messaging

To connect deeply with your potential customers, you need to understand how they think, feel, and talk about their challenges and desires. When your language/content and messaging mirrors their own language, rather than industry speak, it creates an immediate sense of recognition, familiarity, trust and alignment.

Let's take that a step further. People are naturally drawn to those who can articulate their challenges, needs, and aspirations even better than they can. When you reflect your audience's thoughts and feelings in your messaging, when what you say creates a light bulb moment for them, when they feel that yes, this is exactly where they are right now, they see you as someone who understands them deeply and as the right person to help.

Once, at a very specific (hard) stage of scaling my business, someone talked to me about successful entrepreneurs who are so used to doing everything themselves, they become the bottle necks in their business. At that time, that one statement really hit me and made me see exactly what I needed.

Another example; I talk about when people have resistance to sales, they distract themselves and keep busy with ABS (anything but sales) and give some examples of what that looks like. It's very light-hearted and it's gentle, but it's always a section that resonates and sticks in people's minds as they feel seen and understood. They often cite it as the moment they realised they needed to change.
Naming these specific emotions, scenarios, or stuck points, the ones they might not have fully articulated yet, creates instant interest and trust.

How to Understand Your Clients

- Listen to Their Words: Pay attention to the exact phrases your audience uses in conversations, on social media, or in feedback forms. These are the words and phrases to weave into your messaging.

- Ask Questions: Use surveys, polls, or conversations to ask what they're struggling with and what outcomes they're hoping for.

- Research the Pain Points: Look for common themes in reviews, conversations, or even your competitors' testimonials to understand the challenges your audience faces.

How to Reflect This in Your Messaging

1. Focus on Outcomes: Highlight the very specific results they want to achieve.

2. Empathy First: Show them you understand their struggles and their aspirations before introducing your solution.

3. Tailor Your Stories: Share relatable examples or case studies that reflect their journey. Show them what's possible for someone just like them.

4. Highlight Transformation: Speak directly to the "before and after".

Practical Example

Imagine reading this in someone's post or email:

"You're brilliant at what you do. You've built something from scratch, figured out a hundred things no one ever taught you and you've been very successful. But somehow, it's stopped working so well, it feels hard. You've become the bottleneck. Everything still depends on you. You're holding the vision, doing the client work, managing the admin, and trying to keep the sales coming in… and it's exhausting. Deep down, you know it's time to do things differently, but you're not sure where to start."

Or this:

"You say you want more sales… but every time you sit down to do sales tasks, you tidy your Canva templates, rewrite your bio, or make one more tweak to your lead magnet. Anything but sales. Sound familiar?"

These kinds of messages stick because they name something people feel but haven't quite admitted to themselves yet. When you can do that through your messaging, your audience trusts that you understand them better than anyone else, and saying yes to your offer becomes the next obvious step.

Section 5: Make It Simple to Say Yes

One of the biggest barriers to buying is uncertainty either because something is unclear or b because there are just too many options. Uncertainty slows down any decision and introduces doubt. Your offer needs to be structured, clear, and aligned with what your ideal client truly wants.

The right offer, positioned in the right way, so as to be a really easy YES for the right person is critical to your success.

I developed my 8Ps Perfect Offer Framework to help clients develop or refine offers that are both compelling and clear. Use it to map out new offers, or test and refine existing offers you have.

1. PERSON - Who is your ideal client? The best offers speak directly to a specific person with a clear need. Who are you helping, and what do they truly want? Define their mindset, desires, and what drives them to seek a solution.

2. PROBLEM - What urgent, specific problem are they experiencing? Offers that sell solve a real, pressing problem - one your audience is actively seeking to fix. If your offer isn't solving a problem they deeply feel, it won't convert well.

3. PROMISE - What transformation or outcome do you deliver? The best offers are built around a clear, compelling promise. What is the end result you are offering? Your promise should be outcome-focused, not feature-driven and align with the aspirations of your PERSON.

4. PROCESS - How do you take them from where they are to where they want to be? Your method, framework, or approach? Explain your step-by-step approach in a simple way and make your offer feel tangible and real, and like a positive outcome is inevitable.

5. PROOF - How can you demonstrate credibility, results, and trust? Buyers need to believe that your offer will work for them. Use testimonials, case studies, social proof, personal success, and expertise to remove doubt and reinforce confidence.

6. PACKAGE - What deliverables are included in this offer? What is NOT included. Any bonuses or additional support? Any optional add-ons or upsells?

7. PRICING & PROFITABILITY - How do you price in a way that reflects value and feels aligned? Pricing should feel like a fair exchange for the transformation delivered to your client. Underpricing can create scepticism, while overpricing without positioning value can push buyers away.

8. POSITIONING - What makes your offer stand out, and why should people choose you? Your positioning is what sets your offer apart in a crowded market. Why is this offer different? Why should they buy from you instead of someone else?

The Big Mistakes That Kill Sales (And How To Fix Them)

1. Your offer is too broad > Niche down. Specificity sells. A broad offer feels vague and overwhelming.

2. You focus on features, not transformation > Buyers don't care about what's inside; they care about what they'll get from it.

3. You underprice your offer > Pricing too low can signal low value. Charge based on transformation, not time.
4. Your messaging isn't clear > If people don't instantly understand what you offer, they won't buy.

5. You don't give them a reason to buy now > Urgency and exclusivity increase conversions.

6. Your positioning isn't clear > Why should someone buy from you? Clearly articulate why your offer is different and why they should choose you. Your positioning should make your expertise, method, and value stand out so the decision to buy feels obvious.

Section 6: Personalisation, Hyper-Relevance & Risk Reversal

How to build trust, reduce friction, and make it easier for people to say yes.

Personalisation

Buyers want to feel that your solution is designed specifically for them. Personalisation is essential. That means speaking directly to a defined niche, tailoring your content to reflect their language and lived experience, and using examples and scenarios that resonate with their specific industry, role, or challenge. It may also mean segmenting your audience and creating distinct customer journeys, relevant to each segment. The more relevant your offer feels, the easier it is for someone to say yes.

Hyper-Relevance

Beyond personalisation, buyers are also experiencing a bigger picture. Hyper-relevance means connecting your message to what's happening in their world, personally, professionally, economically, and socially. Recognise what's happening in your buyer's world right now - industry shifts, economic pressure, cultural changes, moments of growth or uncertainty. Consider how you can capture the zeitgeist, or a particular movement or moment. When you can create this hyper-relevance, by connecting your offer and your brand to their experience, you move from just offering help, to being seen to offer the right help, at the right time.

One simple way to start to do this is to link your offer or messaging to real-world data. Referencing credible sources, industry research, reports, statistics, or trends builds trust with more analytical buyers and helps you position your offer as a serious solution. For example, you might reference survey findings, research, or even headlines that reflect what;s going on for your clients at that moment. This is an opportunity to cement your authority as an expert, a thought leader and to use data to support your proposition.

Risk Reversal

Buyers are more risk-aware than ever. They research, compare, and want to be sure they're making the right decision. Your role is to reduce that risk as much as you can, by offering as much practical reassurance as possible.

This includes pre-emptively addressing objections and risks in your content, and the way you structure your offers. It may also include guarantees, refund policies, payment plans, or free trials. It should also include social proof, reviews, case studies, testimonials, or evidence of results. These tools reduce buying anxiety, increase trust at each stage, and make it easier for someone on the fence to say yes.

Section 7: Sell with Integrity & Create Clients for Life

Selling with integrity creates a ripple effect of trust and goodwill. When clients feel respected and valued, they're more likely to share their positive experiences, expanding your reach and strengthening your brand. This relationship becomes the foundation for future growth, referrals, and meaningful impact in your clients' lives.

Selling with integrity means putting people first and focusing on service and value. Sales should feel like creating win-win opportunities for you and your clients. Doing this well will be your sales superpower.

Here's how to sell with integrity:

- Focus on service: Shift your mindset from "convincing" to "helping." Ask yourself, *"How can I best support this person?"* This approach naturally removes pressure and creates a more genuine connection.

- Be transparent: Communicate clearly what your offer includes, what it doesn't, and the results clients can realistically expect.

- Celebrate the transformation: Focus your messaging on the outcomes and impact your offer provides.

Tip: Write down three core values that guide your business. Before creating any sales message, ask yourself, "Does this align with these values?" And then consider how it can align even more with these values. How can you inject more of your personality, ethos and approach into the sales process? Consider whether you'd like to be sold to in this way if you were a prospective client? This ensures a great client experience where your values and your integrity shines through every interaction.

Delivering on Your Promise

Here's how to build lasting relationships post-sale:

1. Deliver an exceptional client experience: Go beyond the basics to make your clients feel supported and valued.

2. Check in with clients regularly: Don't assume they're satisfied; ask them. Address any challenges head on and seek to resolve them. Care about their success.

3. Commit to continual improvement and evolution of your service, your delivery and your customer experience. Embrace feedback and learning opportunities that allow you to do this.

4. Happy clients are your best advocates. Ask for testimonials or referrals when you know they're thrilled with your service.

5. Create opportunities for repeat business through additional offers or upsells that build on their success.

Tip: Create a plan that outlines specific ways you'll enhance client experience from onboarding to follow-up. This could include milestones to celebrate their progress, personalised check-ins, or perks for repeat clients.

Client Lifetime Value – Why Selling Once Isn't Enough

Too many business owners focus solely on lead generation. But sustainable, scalable sales, also means a strategy to turn one sale into many. Build trust. Deliver with excellence. Create systems that bring people back.

Increasing client retention by just 5% can boost profits by up to 95%, according to research. Why? Because when someone buys from you again, the cost to sell to them is lower, their spend is often higher, and they're more likely to refer others too.

Checklist: How to Build Long-Term Client Relationships

- Deliver on your promises consistently
- Follow up after purchase to check in, celebrate wins, and offer next-step support
- Build in opportunities for clients to buy again or upgrade their experience
- Stay in touch and keep front of mind between purchases
- Ask for feedback and act on it, showing clients their voice matters
- Recognise and reward loyalty (referrals, bonuses, access, or surprise gifts)
- Make working with you easy, enjoyable, and satisfying

Section 8: Positive Psychology and Entrepreneurial Mindset

Your Mindset Matters

Your mindset as a business owner is one of your most powerful tools. It's the foundation for how you show up, the decisions you make, and how you navigate the inevitable challenges of entrepreneurship.

The science of Positive Psychology gives us the tools to survive these challenges, and also to thrive because of them. Positive psychology focuses on what makes life meaningful, fulfilling, and successful. When applied to business, it emphasises traits like resilience and optimism, and concepts like meaning, purpose, strengths and self-belief, all of which are essential to succeeding in sales and building a business you love.

Here are some core concepts to consider:

- **Resilience:** Setbacks are an inevitable part of the entrepreneurial journey. Not every offer will land, not every prospective client will buy. Not every day will be good. But having resilience means that you have the ability to keep going, knowing that every "failure" is learning, every "no" brings you closer to a "yes" and each challenge makes you stronger.

- **Optimism:** A positive outlook isn't about ignoring reality or toxic positivity; it's about focusing on opportunities rather than obstacles. Stay open to possibilities, even when things don't go as planned and approach problems with curiosity and creativity instead of fear.

- **Self-belief:** Confidence isn't something you're born with, it's something you build. And confidence only happens when you first have the courage to do something without feeling confident. Courage is the foundation of confidence. Each small action you take, each small win you achieve, adds to your sense of self-belief.

- Your mindset is just as important as your strategy and your action. If you work at it, and practise self awareness, your mindset becomes a powerful tool for creating momentum in your business.

Strategies for a Strong Mindset

I'm delighted that my primary school age children are being taught mindset at school; For me, it was something I only started to learn about in my thirties! Wow, what a transformation, what possibility! Building and maintaining a positive mindset takes intentional effort, but it is so worth it, in every area of life, not just business. Here are some practical strategies to strengthen your entrepreneurial mindset:

1. Focus on Your Strengths

Instead of fixating on what you're not good at, lean into what you do well. Your natural talents and abilities are where you'll find the most joy and confidence. Whether it's connecting with people, solving problems, or creating innovative solutions, prioritise the tasks and projects that let you shine. Use your strengths and figure out how to leverage them to propel you towards your goals.

Tip: Write down three things you're naturally good at in your business. Then, find ways to do more of those things.

2. Celebrate Your Wins

Recognising your wins, celebrating them and practising gratitude is one of the simplest and most effective ways to shift your mindset. By focusing on what's working and what you're grateful for, you create a positive mental space that energises you to keep moving forward. Recognising your achievements also helps you recognise how far you've come, which can be incredibly motivating. And tells you exactly what is working in your business, so you can do more of it. I also love looking at setbacks, and things that haven't gone well through the lens of "what is great about this" and seeking the positive whether that's a lesson, a reflection or even just feeling good that I handled a very tricky situation well.

Tip: Start or end each day by writing down three things you're grateful for in your business. These could be big wins, small moments of progress, or even lessons learned from setbacks.

3. Adopt a Growth Mindset

A growth mindset is the belief that your abilities can be developed through effort and learning. It is key to viewing challenges as opportunities to improve, rather than roadblocks. Everything is learning and even if we 'fail' we simply go again, but this time with more information.

Tip: When faced with a challenge, ask "What can I learn from this?" or "How can I use this to grow?" Reframe obstacles as opportunities for growth and experimentation.

4. Visualise Success

Visualising success can improve your performance and motivation. When you take the time to imagine your goals clearly and in detail, you're more likely to stay focused and confident in pursuing them.

Tip: Spend up to five minutes a day visualising what success looks and feels like for you. Picture yourself confidently achieving your goals, and let that energy carry you through your day.

5. Surround Yourself with Positivity

The people you surround yourself with can have a huge impact on your mindset. Seek out mentors, peers, and communities that uplift and inspire you. Avoid spending too much time with people who drain your energy or doubt your potential.

Tip: Find a supportive community of like-minded entrepreneurs.

Key Takeaway: Your mindset is your greatest competitive advantage. When you focus on positivity, growth, and resilience, you'll not only achieve more in your business but also enjoy the journey so much more. Combining a strong mindset with consistent, meaningful action is your greatest route to success.

Final Advice: Go For The Wins AND Play The Long Game

Quick wins feel great, and quick wins in sales are relatively easy to make happen when you do the right things. But long term, sustainable and scalable success is so much more than a series of quick wins; it's about playing the long game. By focusing on trust, value, and relationships, you can build a business that feels good, delivers results, and grows sustainably over time.

All success is possible. For me, for you, for anyone who has the courage to dream big about what they want to do in the world, and the smarts and the consistency go out and make it happen. Let's get to work.

Be Part of the Sales Revolution

We've covered a lot in this chapter. You now know that successful selling is about deep knowing, understanding and connection with your prospective clients. This means understanding how people think, feel, and make decisions, and aligning your approach to match that.

We've looked at the six key principles of sales psychology. You've seen how reciprocity, trust, social proof, emotion, clarity, and value work together to inspire buying decisions. You've seen how to create content, messaging, and experiences that make your audience feel supported, understood, and ready to say yes.

We've also explored how long-term relationships are the true foundation of a sustainable, successful business. Selling once is great. Selling again and again to loyal clients who love working with you, refer others, and stay in your world, that's where real magic (and success) happens and that's when your business feels like a really beautiful special place to be.

And the best part? You don't need to become someone else to sell well. You don't need to use tactics that feel out of alignment. You can sell naturally, using your commitment to client results and connection, and showing up in a way that reflects your values, your strengths, and your personality. And when you do that, that's when selling starts to feel easy, exciting, even fun. (Yes, really!)

Buyers want to find solutions to their problems. They want to buy. They want to trust you and feel confident that you can genuinely help them. So build that trust, show up with value and consistency, and refine your process to make sales feel like a natural, almost inevitable next step rather than a hard sell.
This is the sales revolution: a movement away from outdated models and into a future where great businesses thrive by building trust, creating connection, and leading with integrity.

So here's my invitation to you: Take what you've learned here and use it. Review your sales process, tune into what your audience needs from you right now. Start applying psychology. Start making small shifts. Start showing up as someone who understands their audience deeply, including how people really buy, and who knows how to support them through that journey. You don't have to overhaul everything at once. Just begin. Take one step. And then another. Momentum builds quickly when you focus on the right things.

This is your time to lead.

Welcome to the Sales Revolution.

About Me

I'm Anna Payne, a sales expert and business growth strategist, entrepreneur, and author of the bestselling book Everything You've been Taught About Sales Is Wrong (*Probably). With more than 26 years of experience in sales, leadership, start-ups and entrepreneurship, I've helped thousands of business owners to make more sales in a way that feels good for them and their clients. My approach prioritises value, integrity, and long-term relationships. I believe business should feel fun and create ultimate freedom and fulfilment, whatever that looks like for you. For me that means spending time with my family, travelling, and of course dreaming big about the future. I'm making that success, impact and freedom a reality for me and on a mission to support anyone else who wants that too.

Ready to Take the Next Step?

If you found this chapter helpful, I have so many additional resources, tools, templates and trainings (both free and paid) to help you, whatever stage of business you are at, and whatever your next sales goal - visit www.anapayne.online/everything
And I'd love to connect with you on social media: drop me a message and let me know you've read this book, or pop me an email at
anna@annapayne.online and tell me your biggest takeaway.

Maria-Ines Fuenmayer

Conscious AI & Ethical Innovation. Pioneering the integration of AI in brand and creative ecosystems with a strong focus on ethics, inclusion, and human-centered design.

AI for the Rest of Us: Desmistifying AI

To my beautiful Mérida. Your arrival didn't just make me a mother; it cracked me open in the most beautiful and transformational way. You've helped me become the fullest, truest version of myself. You've shown me the meaning of resilience, and through your eyes, I've learned to imagine a future filled with more hope, more wonder, and more truth, for me, for you, for us.

Being your mom is the greatest privileged of my life.
Yours always, Mami.

@envisionedbrands

AI FOR THE REST OF US: DESMISTIFYING AI

Introduction

When my daughter Mérida was born, her arrival was anything but typical. Due to complications at birth, she had to be rushed off to receive life-saving care before I ever got to hold her. Today, I'm grateful that she's a thriving, inquisitive and empathetic little 4 year old.

The reason her story is relevant to this chapter, is what the yearning of not being able to hold her after her birth left in me and the subsequent chain of events that transpired and led me to where I am today.

Let's travel back in time to the year 2020, the world was in lockdown, and life as we knew it had come to a halt. Not only was the world completely different out there, but mine had flipped on its head as well.

I had become a mother. And yes, all the clichés came true.

In the quiet hours of feeding and rocking the baby to sleep, the only connection to the outside world being the internet, social media and well, my phone. I began to hear whispers of a new technology rising. Artificial intelligence.

I'm a geek at heart, always have been, so naturally this caught my attention. I kept visiting the dark corners of the internet and one day, decided to give it a try.

Following my 30 years as a photographer (10 of those as a personal brand photographer) my natural curiosity led me to try something called generative AI, (that's creation of text, images, music, or even video, using machine learning models.)

The first image I created was for a "Latin woman with big curly hair holding a baby on her chest, being surrounded by the universe" While this image is far from perfect, its abstract-ism is precisely what became the most cathartic moment in my life.

Personally, I realized how much I had yearned for that moment I never had, to hold my newborn baby and welcome her into the world. But, it also moved me tremendously. I realized right then and there, the potential this new technology could have.

Remember, this was the time when people couldn't travel, couldn't be together and while other photographers had come up with creative ways to continue to create remote photoshoots, I thought to myself. This goes even beyond a 'remote photoshoot' this wouldn't even require clients to be in the room or on a call even.

This wasn't just about creative innovation, this was disruption.

And even if I couldn't name it then, I felt it: AI was different, I sensed its potential. Not just to disrupt the way we work, but to democratize who gets to lead, create, and be seen.

After a few years of using it I can tell you now. AI is NOT a trend, it is not just a tool, but a turning point. It's an equalizing force like we hadn't experienced in a generation, maybe ever.

The internet gave us access. AI gives us agency.

In this chapter I want to inspire you to learn, understand, and maybe make you curious about AI, its potential, implication and most importantly, I want to empower you to understand it as a partner, a force to amplify not only your business, but your life in general.

I will cover topics related to the understandable doubts, caution and even fears around AI. Because I won't be coming from a 'let's embrace it without questioning it' perspective. But I will also help you see the other side of the coin and how disengaging from it is also not an option in this paradigm shifting revolution we are in. Because if you take nothing else from this chapter, take this:

AI is not changing our world. It already DID.

I want you to leave this chapter feeling curious, and excited about trying AI. But I will also show you how to do so in a strategic way, so you are not just collecting AI tools as shining objects but you are doing so from a place of knowledge and discernment to help you start thinking as a disruptor in your industry rather than a trend follower.

Before we dive in a few basic terms we will be using in this chapter:

• **LLM (Large Language Model):** AI trained on massive amounts of text to understand and generate human-like language. Think: ChatGPT, Claude, Gemini, etc.

• **Generative AI:** AI that creates new content — text, images, video, audio — based on learned patterns, allowing creators to scale faster and smarter. • Custom GPT's: Specialized versions of language models tailored to your business, brand tone, or industry-specific tasks — like your personal AI assistant.

• **Agentic AI:** AI systems that can take actions, make decisions, and operate autonomously toward goals — e.g., scheduling posts or tagging content without prompting.

- **Automation:** Using AI to handle repetitive, manual tasks like client onboarding, follow-up emails, or financial summaries — freeing you to focus on strategy and creativity.

- **Low-Code / No-Code Tools:** Platforms that let you build powerful AI workflows or apps with minimal (or no) coding — democratizing access to innovation. • **Bias in AI:** The inherited prejudices from biased data — a critical concern when building ethical, inclusive, and representative brand assets. • **AI Ethics:** Guidelines ensuring that AI is used fairly, transparently, and responsibly — especially vital in branding, hiring, and client interaction. • **AI Safety:** Practices that ensure your AI tools behave predictably and avoid unintended consequences or harmful outputs.

- **Data Privacy:** Ensuring that personal or client data is handled securely and in compliance with regulations like GDPR or CCPA — especially relevant for CRM, transcriptions, or email automations.

Part 1: Understanding the AI Revolution

Unless you have been living off the grid, you have not been able to avoid AI. It's on the news, on the radio, your phone, your feed, embedded in every single app and software that we use for our businesses. It can be overwhelming and fascinating all at the same time.

But here's the nuance that I rarely see reflected in mainstream narratives: to truly understand the magnitude of what's unfolding, we need to get clear on something first.

Yes, AI is a wave of disruption, yes, it is fundamentally different from the internet, social media, or even mobile technology before it. What AI is NOT, is a trend. AI is not the future. It already

IS here. And, it's here, to stay, and we need to understand it whether we are ready or not.

Before we get into some specifics, I wanted to share some of my unique perspectives on how I've learned to view, interact with, and chosen to impact its development.

Concerns: I want you to read these words from the premise that while I'm an optimist when it comes to AI, I recognize and in fact, I advocate and encourage our engagement with it with the understanding of its biases, ethical, and security concerns and considerations.

Impact: While I will be covering mostly AI's impact on business, know this. AI is permeating everything in our lives, and while it will take time for even our nervous system to come to grips with it, it's calling us to also be open minded in the understanding that it not only requires us to do business differently, but to BE different. And this is not necessarily a bad thing, as a business partner AI has the potential to free, streamline and optimize our business like we've never even fathomed before. The question I want to pose here is. What would you (truly) do with this newfound freedom? Work more? Or actually take time to BE. Wasn't that why we started our business in the first place?

Knowledge: AI is not only a new(ish) realm but is evolving faster than even we the experts can keep up with. By no means is this chapter meant to be an all encompassing, all inclusive or exhaustive educational resource on AI. In fact, I caution you to not feel, after reading this chapter, that you have to go off and become an AI expert yourself. I always insist that brand alignment and your zone of genius trumps AI. You don't need to have an AI offer or become an AI expert to take advantage of this AI innovation.

Potential: Finally, I want you to read these words with your heart open, and the excitement of a 4 year old, because the future is wide open and it's exciting and WE get to shape it. For the first time in history, access to tools and resources are no longer the exclusive domain of large corporations and big budgets. This is not just innovation, this is power shaking, paradigm shifting in the making. And that means opportunities for each and every one of us.

Part 2: What AI actually is (and isn't)

Most of the AI you'll interact with today (ChatGPT, Claude, Gemini, and image generators like Midjourney or DALL·E) is powered by something called a Large Language Model (LLM). In simple terms, these "models" are trained on massive amounts of text and data pulled from the internet. That includes books, articles, websites, forums, etc. All of which carry the biases of the people and cultures that created them in the first place.

This matters tremendously.

When we think about it, most of that data was created in the Global North (primarily English-speaking, Western, and white-dominant contexts). Which means the outputs AI gives us are not neutral. They are shaped by existing worldviews, assumptions, and exclusions.

This is why our role as a conscious creator and entrepreneur is critical. We must engage with AI not passively, but intentionally. And understand that we also carry our own biases. That means we need to ask better questions, and use our own discernment when we receive outputs, especially in areas like identity, ethics, safety, and representation.

On the other hand, it's important also to understand that LLMs are just one part of this evolving space. Most of what we call "AI" today (writing tools, image generators, video summarizers) falls under the umbrella of generative AI. These are the tools most of us will interact with regularly, and this is where I will focus most of our time here.

But know this, that innovation is quickly moving toward the next phase: agentic AI. These are systems that don't just generate, they take action. Think AI agents that schedule your calendar, tag your content, manage your inbox, or even make business decisions on your behalf.

I'm going to show you how to use AI as a strategic partner and not only a glorified virtual assistant. Because, we are not in a 'content revolution' we're entering an intelligence orchestration era. An era where content volume has made content a commodity adding to the noise and where personal branding and authenticity has become and will increasingly be the single most valuable currency you own.

Part 3: Safety, Security and Ethical Considerations

While AI offers incredible potential, it also introduces new considerations around ethics, security, and intellectual property. Let's address these practically:

Protecting Your Intellectual Property

Your creative work and business methodologies are valuable assets. Here's how to use AI while protecting your IP:

- **Practice Strategic Feeding:** Never upload your entire proprietary framework, course curriculum, or business methodology into a public AI tool. Instead, break it into conceptual chunks, removing your unique terminology and process steps that make your IP distinctive.

Practical Example: A coach I worked with needed AI assistance with her signature program but was concerned about IP theft. We created "shadow versions" of her frameworks, teaching the AI the structure and purpose without the exact proprietary language and sequencing. The AI could still help generate aligned content without exposing her complete methodology.

- **Use Dedicated Instances:** When possible, use custom AI instances (like a Custom GPT) that aren't training on your inputs rather than public versions. Many enterprise solutions now offer this feature.

- **Consider NDAs and Terms:** If working with AI developers or consultants, use NDAs that specifically cover AI training data and generated outputs. The legal landscape is evolving rapidly here.

Data Security and Privacy

- **Client Confidentiality:** Never upload identifiable client information to public AI tools. Anonymize case studies, remove names, and alter identifying details before using them for AI training or analysis.

Practical Example: A therapist wanted to use AI to identify patterns in client sessions. Instead of uploading raw transcripts, she created composite profiles and generalized scenarios that captured the essence without exposing confidential information. This maintained ethical boundaries while still leveraging AI's analytical power.

- **Audit Data Flows:** Regularly review which platforms have access to your business data. Create clear policies about which information can be used with which AI tools.

- **Local-First Options:** Where possible, explore AI tools that process data locally on your device rather than sending it to external servers. This is a rapidly growing category of tools.

Ethical AI Usage

- **Transparency with Clients:** Be clear about where and how you're using AI in your business, especially in client-facing contexts. This builds trust and sets appropriate expectations.

Practical Example: A writer updated her services page to include a "My Relationship with AI" section that outlined exactly how she used AI (research assistance, editing suggestions) and what remained 100% human-created (core concepts, voice, final decisions). This transparency actually increased her bookings, as clients appreciated her thoughtful approach.

- **Content Verification:** Establish a verification process for AI-generated content. AI can "hallucinate" or present false information confidently. Always fact-check important claims, especially in specialized fields.

- **Representation Matters:** Actively counteract AI's inherent biases, especially around gender, race, and cultural perspectives. Review outputs with an inclusive lens and provide specific guidance for diverse representation.

Balance and Boundaries

- **Define No-AI Zones:** Identify which aspects of your work must remain purely human. Perhaps it's the heart of your coaching calls, the conceptual foundation of your art, or the personal touch in client communications.

Practical Example: A photographer who uses AI for many business operations established a "sacred circle" around her creative direction and emotional connection with clients. She created a simple decision tree: "If it's about artistic vision or human connection, it stays 100% human. If it's about efficiency and consistency, AI can assist."

- **Regular AI-Free Time:** Schedule regular periods of working without AI assistance to maintain your own creative muscles and critical thinking. The best AI users are those who don't become dependent on it.

Remember: Ethical AI use isn't about perfectionism, it's about intentional, informed choices. The thoughtfulness you bring to these considerations is exactly what will set you apart in an AI-saturated marketplace.

Part 4: Reframing "how" to use AI

Now that we've established that you're not going to be using AI like the rest, let's get to it, shall we?

Yes, you already know you can use AI to help you write: emails, captions, landing pages, and all the usual suspects. But we're going beyond the basics.

From this point on, you're going to think with discernment and strategy. You're going to resist the urge to collect one more

"ChatGPT prompt" thinking it'll magically unlock your next level.

Because here's the truth: Prompts alone won't get you farther than where you are right now.
What will?

Creative, outside-the-box, vision-aligned uses of AI that go beyond task automation. That's where the magic and the true leverage lives.

So let's explore some unexpected, innovative, and deeply strategic ways AI can support not just what you do, but who you're becoming as a leader, brand, and business.

Brand Memory

Most of us forget how much gold we've already created. AI can help you codify your legacy (past content, client stories, voice notes, even product ideas) and organize them into usable, living assets.

Practical Example: Create a "Living Vault" using AI to catalog and make searchable everything you've ever created. Upload transcripts from your best podcast episodes to Claude or ChatGPT, then ask it to extract your unique frameworks, client stories, and analogies. I did it for myself and was able to codify 700+ pieces of content and have created new content, new frameworks with all the gold already in existence.

Tip: Use ChatGPT or Claude Project feature to keep all the background information handy for future use.

Thought Partner (Not a Copy Machine)

Use AI to clarify, challenge, and expand your thinking. Treat it like a collaborator that helps you explore new angles, test strategic ideas, and refine your positioning, not just spit out posts.

Practical Example: When updating my AI photography packages last year, I felt stuck in the same pricing model everyone uses. Instead of asking AI to "help me price my photography services," I prompted: "Challenge my assumptions about photography pricing models. What approaches exist outside the standard hourly/package structure that could better reflect value?" The AI suggested things I hadn't thought of before. Now, this does not mean you have to agree and implement, merely that it opens you up to things you may not have previously thought of.

Tip: Use custom instructions and provide it with very specific instructions on how you want it to answer you. Ask it to be critical and not a cheerleader (AI is trained to basically be a people pleaser by default). Also in the paid version you can use Deep Research for better results. Perplexity is also a very good tool for this.

Consistency Engine

You don't need to create more, you need to reuse smarter. AI can track, repurpose, and translate your ideas across platforms while maintaining your tone and values. This helps build a cohesive presence without more hustle.

Practical Example: For a product launch, I created one comprehensive brief describing my offer, ideal client, and positioning. I fed this to AI and requested it generate 30 days of content—not as isolated posts, but as an interconnected narrative arc that built anticipation. Each piece reinforced my core message while addressing different objections and highlighting different benefits.

Tip: Look for your high performing and most engaging content and ask it to turn them into different assets. A podcast into blog posts, IG captions, carousels etc.

Systems Integrator

This is an advanced one but it's good to keep in mind and start helping you think of 'all' the possibilities. Your genius gets stuck when your systems don't talk to each other. AI, especially when paired with automation tools, can stitch together the parts of your business (content > operations > data > delivery) so you can work from clarity, not chaos.

Practical Example: A wedding photographer I mentored was spending 20+ hours weekly managing her business systems manually (even though she was using CRMs). Client inquiries came through her website, bookings were tracked in a spreadsheet, content was stored across Google Drive and Dropbox, and delivery happened through yet another platform. We built what she calls her "AI Command Center" a custom system using Make.com (an automation platform that integrates all the pieces together).

Tip: From now on start gathering all your past and future content, and start paying attention and creating standard operation procedures manuals (AI can help with this too) in a central location because with a few automation you can create a potent "brand brain" that can help you start from 80-90% instead of 0% every time you are working on a brand asset.

Brand Voice Guardian

AI can learn your tone, values, and unique brand voice, it can help you protect and express that voice across every touchpoint. This isn't about making it 'sound like you' it's about NOT sounding like everyone else using the same recycled prompts. It's about training AI to sound like your brand, so that everything carries your frequency.

Practical Example: I created my AI Brand Voice Guardian by developing three key documents: a voice guide detailing my unique writing patterns, a "banned language" list of industry jargon, and a collection of high-performing content tagged by tone. After uploading these to a custom GPT, my team produced launch content that clients immediately recognized as "this is so you," while saving hours of editing time. This doesn't just maintain my voice; it actively protects my brand integrity across all channels, even as we scale.

Tip: Go beyond training a Custom GPT with a few posts. Feed it your brand strategy, tone of voice guide, messaging pillars, brand archetypes, and customer journey insights. If you don't have those defined yet, consider this your invitation to prioritize it, because once your AI understands your brand deeply, it becomes your most aligned creative collaborator.

Mirror for Expansion

When prompted with intention, AI reflects your clarity (or lack of it) back to you. It surfaces the edges of your thinking. It reveals your gaps. It helps you grow into the version of you who doesn't just run a business, but builds an ecosystem.

Practical Example: Here's how you can use AI as a mirror right now: Take your last 5-10 client testimonials or social media comments and paste them into ChatGPT with this prompt: "Analyze these responses to identify: 1) What clients value that I'm not prominently featuring in my marketing, 2) Emotional patterns in their language that reveal deeper needs, and 3) Any contradictions between what I think I'm selling versus what clients say they're buying." One coach I worked with discovered her clients barely mentioned her curriculum (which she spent months perfecting), but repeatedly praised how she "made complex concepts feel manageable" and "created safety to experiment." She immediately rewrote her sales page to emphasize these emotional benefits, created a simple self-assessment quiz for prospects to identify their "learning safety" needs, and saw conversion increase. This mirror technique costs nothing but consistently reveals the gap between how you see your business and how your clients experience your true value.

Tip: This doesn't only apply to business, but as conscious humans when we are engaging with the LLMs we are also contributing to its future training so thinking critically with it it's also important.

Ask it to:

• Reveal blind spots in your client profile, offer, or sales messaging. • Show where your assumptions may be excluding or alienating audiences. • Check for emotional sensitivity, cultural relevance, or bias in your content.

This is how we start using it as a tool for personal and collective evolution not only as a shortcut.

Part 5: Applied AI

I've seen a lot of people jumping on the "AI teaching" wagon lately, mistakenly treating AI as a trend they have to ride so they won't be left behind. But you and I have already established that we are not here to turn ourselves into bonafide AI experts (unless it genuinely aligns with your brand, your zone of genius and your long term vision).

Instead, you are here to use it strategically, critically and with discernment, as someone who understands it not as a gimmick but for the potential it can have to transform your business. That's an entirely different category of leadership.

Believe me, I get the temptation. AI feels like a low-handing fruit right now.
But here's the truth. If you have been in business for a few years, you have built trust and a brand reputation, jumping into AI just because 'gurus' who've been using it for two months (if that) promise they hold the key to 'unlock its full potential and quantum leap you into millions' it's a gamble. And to be honest? It's not worth betting your brand equity and reputation on that.

And if you are in the early stages of business. Here's what I want you to know: unless it truly makes sense to sell AI as a part of your business model, the future won't belong to those selling isolated tools or tactics. It will belong to those creating integrated systems, experiences and solutions that are intelligent, experiential, aligned and strategic.

Wherever you are in your journey, I'm going to give you enough food for thought to help you engage with AI from your center, not someone else's playbook.

So let's turn all these insights into practical applications. Because it's one thing to know the potential of AI. It's another to actually build with it, intentionally, and in service of your genius.

This isn't about doing more. It's about building a business that moves at the pace of your clarity.

Let's start by mapping out where AI fits into your ecosystem.

1. Start With Your Genius Zone (an audit of YOU, not just your business)

Your goal isn't to outsource your brilliance, it's to stay in it longer. So let's flip the script.

Ask yourself not what AI tools can I use for…but:
- What are the things only I can do in my business?
- What part of my brilliance feels under-leveraged?
- What drains me but is necessary for things to run?
- What do I keep repeating, explaining, or recreating?
- What valuable content or knowledge am I sitting on that isn't being used?

This isn't just a productivity audit, it's a creativity, energetical one as well.

Note the outputs and here's where you can let AI hold the repetition, the sorting, so you can hold the vision, the nuance, the direction.

2. Create Your Aligned AI Stack

Based on the result of your audit then we can start (strategically) thinking of where and what we are going to delegate to tools, automations and AI in general.

Function first. Tools second.

It should reflect how you work and what you actually need, not what's trending. This will only cost you dearly in subscriptions never used and precious time learning them.

Here are four core areas every small business can enhance with AI.

CAUTION: You don't need all of them right away. Start where the friction is highest. Some of these tools are too advanced for beginners and not needed as you start to dabble into AI. I'm however creating the full picture so you understand the lay of the land.

Content & Visibility

- Repurpose live content into newsletters, carousels, and blogs
- Generate ideas and outlines in your voice
- Use image generators to visually express your frameworks
- Tools: ChatGPT, Claude, Jasper, Midjourney, Krea.ai, Descript

Client Experience

- Auto-generate onboarding documents and welcome emails
- Build resource libraries powered by Custom GPTs
- Analyze intake forms to generate personalized journeys
- Tools: Make.com, Notion AI, Tally + Airtable + GPT, Custom GPTs

Operations & Admin

- Auto-organize and tag content libraries
- Summarize meeting notes or voice memos into action plans
- Generate weekly check-ins and CEO dashboards
- Tools: Notion, Airtable, Make, Google Workspace + Zapier

Strategic Thinking & Decision Making

- Use AI to test different framings for your offers

- Get feedback on positioning, pricing, or copy
- Prompt it to act as a coach, a strategist, or even a client
- Tools: ChatGPT Custom Instructions, Perplexity, Claude, Anthropic's Opus 3.

Design Your Feedback Loop

One thing that I don't hear a lot of people talk about is a term used in the LLMs training called sycophancy. It's basically a 'phancy' word for pleasing people. AI is basically trained to achieve the goal, so if left unchecked it will become your cheerleader and that's not the best use of its potential. So it's important for you to remember that AI gets better the more you teach it, but only if you correct it. So be bold (it won't get offended).

If you're not getting the output you want, try:

- Asking it to remove fluff or filler
- Giving it examples of your language and structure
- Feeding it context: "Here's who I'm speaking to. Here's my philosophy. Here's what matters to me."

AI doesn't just need prompts. It needs parameters. And it needs your discernment.

And if you've trained a Custom GPT or created a brand brain, give it feedback often and be specific. That's how you train it to think with you, not just for you.

Part 6: The Unshakable Framework - Leading with Identity in an Age of AI

For better or worse, one thing is true: AI has created a lot of noise. It's made content a commodity. The hustle culture to produce more, faster, and everywhere has only intensified, because now, with AI, you can.

And yet, in a sea of automated outputs and algorithm-chasing sameness, identity, and therefore, authenticity has become the currency of the day. And that is good news for the 'rest of us'. In this era of overproduction and manufactured relevance, resonance is the real revolution.

And that's the difference between those who ride the wave and those of us who lead it. Because when the landscape is shifting beneath us, platforms, formats, expectations, what becomes non-negotiable is who we are at the center of it all.

This is the lens I've used to guide both my own journey and is the foundation I've built inside my work with visionary entrepreneurs navigating innovation. I don't always call it a framework. It's more of a grounding, a compass to navigate innovation through alignment, not anxiety. A move from fragmented brilliance into integrated resonance. I think of it in three core layers:

1. SELF: Identity First, Tools Second

Here's what I tell my clients all the time. No amount of artificial intelligence can out-clear non-clarity. If the foundations of your business, your brand are not set, not clear. If you are not grounded and convicted on your place in your market, AI will only continue to scale that.

The most powerful use of AI begins with identity. With you.

With your lived experience, your embodied values, your point of view. You are already a category of one, that's what you need to ask AI to support.

This is why I say: **AI should never be your brand voice, it should be your brand echo.**

So, identity, clarity, conviction first, tools second.

Next time you are tempted to ask: What can I automate? What prompt will give me the best output?

Get back to: What do I want to be known for? What do I never want AI to touch in my business? What part of me am I no longer willing to outsource?

When you lead from identity, the tech bends to you. Not the other way around.

2. STRUCTURE: Systems That Support, Not Replace

AI is powerful, yes. But not all friction in your business is a "tech" problem.
Sometimes what you need isn't another tool. Sometimes what you need is integration.

I see so many brilliant entrepreneurs duct-taping together AI tools, hoping it will magically solve their overwhelm. But what they end up with is fragmentation at scale. More tabs. More tasks. More complexity disguised as innovation.

Here's what I want you to consider instead: You are not here to build a content machine. You're here to orchestrate an intelligent, intuitive ecosystem.

Let AI be the glue between your workflows, not the architect of them. Use it to:

• Close the loop between your ideas and your visibility

- Bridge the gap between your zone of genius and your backend operations
- Free up the mental space to focus on the moves only you can make

The goal shouldn't be to use more AI, but to use it where it creates resonance, not resistance.

3. SIGNAL: Resonance over Omnipresence

AI has made omnipresence seductive. Post more. Post faster. Be everywhere. But visibility without intention is just digital noise.

This is the new temptation: to chase volume, to gamify growth, to show up in ten places with the same recycled message. But it's not volume that cuts through. It's vibration. Resonance.

In a world where It's becoming increasingly difficult to discern what's real from what's generative, identity and embodiment will reign supreme. And that my darling, is good news. The rise of AI means anyone can look polished. Anyone can sound clever. Anyone can generate content at scale. But only those rooted in clarity and conviction will be able to create connections that stick.

Because here's the truth:

- Looking like a leader ≠ leading. (i.e. pretty images ≠ success.)
- Sounding wise ≠ being embodied. (i.e. clever words ≠ getting solid client results.)
- Publishing daily ≠ having a presence. (i.e. constant output ≠ meaningful impact)

AI can mimic visibility. But it cannot manufacture essence. And presence isn't about being everywhere, but about being undeniably you wherever you choose to show up.

This is the real power of AI when paired with strategic, leveraged presence: it helps you show up where it matters, not just where you can. It helps you show up deeper, not just louder. It allows your essence to echo across platforms without dilution, so your brand presence is felt, not just seen.

True signal comes from alignment. It's built by expressing your depth across multiple mediums without diluting the message. And that's exactly where AI shines. When trained well, it doesn't mass-produce content, it translates your truth. It doesn't erase your originality, it amplifies it.

AI allows you to repurpose your most meaningful ideas, reflect your deepest positioning, and maintain consistency without creative burnout. But it cannot replace your essence. That's the work only you can do.

So when you're building your brand presence with AI, don't ask: How can I be everywhere?

Ask instead: How can I create resonance, everywhere I choose to show up?

Because that's the future of visibility: not omnipresence. But leveraged, embodied presence.

To me, this is what being unshakeable in the age of AI really means.

To be unshakable isn't about resisting innovation, it's about staying rooted as the landscape shifts. It's knowing what's yours to hold, what's safe to delegate, and what must remain human. It's not about doing more, faster. It's about being so grounded in who you are and what you stand for, that no trend, tool, or algorithm can throw you off center. In a world chasing omnipresence, being unshakable means choosing intentional resonance over frantic relevance, and letting your essence become the loudest signal in the noise.

That's how you move from Fragmented Brilliance™ to Integrated Resonance™. From noise to knowing. From burnout to brilliance. From urgency to unshakable.

Because this revolution is just getting started, and you need to build resilience, strategy and conviction to innovate not WITH AI but in spite of it.

Part 7: Closing thoughts.

So, now that you know everything there is to know about AI… just kidding.

It would be impossible to compile all the knowledge into one chapter. We've only scratched the surface. But I hope this has offered enough clarity and insight, and that you receive it as an invitation to begin engaging with this technology not just as a tool, but as a turning point.
Every force of transformation in history has brought with it both breakthroughs and collateral impacts. AI is no different. It offers access, amplification, and acceleration. But what we do with that access, that's what will define us, as individuals and as a human race.

What I am adamant about is this: we cannot let fear, or fascination, pull us out of the driver's seat. We still have agency.

And we cannot afford to navigate AI as if we don't, or worse, allow its future to be shaped solely by a narrow, privileged elite.

This is especially true for women, people of color, and historically underrepresented voices. We cannot sit on the sidelines while new systems of power are being designed in real time without true and wide representation.

As a mother, I feel this deeply. I refuse to let my daughter's world be shaped by a handful of billionaires or the invisible hand of algorithms. I want her future, and the future of all our children, to be shaped by truth, integrity, and diversity. By people like you. By people who care.

That's why I wrote this chapter. Not to turn you into an AI expert, but to offer you a different lens. One that's rarely spoken about, yet more vital than "how to prompt ChatGPT to sound like you."

I wrote this chapter to show you how to pair your soul with your systems. To remind you that your presence matters more than your productivity. And to help you move from fragmented brilliance to integrated resonance, not by becoming more machine-like, but by becoming more fully yourself.

AI gives us, for the first time in history, the power to rival the infrastructure of corporations. To compete on equal footing with deep pockets and endless budgets. To automate what drains us. To extend our reach. To codify our legacy. And to build businesses that scale our truth without burning us out.

But power without discernment is just more noise. That's why your presence, your identity, your values, your clarity, must lead.

The future will not belong to those who use AI the most. It will belong to those who use it most wisely. So take the time to root in your truth. Build your systems with intention. Define what presence means for you, not as omnipresence, but as resonance. Let AI hold the repetition, so you can hold the vision. Use it to echo your essence, not replace it.

Being unshakeable doesn't mean resisting change. It means holding your center within it. It means shaping your future with discernment, not fear. With presence, not pressure. And that's exactly what this moment demands of us.

The future is bright and exciting. But it is not inevitable. It's ours to shape, but we need to stay awake, engaged, and deeply unshakably ourselves.

Thank you for walking this path with me. Now, go lead.

Nic Davies

Productivity, efficiency and life logistics mentor and expert. Vintage lover, up-cycler and life long multi-passionate creative

When You're the Backup Plan, the Safety Net, and the CEO

"Better to have a plan and change it up, than to have no plan at all."

"Buy the notebook."

"Write it down."

Instagram - @platespinningacademy

WHEN YOU'RE THE BACKUP PLAN, THE SAFETY NET, AND THE CEO

I often think about how people manage to build and run a business whilst doing all their life stuff at the same time. I know it can be a magical way to create a purposeful life as it's what I'm doing too. And there's one aspect of it that always hits hard with me.

How many social media posts have you read from people you admire and look up to, that talk about having immense gratitude for their family support? I see them often, and I read them with bittersweet emotion. Comments that stand out for me go something like this:

"I am so grateful my mum was able to collect the kids from school for me today"

"I dread the school holidays, but I'm glad we've got grandparents to help"

"There's no way I'd be able to run my business without the support of my mum / dad / sibling / any other relative that happens to be on hand"

"I wouldn't be able to run my business without my family. I don't know what I'd do without them having their hands at my back"

And it's that last one that always cuts a little too deep with me.

I am glad that so many people have their family genuinely supporting them through their business and life journey. They certainly lighten the load, helping with undertaking the school run so you can get to work a bit earlier, or on time. Turning up with a home cooked meal when you're at capacity but also

217

need to focus on your next work deadline. It's having someone on hand to collect the kids from school early because they're sick, and you have a client call booked. Leaning on your mum for support, when you're having a bad day. Knowing they've "got you", even on those days when the rest of the world hasn't.

But what happens when family support doesn't exist? How do people who don't have that network (for whatever reason) manage to build a business at all? If you see successful people talking about how grateful they are for their family, how would they be managing without that family support? Would they have been as successful? Would they even be in business? It's an interesting question.

I've had the complete and utter misfortune in life to be dealt a shitty hand when it comes to family. My dad died at 53, and mum at 63, although any support from her prior to that also came in toxic wrapper. I was 27 and 37 respectively when they departed. I have two siblings – I know where one of them is, yet I've never been a real part of their adult life. I have no idea where the other is, and even if I did, it would make little difference as that relationship was fractured in our teenage years through intimidation and physical violence.

I've never had the true luxury of making a phone call to ask for genuine unconditional help. It's a bittersweet pill I regularly swallow, knowing that I'm in an Entrepreneurial world full of people making impactful, positive headway, and building financial freedom, and yet I often ask myself why I find it so difficult to do the same without getting stressed and falling ill. Feeling like a failure is a regular occurrence, despite me truly knowing otherwise. The feelings still rise and take my focus away from important things. I'm also aware that I'm not alone in feeling like this. Life does its thing to everyone. No one is immune from curveballs, large or small.

If you don't know my story, I'm Mum, Step-Mum and Nana Nic in a complicated and multi-layered large, blended family. There are a lot of children, although they are now all mostly teenagers and young adults. It's been a difficult task to stay focused on building any form of business, as there's always the aspect of clock watching to see how long I've got before various school runs. Then the interruptions with phone calls from school as there's been "another" incident. Or someone is sick. Raising children who've lost a parent can often feel like an impossible task. Their childhood is complicated, and the odds are against them from the start, coming under the banner of having ACE (adverse childhood experiences). It's not a straightforward linear journey. It was never going to be.

And yet, I still find a way. Always. I find a way through, even if it means an hour of snot crying and wailing into a cushion. I give myself space, allow the feelings to flow, complete the stress cycle and then pick myself up, dust myself off, and get back on the horse. It's safe to say that the odds tend to feel hugely stacked against me being able to build a successful business and leave a legacy. With such a complicated set up and no other family support, it feels almost impossible.

But there's one sure thing in my life and that's the fact that I will NEVER give up my Entrepreneurial journey. It might take me a lot longer than others, but this is my road to travel, and despite my regular frustrations, I need to ride it without falling off permanently. My Entrepreneurial spirit animal is the Tortoise. I see them everywhere I go!

So how have I managed to build such robust resilience into my life? That's an interesting question, with many answers. It's not just been one single thing. No one magic answer. It's a combination of lots of decisions, research, mindset work, a bucket load of therapy and lots of healing! And here's the kicker... the work is never done. There is still so much to do. I still get a lot of things wrong. But I use every moment as a point of learning, and with each block I hit, I find a way to smash through it or round it. Standing still in front of it forever isn't an option.

If there was ever a competition for the number of times someone has hit burnout, I'd likely be a good candidate. I've crossed Burnout Bridge more times than I'd ever want anyone else to. It's taken a while for me to come to terms with the fact that it's how I'm wired. I've always sailed close to the edge. It's a challenging route to take. A narrow path that myself and similarly wired creative pioneers travel along, flitting between being all in, hyper focused, motivated and driven, to then finding ourselves exhausted and out of energy. Wondering that despite our intelligence and need for a healthy work life balance, we still don't feel we have achieved our optimum capacity yet.

Whilst I make light of the fact that I flirt with and fall into burnout on a regular basis, it's also not something I'd recommend as a particularly desirable lifestyle choice. It's my way of acknowledging who I am, how I function, and that I will likely always be tweaking and changing course, hoping I've not overdone it again after being on a roll and making good progress.

I also know what it feels like to lie on the sofa for four years, staring up at the sky, watching the clouds go by along with the rest of the world, wondering when I'll get my time to shine. Because my body doesn't always work so great. It gaslights me regularly. I've a history of Chronic Fatigue, and Fibromyalgia in recent years, as well as being five years post heart attack (which is enough on its own to contend with). I accept that I'm susceptible to chronic illness, and as I get older (along with menopause), I become more flexible with my approach to life, knowing I may need to change my schedule quickly, should my energy or pain levels suddenly change. It is extremely frustrating, and some days

I believe life would be easier if I just signed up for social security benefits, and accepted defeat. Live a quiet life with a "pottering at home" routine, watering my houseplants, reading the latest celebrity gossip, and gaslighting myself into thinking I that never had any big plans to leave a legacy anyway.

Yep. That's not me, and it never will be.

When I look around at my extensive business network, I see regular similarities in working patterns, and know that despite my struggles, I am also here as an amplifier to help others. And what I have learned over the last few years is that there is a distinct difference between working through a crisis, where life is temporarily thrown into disarray. And then that becoming the norm, the default. Then years down the line we find ourselves still living life in firefighting mode. Just "getting through" to the next day, without any longer-term plans.

Firefighting mode in a crisis is expected for a short while. Imagine a huge curveball has been thrown into your life. Everything changes, priorities suddenly become sharper. Making sure everyone is fed and watered may be the only priority for the day, and not much else. But when the crisis is over, we need to get back to normal. Or perhaps it's been a life changing curveball, and you now must work hard to find your new normal.

Unfortunately, many of us find ourselves accidentally living in survival mode for years, and we simply aren't wired to live that way without it causing immense pressure on our physical, mental and emotional health. Similarly, we end up in this mode as Entrepreneurs. Working hard now, so we can take it easy later. If you've stepped up to the role of business owner / Entrepreneur / CEO – however you identify yourself, you may already realise you've taken a courageous step that most won't do. Building and running a business is not an easy life, despite many influencers showing their glamorous "laptop lifestyle" and talking about only needing to work for 15 minutes each day. Let's say that was true, I'd pretty much guarantee they'd have already worked regular sixteen-hour days over several years, pulling all nighters to meet deadlines, and cried themselves into a mess on a regular basis to be able to get to that point. There are few that can truly claim the Holy Grail of Entrepreneurship that is time and financial freedom. It's not actually what it's all about for the majority.

Getting to that point is far from glamorous. It's not a breeze. It's graft. Hard work. It's beyond exhausting and will test your patience and resolve to the absolute limit.
You'll need nerves of steel to ride the cashflow rollercoaster without falling into debt. You'll forget to eat and drink. You'll engage hyperfocus mode, get on a roll and then realise you haven't moved for hours, and your legs have cramp. You're completely dehydrated and feel terrible, sporting bags under your eyes and you might not have showered for a few days. But... you got that website built, right? You built the sign-up form, and it's all connected to your chosen software system. You wrote three months' worth of social media posts in one sitting, and the weight from your mind is lifted!

Does that sound like a fair exchange? Hmm, I'm not so sure. If feels like that in "keeping up" with the Entrepreneurial Jones' you put yourself physically, mentally and emotionally through the wringer just to show up consistently online. You haven't got time to sleep properly because you've got just as much again to do tomorrow, so you grab a few hours between 2am and 6am, and then you're back on the hamster wheel, hoping that today is the day you have your big breakthrough. Hoping those high paying clients you've been praying for, finally reach out and tell you they want to work with you.Whilst I've worked through the night on a few occasions, and I've had laser focus for hours on specific projects, I know only too well that this is NOT a sustainable way of working. Is it any wonder we are burned out if these are the expectations? Stepping into the Entrepreneurial world is literally stepping on to the world's worst rollercoaster. It's adrenaline filled from day one, you don't know when the next turn is, you don't know when the next drop is, you're up, down, and all around. You hang upside down at times and by the time the ride is finished, you're wondering where the time went and realise you're right back where you started, with nothing to show but the fallout from adrenal fatigue, a bad hair day and high blood pressure.

Okay, I'm not saying all of this to put you off. I'm saying it because it's real. It's true, and it's downright dangerous if you're not strapped in properly. Most people I work with have fallen into business ownership accidentally. It was never in the plan, or if it was the timing was inconvenient with employment ending abruptly. Many have left toxic work environments because they just could not deal with it anymore, or they've had enough of the patriarchal bullshit. Whatever the reason, they don't "fit" into employment, and struggle with feelings of despondency and failure. I know how this feels as it's something I've had to work through. But put simply, employment is not for everyone. Whilst a lot of people are happy with someone else dictating their time and salary, It can also be a restrictive and soul-destroying option for many others.

The same goes for running a business which is also not for everyone. But for those that feel called, we need to be taking extra care of ourselves to make sure we don't burn out. Stress has sadly become the norm for many, and 21st Century lifestyles are something we have not physiologically adapted to.

I've implemented many strategies into my life to help me create resilience whilst I undertake my business journey, and I'd love to discuss three of them with you. I'll be covering:

1. Creating Your Own Employment Contract
2. Parenting Yourself
3. Carving Out Your Creative Time

So, if you have fallen (or however it's happened) into Entrepreneurship, you might be at a point where you're thinking "okay, where is my entrepreneur manual?" You could really do with one because you're not just undertaking one role now, you have EVERY SINGLE HAT of business to wear. Here are examples of some roles a business owner takes on when they first start up on their own:

- **CEO** – you oversee absolutely EVERYTHING! You are also responsible for everything. You make all the decisions and manage every aspect of the business. You also can't afford to pay anyone to do any of the work yet.

- **Finance Director** – responsible for all income, expenditure, cashflow and forecasting. Creating a financial strategy to make sure you stay out of debt, and don't go out of business. Budgeting, making positive financial decisions, accounts, adhering to tax deadlines and ensuring everything is done correctly.

- **Operations Manager** – undertaking all the organising of systems, analysing what works and what doesn't, creating new systems and implementing them, testing them, creating user manuals and back ups for when it all goes wrong. Creating efficiency and better productivity. Creating reports and looking at continuous improvement. Procurement and/ or creating products.

- **Sales Manager** – responsible for negotiating all sales, creating and meeting targets, motivating the sales team (which is just yourself right now), finding new and different ways to sell. Looking at consumer trends, creating new relationships with potential and existing clients. Creating reports and forecasting

- **Marketing Manager** – responsible for creating the company vision and brand. For creating marketing campaigns, engagement with potential clients, exploring new networking opportunities, looking at where to gain more exposure. Looking at potential collaboration work, and generally making the sure the company message is in line with its values, and that it is visible to the outside world in order to be discovered.

- **Administration Manager** – making sure that all admin tasks are done. Whether that's emailing clients, creating newsletters, writing letters, dealing with incoming correspondence, creating and maintaining filing systems, keeping documents filed securely, dealing with GDPR compliance, making sure the printer is in good working order, that you've not run out of ink or paper, and keeping a healthy supply of multi coloured post it notes within reach at all times (as these are ESSENTIAL for the budding Entrepreneur, along with numerous notebooks with varying cover designs).

- **Project Manager** – making sure all client work runs smoothly and meets all deadlines. Planning work in so you're not completely overloaded and making sure the standard of work is good enough.

- **IT Manager** – making sure your desktop computer and/or laptop is up to date, that all files are backed up, and any potential hacking is to a minimum. Dealing with passwords for probably at least 20 different software applications, and having some sort of contingency to continue working, should the "blue screen of death" appear on your computer.

- **Customer Services** – dealing with enquiries, complaints and prospective clients. Working to the level of standard you've decided upon, and dealing with negative Google reviews, should they occur.

Some list, right? It's a lot. In fact, it's impossible for one person to do all those things. But we still try. And the worst part? There is one more. Possibly the most important one, and it doesn't get discussed enough:

- **Human Resources** – The HR department. The one that looks after all personnel, the one that deals with employment contracts, payroll, ensuring that working conditions are fair, and that no one is exploited. The department that deals with appropriate training for staff, as well as compliance with legal regulations. The department that deals with long term sickness, as well as policies and procedures for when life curveballs hit their workforce, and they can't show up for work.

And it's this department / hat I want you to focus on. Because HR isn't top of mind when we start up in business. We just want to get on with the bits that we are good at, and not the boring stuff.

Be honest, was this the first thing you considered when you decided to step into the business ring? It's a huge missing part of the piece, and it's one of the many reasons that Entrepreneurs end up in burnout. We are simply not looking out for ourselves, where a HR department within an employment capacity would be expected to. So what's the answer? In its simplest form, we create it for ourselves.

CONCEPT NO. 1 - CREATE YOUR OWN EMPLOYMENT CONTRACT

One of the first things we do when accepting a new employed role is to sign an employment contract. This helps the company we work for to comply with employment law. This covers some of the following, and is put in place to:

- Ensure a healthy and safe working environment
- Ensure employees get adequate breaks
- Clarify where everyone stands with regards to holiday and sick pay
- Ensure a minimum working wage, and any overtime enhancements
- Ensure a maximum hourly working week
- Protect from bullying and harassment in the workplace
- Ensure suitable training for the role expected
- Provide suitable PPE if required, a comfortable working environment, access to fresh air and light etc.
- If you're sat at a computer, ensuring regular checks are required for posture. Possibly offering regular eye tests, and/ or physiotherapy sessions for any back pain caused by sitting for long periods
- Dealing with grievances and complaints. Ensuring fair treatment for all

But how many of these do you consider when working for yourself?

Would you want to work for someone who didn't offer paid holidays, or sick pay? What if they asked you to work a twelve-hour day? Erratic working patterns, last minute changes to your workload. Insufficient breaks, or just general intolerable conditions.

What about if you need to pick the kids up from school if they're sick? What if that's a no, and you'll lose your job if you do?

Who would want to work for an employer like that? I don't know anyone that would even get away with those kinds of working conditions. Yet when we work for ourselves, a lot of us put ourselves into this exact environment. We don't allow ourselves healthy working conditions to thrive in. We aren't even meeting our basic physiological needs some days.

It's a tricky trade off. One the one hand we want to work hard to build our business, and the message we hear is that "you get out what you put in". But over a longer time period if we keep putting in with long working hours and not enough rest or even eating properly, what are we getting out of it? I'll tell you what we get. We get stress. Inflammation. Fatigue. We get sick.

Why do we expect that we can just carry on working like this regardless? If we are not providing ourselves with even the absolute basics, then we have just signed what could be the worst employment contract ever. And it's all our own doing.

So let's look at creating our own employment contract with ourselves. It doesn't have to be fancy or complicated. It can be as simple as an A4 sheet of paper with bullet points on it. See it as a commitment to treat yourself with decency and fairness, and no less than what you'd expect from an external Employer.
State how many hours you'll work in a day, decide on a weekly maximum. Lay out your breaks and time off. Write down in advance what you'll do if you have kids at school that are sick and need to be collected. What's the contingency should that happen? And decide this in advance, otherwise it adds a whole extra layer of stress to a day with a sick child.
What about a dress code? I know I feel more productive when I'm not lounging around in yoga pants. It doesn't need to be

super strict or smart. But perhaps wearing specific "workwear" that only you know is workwear. It'll also help your brain to adjust and focus when you are in work mode, and when you are not. My "go to" work uniform is a casual t-shirt or top, jeans and trainers. Nothing fancier than that.

Give it a try. See what works for you. Put it in your diary to review it every quarter and change anything that isn't working.

CONCEPT NO.2 – PARENT YOURSELF

Growing up our parents always chose our bedtime, what food we ate, when we ate, what we did, where we went etc. Working for someone else requires working within their framework, which goes so far as being told when to take your lunch break, when to start work, finishing time and permission for booking annual leave. As a business owner, we have free reign to do what we want, when we want. No one is going to stop us!

And that can be a big problem. Because no one is checking on our working hours. No one is telling us when we can take time off. We don't have parents supervising our bedtimes, screen time, and making us three decent meals a day. We're on our own, and it's a dangerous place to be when all you want to do is the fun part of business building without a sensible structure in place.

We DO need to be parented on this, and as I've pointed out in the previous section with the employment contract concept, we also need to create a parenting framework for ourselves. We are no good to anyone if we're not keeping tabs on working late and not eating properly. I call this the unsexy self-care part of adulting! If you're aware of Maslow's Hierarchy of needs, right at the bottom of the pyramid is the foundation layer. The things we need to stay alive. Our basic physiological needs in the form of food, water, shelter and warmth. Without these things humans cannot survive very long.

So imagine you're in hyperfocus mode. You're in the zone, and on a roll. You are oblivious to the outside world as you churn out your very best work on whatever project you've harnessed the energy for. Hours go by and still you're working. You are on fire! The dopamine from seeing your project take shape spurs you on. You want to continue and are reluctant to stop.

And then reality hits when you realise you haven't moved from your office chair for around four hours. You're dehydrated from lack of fluids as it simply hasn't occurred to you that you need a drink. You haven't eaten. Your legs are stiff as you've not even got up to use the bathroom (because you've not drunk anything other than caffeine). You've been that pre-occupied with your work that all your basic needs have gone out of the window. You're in a bit of a state, feeling light-headed and spaced out.

As a one-off, we can probably cope with this. Go to the bathroom. Get some fluids down your neck, and some food. Stretch your legs and look out of the window to focus your eyes on something other than a computer screen. Then you're good to go again.

But doing this on a regular basis is a recipe for disaster. Our bodies need hydration and fuel in the form of proper nutritious food. Our bodies need movement for all our internal systems to work properly. Working like this on a regular basis is not sustainable.

Now add in some late bedtimes for good measure. You've been so busy with work that when you finally clock off for the day, you want some wind down time. And I'm guessing a lot of that time is spent scrolling social media. Yet more screen time! Your eyes hurt and you feel tired. But you go to bed and your brain can't switch off. Your mind is racing with every thought and worry of the day. You've not had a proper wind down period, so your mind is still churning over work stuff. You give up on sleep so you get up and back to the computer. May as well do some more work if sleep isn't happening eh?

Please, don't.

It sounds extreme, but this is what life can look like for the modern Entrepreneur if we don't put proper boundaries in place. We desperately need to parent ourselves. Give ourselves a proper bedtime. Put routines into place. Eat proper food at the right times and in the right portion sizes. Stop snacking on crap food just because it's there.

And if part of your wind down routine also includes opening a bottle of wine or a couple of gins? STOP!

If you want to take your business seriously, then you also need to take your health seriously too, in all its physical, mental and emotional forms. Your business won't build itself. It needs you to be on top form to make it all happen. We've already discussed how many hats/roles there are as an Entrepreneur. The odds are already against us and we don't need to make it more difficult by erratic bedtimes and mealtimes, combined with a lack of proper hydration with alcohol thrown into the mix. I guarantee you by parenting yourself you will function better than you ever have before, and you are more likely to succeed. Because that's part of the plan isn't it? Success?

Put strict boundaries in place as to when you will stop work. Set timers on your phone. Program your computer to switch off at a certain time. Stop all screen time an hour before bed. Set yourself an early yet realistic bedtime. Put a proper bedtime routine together. Let your body wind down naturally.

Get a head start on the morning by doing a little bit of prep in the evening. This could be getting packed lunches ready, taking a shower in the evening rather than morning (I realise we will all have our own preferences for this), jot down a little task list to get it out of your head and you won't forget.

BEDTIME ROUTINE

Decide on your time for lights out and stick to it. Whatever is outstanding on your task list, you'll tackle it better after a good night's sleep. If you are genuinely struggling with sleep, look at using some sleep hygiene apps, where you can get tips and advice on the best way for you to get sleep, and the use of trackers to see how you're getting on. What has worked for me is an alarm on my phone at 9pm to make sure I'm off all screens. I shower in an evening which helps me to wind down. I have a cup of decaf tea before bed, and a second alarm goes off for my lights out at 10.30pm.

MEALTIMES

Look at your diet and visualise your food as fuel. If you put cheap quality fuel into a car engine, it won't run well. Likewise, if you eat crap, your productive output will match. Try and fit as many nutrients into your diet as you can. I always go with as many vegetables and fruit as I can manage, with lots of protein and just a small amount of carbohydrate. This will be different for everyone, and I've found my optimum diet for my age and health conditions. If I get it wrong, I end up with crashing fatigue around 3pm and I need to stop whatever I'm doing and rest.

To make mealtimes less stressful, put some form of menu/meal plan into place. If you know in advance what you're having, it helps you reclaim badly needed headspace. There'll be less arguments about what to make, and it'll help reduce daily decision fatigue. If stuff needs taking out of the freezer the day before or in the morning, set a reminder on your phone.

One of the easiest meals I make for myself takes less than five minutes, and there is no prep or cooking! It's a ready cooked chicken breast, a generous dollop of hummus, pitta bread, pickled beetroot, mini plum tomatoes, cucumber chunks and a couple of torn lettuce leaves. I love the fact that it's almost all "open and serve". I feel good after eating it, knowing I've given my body a decent meal in less time than it takes to order a takeaway.

Another quick and easy meal is jacket potatoes – an hour in the oven and everyone has different toppings. I always cook extra for the day after. They're reheated quickly and provide me with a quick and balanced lunch, instead of reaching for more bread for a sandwich.

MOVEMENT

Don't forget to move! If we don't move our bodies, a lot of our internal systems stop working properly. We need regular movement, and this easily done with phone reminders. My smart watch prompts me every hour I am sat to make sure I get up and walk around. Your movement doesn't have to be full on exercise, but some gentle stretches and moving about is enough. Dance if you feel like it, but make sure you move at least once every hour.

This all takes discipline but it's for the benefit of myself and being able to function. I have no one enforcing what I eat and when, or what time I go to bed. I need a CEO head on, not a teenagers head, who wants to stay up late. Be a parent to yourself. You'll need it to keep those boundaries in place. But as your own parent, don't ever punish yourself. You deserve understanding, compassion and unconditional love. Forgive yourself when it doesn't go to plan. Reset and try again. You want the very best for you.

ANCHORS

If you're struggling to stay motivated to do this, look at some anchors to help you. These can be simple things written down and kept visible on the wall or anywhere you will see them regularly. These anchors are the reasons why you are building and running your business. These could be around having financial freedom, or just having the freedom to be flexible with your time. They could be around supporting your family, being available for your kids where a full-time employment role wouldn't facilitate that. Or perhaps you are working towards a big life change. Earning more money to be mortgage free, or perhaps to get a mortgage and away from renting. Whatever those anchors are for you, get them written down and up on display. Each time you feel yourself slipping back into less helpful habits, look at them and remind yourself why you are parenting yourself. It's not about being mean to yourself, it's about being meaningful and giving yourself the best opportunity.

You deserve to have an amazing life. If that means self-enforced boundaries, then it's worth it.

CONCEPT NO.3 - CARVE OUT YOUR CREATIVE TIME

I'm a naturally creative person. I always have been. As a small child I was always colouring in with crayons in numerous colouring books. I would draw and create patterns with anything I could find. I would daydream. I read many books and took myself off into different fantasy lands. I learned to play guitar and always regretted not continuing into adulthood. As I got older, life got in the way, and it became more difficult to stay creative. But I always found myself little projects here and there. Mostly upcycling projects (before upcycling became a "thing"). I'd see something and want to turn it into something else. I loved the transformation of a piece of furniture, or even a house refurbishment on a larger scale. I designed gardens from scratch and loved interior design. Anything to bring colour and flow to my life.

I always thought that's how everyone functioned. I didn't realise it was part of a stubborn yet wonderful creative streak that thankfully still stays strong today. And I recall periods of my life where I wasn't expressing my creativity, and those were far more darker and difficult days. It's not something I was aware of at the time or thought about until the last few years, where I've undertaken a lot of self-development work and learning about myself and how I function in the world.

The golden thread to me having a content life has always been to have creativity by my side. To always have an outlet, regardless of what it was. I'm curious about how I work and getting the very best out of myself, so by really doubling down on what is going on whenever my mental health starts to dip, one of the patterns I uncovered was that whenever I got busy with business / life / curveballs etc. I would push my creativity to one side to focus on whatever needed doing. This sounds like common sense, doesn't it? My knitting / painting / writing can wait if essential housework needs doing, or the accounts need reconciling. If the kids need additional support and have things going on, we put down our creative tools and deal with the priority. That's to be expected. I mean I can't justify knitting while my world around me is falling apart!

But what's important is to make sure that once the essential tasks are done or when the firefighting is finished, is that we pick our creative tools back up, and have that time for us. I've realised that I'm more than likely the owner of a neurodiverse brain. At the time of writing, I don't have any official diagnosis, although I have very close family members who do, and I recognise similar traits that I see in myself. One of those is have a "disco brain", as in, it never stops. It's never quiet. There are always thoughts popping up, and having tried traditional meditation, lying in a dark room, and all the other things we are told to do, that still doesn't work. But what does work for me is creativity.

The ONLY time my brain is silent, is when I'm creating. I get to zone out and focus. I forget everything else that's going on, even if it's just for a short time. I come home to being myself again in a crazy busy world.

Being a multi-passionate creative, the norm for me is to have a dozen or more different projects on the go at any one time. Here are just a few of them:

- Knitting – mostly scarves and smaller projects these days, I knit with three strands to give a chunky multi-coloured look and texture
- Pen drawings, Zentangles and free flow organic shapes. Then painting/colouring them in different themes
- Colouring Books (the grown-up kind with fine liner pens, not crayons)
- Mixed media wall artwork and sculpture
- Sewing – machine work only, I don't have the patience for hand sewing any more
- Refinishing and repainting furniture
- Refurbishing and restoring small wood homewares (bowls, candlesticks etc).
- Blog and book writing
- Podcasting for the Platespinning Academy Podcast
- Planning and organising (yes I'm claiming this as a creative pursuit as it clears headspace and motivates me)

I'd also love to have a go at:

- Pottery – slab vases and wheel work
- Wood turning and carving
- Making solid wood furniture
- Crochet – I learned when I was very young but lost the skill
- Singing – as in learning to do it properly with breathwork and vocal strengthening
- Picking up the guitar again, and learning to play drums

My previous creative pursuits include:

- Gardening – landscaping and growing from seed
- Decorating and all flavours of DIY around the house
- Cross Stitch and Embroidery
- Mosaic and Mural work
- Prop and backdrop design and creation for a local amateur theatre group

I've lived and continue to live a truly creative life. I have an upcycling workshop where I renovate and repaint furniture and homewares. It's my happy place, and despite me not using it as much as I want to, I can always tell when I've had a fulfilling time there. The day after I am generally more productive and efficient than if I'd have muddled through without it.

I've learned to recognise the signs of when my mental health is starting to dip, and when I stop myself and assess what I've been doing, it's usually down to having had an extended break from creative pursuits. I've had an instance recently where my mental health plummeted, and I was concerned that I was heading for a level of depression I've not had for years. I sat, got curious, and realised I'd not been in my workshop for over two weeks. So, the next day I got in there and within 24 hours, I'd turned things around and got myself back on track. 24 hours is all it took, and I was grateful I was able to join the dots and realise what I needed.

Whatever schedule you work to, please make sure you make time for whatever your creative activities are. Daily is ideal, but if that's not possible, then definitely make it a weekly thing. I keep smaller projects to hand at home such as drawing pads and knitting, knowing I can't just nip to the workshop for an hour of painting as it's not located at home. But little top ups here and there of creativity help me to feel balanced and keep my mental health in check.

Consider what creative activities you can implement to keep your life balanced. Think about the times when you feel overwhelmed. What do you do? I'll bet the first thing that comes to mind isn't to go and knit / draw / paint. But maybe it should be, particularly if you find traditional meditation difficult.

Think of it as a little reset in your day. It could even be something as simple as ten minutes of writing, whether that's journalling, fiction or even poetry. Anything to take your brain away from business and life for a short time. If you also identify that your brain is only silent when you're creating, then give it the rest it so badly needs.

And if you think you don't have time for creativity in your life, then it's even more important that you do make that time. I guarantee you'll work better on all the other stuff once you've integrated it into your schedule.

SUMMARY

Having focused on just three areas of the big jigsaw of building and maintaining resilience as an Entrepreneur, I am aware that there are so many more pieces to the puzzle. There are no guarantees on this journey either. Building a resilient lifestyle to deal with overwhelm and avoiding burnout can be such a difficult thing to do as a business owner. Many of us are wired in a way where we don't have an off switch (note; My DNA has been screened and yes, this is an official thing!). But if we know this is how we roll, it can be the first part to help in tackling the less desirable aspects of Entrepreneurship.

Navigating the pitfalls and doing what we can to avoid them.

There is so much more to getting this work/life balance thing nailed. Progress isn't linear. You will have setbacks; you will make mistakes. But keep at it, and keep trying, even when you hit a block. Have a go at implementing the three concepts I've discussed, and then look for other ways to change things for the better to facilitate creating the life you deserve. You absolutely deserve the best chance possible, don't ever settle for less.

Productivity, efficiency, logistics and creating your tailored work/life blend is definitely something I can help you with. If you want to check out my online resources (including my podcast, or working with me), check out the QR code below.

Danielle Thompson

Danielle runs Goldspun Support and is an experienced business owner with over a decade of ops experience, a skill for nagging (nicely) and 16 years of marketing know-how. She's a best-selling author, podcaster, aspiring poet, cross-stitch fan and lover of Malibu (drink not place). Neurospicy, GSOH and all own teeth.

The Comparison Trap: Guarding Your Mental Health in the Age of 'Success Porn'

This chapter is dedicated to all of the people who believed in me, I couldn't have done it without you helping me believe in myself.

Instagram - @goldspunsupport

THE COMPARISON TRAP: GUARDING YOUR MENTAL HEALTH IN THE AGE OF 'SUCCESS PORN'

"Comparison with myself brings improvement, comparison with others brings discontent." Betty Jamie Chung

Have you noticed how many posts there are online that sugar coat people's success stories, humble brags from people online showing off how easy everything is for them, how quickly they can make x amount of money or how many hours they don't work a week. That deluge of perfection is what I call 'success porn'. We used to be inundated with images of people that were impossibly beautiful, but now they're impossibly successful too and frankly it's all a bit much.

Let's be honest, we've all seen posts like this, and we've all felt the impact of them.

Sitting on your sofa at home scrolling through hours of this type of content can be exhausting, feeling like you're not doing enough and always desperately trying to do more. Filled with self-doubt because everyone else seems to be doing it better, more easily, quicker. It's soul destroying to look around and feel like every single person in the world has it figured out except you.

I'm here to tell you that it's all crap – not the way you feel of course, but the way people are showing up.

The problem with today's internet landscape is that it is awash with people who want you to buy from them and rather than using ethical tactics and the truth, they use fear tactics which make you feel like you're not good enough or that you're not doing enough so you have to buy from them to solve all of your 'issues'.

Imagine your mind being told every single day that you're not enough (which it is) and the impact that that would have on your belief systems, your self confidence and your mental health.

The good news is that the comparison trap does not have to be a bear-pit that you cannot climb out of. There is no reason that posts like the above should be nothing more than a chance to roll your eyes and count your own blessings.

And that's why I'm going to show you how to ditch the comparison-itus and protect your mental health on a daily basis to become the strongest, most confident version of yourself, focussed on your own success.

I imagine as you're reading this that you're probably thinking that it's okay for me to say all this, I sound confident, how I literally sound like the last person in the world who could 'get' you and how you feel. Listen up reader, between you and me I'll let you into a secret. When I was younger, I was incredibly shy, I was always that child that wouldn't leave their mother's side – heck, I didn't even go on a slide until I had my own children because I was too scared to step away from my mum. Can you imagine that, amplify it and then throw me into running my own business. I sometimes wonder how I did it.

I can honestly say, without hesitation, that every single move I made in the early days of my business was out of my comfort zone and even now, a decade later, there are still times when I am terrified (mostly when networking or making phone calls) but I have learnt tools and strategies to help me overcome my natural shyness and I have had to work hard to build mechanisms to mitigate my natural urge to compare myself to every Tom, Dick and Harry on the internet.

So, are you up for learning how? Good.

My Story – The Unfiltered Truth.

When I started my business over 10 years ago, it was as a way to survive after the corporate world almost killed me.

At that time, I was at my lowest ebb, completely burnt out and utterly traumatised, suffering PTSD, my depression triggered and terrified of the future. Starting my own business was a chance to live my life differently but it wasn't an easy, or even conscious, choice.

There were many catalysts to my giving up a solid career path and a 9-5 (well more like 8am-8pm) but the most significant one was about a week before I walked out of my role.

I came home at 7pm, literally at bedtime for my two children. My son was already asleep, and my daughter should have been on her way. However, as I walked in the house, tired and stressed, I found my daughter sat on the stairs crying. I asked her why she was so upset: "why don't you love us enough to be at home mummy?"

That right there nearly ruined me. I worked because I thought my children needed things, although I also worked because I enjoyed it. It turns out that all those hours and all that money are pointless if your children don't think you love them.

The funny thing is, I'm a perfectionist, I was focussing so hard on earning money, being good at my job, remembering all the birthdays, making sure the cupboards were never empty and that we never ran out of toilet rolls that I forgot to focus on my actual life.

My daughter's words haunted me until the day I walked out of my job- one of the bravest and most stupid things I ever done. I honestly rarely surprise myself- I'm usually so utterly predictable but this was out of character and really showed how far I had been pushed. It's a long story and not really one for public consumption but needless to say, in a most uncharacteristic and melodramatic fashion I made my exit from my corporate career, and I've never looked back since.

I could tell you that from that moment on it was all sunshine and roses but that's not real life. For three weeks' I think I either cried or slept: my brain needed to adjust, I'd never not worked, and it was a shock to my system. I was scared: of the mortgage; of my family's expectations; and of what people would think of me and that pressure almost crushed me.

I built my business to help other people balance their lives, so they never feel the way I did all those years ago – burnout, overwhelmed and with no idea how to escape. I love doing that for people, it makes me happy, just as much today as it always has.

On top of that I could do the school run, chaperone school trips (okay, it was once but they made me wear a hi vis vest so you can understand why I've not been back), take days off when I need to, get my hair done in the middle of the working week (shock, horror) or even take a random afternoon nap. It's a totally different life to the one I was leading and the one I would still be leading now if I had not made the change.

Sounds idyllic, doesn't it? Like I've got it all sorted and that everything is perfect now. Yeah. It's not.

That time I spend in the hairdresser; I'm often writing blogs on my phone or doing research. Those naps are just displaced time, so I sometimes sit in the evenings with my laptop open. Those school runs mean I have to squeeze meetings into a 9am-3pm day which is sometimes a struggle (especially with international clients in different time zones).

I think the saying goes that we start our businesses, so we don't have to do the 9-5. The truth is we start out businesses so we can do the 9-5 on our terms, at our pace and around everything else we do. It's hard work, it's 24/7 but it's rewarding.

Anyway, back to the timeline. For a long time, I stayed small, healing my wounds from my corporate role and working on building my confidence back up and at the same time my business stabilised.

Abraham Maslow, renowned American psychologist said: "In any given moment we have two options: to step forward into growth or step back into safety."

I think that is one of the most powerful things about life. We have choices and although they're not always easy or straightforward, they are there. Please understand me, there is no shame in stepping back, keeping yourself safe and looking after yourself. I've done it, I did it for years and it was the right choice for me.

But I'm no longer doing that, I'm stepping forward. I'm embracing growth and change, and the next phase of my life and I could not be more excited about it. I want to help you get to that place too, to understand and recognise your power and your confidence and to step forward.

Why We Compare – The Psychology Behind It.

Look, I'm a human, you're a human, we're all human here. Human nature is pretty straightforward, we're all driven by the same impulses and the same programming and although our behaviours can be coloured or heightened by our life experiences,

245

our knowledge of trauma or our external influences the starting point is the same.

From an evolutionary perspective we are hardwired to compare ourselves to others. Back to our cave men predecessors, comparing ourselves to our surroundings allowed us to assess threats, understand social status and ultimately survive. As part of a community or a wider group of people we want to belong, being excluded is something we fear (because being out there alone in the wild makes us vulnerable) and conversely, we are pre-programmed to fear anything that is different or that stands out because it doesn't fit our expectations and might therefore be dangerous.

In the modern world we are being constantly overwhelmed with a picture-perfect view of what life looks like. You're no longer seeing your neighbours go about their everyday, unfiltered lives. You're seeing what people want you to see – the polished, curated perfection they want to show off to the world. Although we do exactly the same ourselves, and therefore know the truth, our brains process the information we see as the full story, and not the edited highlight reel it is.

Your lizard brain is desperate to fit in and when you're surrounded by 'evidence' of how much better everyone is doing is it any wonder that your cave-man brain panics and thinks you're going to fall victim to danger? Not being good enough is the modern equivalent of that fear, anxiety and depression, overwhelm and burnout are all symptoms of a society where we simply don't feel safe because our brains are telling us we're not doing enough to survive, let alone thrive.

Then if we layer in the myth of a level playing field, we're suddenly even more unbalanced. If I have two friends, one in her 20s and one in her 60s (whilst I'm in my, ahem, 40s) should

I expect us all to be at the same place in life? Should I have my mortgage paid off like my 60+ friend or be able to travel the world working anywhere like my 20 something, child-free friend? No, that's crazy. Does the logic stop me comparing and wondering why I can't indulge my wanderlust or why I haven't been more sensible with money and paid off my mortgage yet? Nope.

By believing that everyone is starting from the same point with the same resources, the same experiences, the same ideas you're already disadvantaging your cognitive processes. You will never measure up if you believe we are all the same. The truth is you may never know everyone's back story, there are clues and there might be evidence out there if you Google stalked enough but you don't need to do that. What you actually need to do is to recognise that this is your story – not theirs – and to remove your belief that you should be where they are because you both started from the same place.

As if that isn't all enough let's look at confirmation bias. That's the way your brain looks for evidence to support the things it already believes. So, if you believe that you're short and everyone is taller than you, your brain will seek out all of the tall people in a room, ignoring the shorter ones to prove that you are vertically challenges.

How does this look in real life and as a business owner? Well, if you're sat there every evening thinking that you aren't earning enough for your business or you're not putting enough effort in and then you see reels that show 'how I made 6 figures in 6 weeks'; 'my side hustle paid off my 10k debt'; just look at me working from this beach with my Prada sunglasses and Macbook'.

It's not a surprise you're going to start to think that every other person out there is doing better than you. You won't notice the real stories, the raw authenticity or the genuine people because you'll be so caught up 'proving' to yourself how badly you're doing.

Finally, you need to face the fact that as a business owner you are doing something scary – as entrepreneurs we're often sailing in uncharted waters and as the maps always say, there be monsters 'ere. Well, the maps weren't wrong and although you may have expected those monsters to be sales shaped, networking feeling, the texture of financial worries I don't imagine you ever thought that monster could be your own inner critic, hooked on comparing yourself to others and beating yourself up for not being enough.

The good news is that all of this is normal, especially this last one. It's all a key part of figuring out who we are outside the identity of a career, away from other people's expectations and into our passions. The bad news is that if you don't recognise and address these behaviours they can start to dilute your uniqueness and lead us away from our authentic selves.

The Hidden Cost of Comparison.

Hopefully you've started to recognise some of your own thought patterns in the things I've been sharing and hopefully you've not been beating yourself up for being a perfectly normal (evolutionarily speaking) human being.

Let me expand a little now to show you the impact that these thought processes can have on your mental health because that's the hidden cost of comparing yourselves to others on the regular. But it's not all doom and gloom because as wonderful clever humans we can develop awareness and the minute we're aware we can start to implement tools to combat, redirect and rewire our thoughts. More of that later though.

These are the impacts that comparison can have on your mental health:

- **It Destroys Confidence and Clarity**

The constant comparison can cause you to second-guess decisions or the path you're on which can lead to a crisis of confidence and a lack of clarity. In this place you don't trust your own instincts or ideas and you look for external validation such as buying expensive courses or relying on what 'everyone else is doing' to guide you. This could mean you change direction often, chasing what's working for others instead of forging your own path.

Constant comparison keeps you second-guessing every decision or, at its worst, not making decisions at all and over time that will chip away at the trust you have in yourself.

- **It Drains Your Energy and Focus**

The mental load of comparison is heavy: scrolling, analysing, overthinking, second-guessing, staying stuck, chopping and changing. All of your energy goes into this process, the process of watching and comparing and that will leave little for yourself and your own pursuits.

This cycle leads to distraction, decision fatigue, and burnout.

- **It Builds Invisible Walls Between You and Others**

I'm a firm believer that there is no competition, there is space for all of us and through collaboration and community we build strong businesses but when you're stuck in the cycle of comparison, you start to see peers as competition, not community.

249

Events such as networking start feels threatening or frightening, not collaborative which leads you to isolate yourself because you're ashamed or feel 'less than' the people around you.

Negative emotions like resentment, envy, or shame are commonplace and not all helpful for growth (business or personal).

- **It Fuels Imposter Syndrome and Perfectionism**

The standards we set for ourselves are the highest, although they can be based on learnt behaviours as a child they are also influenced by factors in our adult lives. Once you set yourself impossibly high standards or procrastinate out of fear of not being 'good enough' you are stifling growth and creativity.

Comparison makes you feel like a fraud by thinking "I don't belong in this space"; you start to believe that you need to "catch up" before you can show up. It all reinforces the lie you're telling yourself that there's a perfect version of you out there, but you just haven't found it yet.

- **It Warps Your Business Decisions**

Every business is unique, there is no one size fits all but when you're comparing yourself constantly you end up doing the things you think you should be doing, rather than what works for you and your business. You'll have copy that isn't aligned with your values or audience, you'll have pricing, a brand, and an ideal client based on what others are doing instead of what works for you. You'll say yes to things that drain you, just to feel like you're keeping up with the Joneses.

But worst of all. You'll lose sight of your own goals and start chasing someone else's definition of success. And that will always feel uncomfortable, like you're wearing the wrong size shoes.

• It Freezes You in Place

Analysis Paralyis is a thing. Plus, it's fun to say. Not so fun to live with though. Your brain is telling you, "Why bother? I'll never be as good as them" so you hold back from posting, launching, or showing up because it'll never measure up to what you think perfect looks like or what you should look like.

You stay small out of fear, with comparison shrinking your courage and you put your ideas and dreams in a drawer out of site because they don't measure up.

• It Damages Your Mental Health

As someone who has suffered from mental health problems since my teenage years, I am especially sensitive to the impact that comparing myself can have, it leads to anxiety, low mood, exhaustion, chronic stress.

And back to that lizard brain, because we believe we're different, we don't fit in and that we're not doing enough, we feel vulnerable and that triggers our stress response (better known as fight/flight/freeze). So, you're left with running away from everything, hiding from everything, not doing anything at all or setting fire to it all (metaphorically speaking).

This all builds into a vicious cycle: you feel bad > so you compare more > and that makes you feel worse.

Do you recognise any of these in your own thoughts?

Mental Health in Business – The Silent Crisis.

Although mental health is becoming more of a talked about topic there is still a lot of stigma around admitting that we're struggling, especially in the online world. That creates a vicious cycle of not talking about it because you think you're the only one and then the next person sees you not struggling and assumes they must be abnormal and so they keep quiet too. You can see how this cycle continues ad infinitum.

You're sitting there feeling like you're the only one whilst you suffer with feeling lonely – not just physically but emotionally as well. And then overwhelm, burnout and exhaustion become hallmarks of your day, and you can end up assuming that that is your identity – that you are just permanently tired and that that is normal. But that is your brain building unhelpful neural pathways that create self-fulfilling prophecies in your body – say you're tired enough and you'll believe it.

The isolation you can feel as a small business owner just compounds this, you can feel alone in with your thoughts whilst the online world shows your nothing but success and coping. Even you are posting your highlight reel online and hoping no one will notice how much you're struggling.

I'm going to take you through some of the elements of what being an entrepreneur can do to your mental health and why, as business owners, we're especially vulnerable.

The Entrepreneurial Load

When you work a 9-5 job you have set tasks, set times and the likelihood is that you will have set reporting lines, so you know where your job ends and someone else's begins. You have teams to support, people to learn from and you know where to go for help. Running your own business isn't like that, even with a team in place you are still expected to carry the mental load for everything – from one end of the supply chain to the other and everything in between.

You're a jack of all trades pulled in a million directions – most of which are away from your zone of genius and the reason why you started the business in the first place. You're not unique in feeling like it's too much or for getting frustrated when a 'simple' job takes you ten times longer than it should because you had to keep googling what to do.

Compounded with no sick leave, no respite and the constant external pressure to be successful you have heavy burden to carry.

Anxiety & Overthinking are normal.

It's likely, especially if a lot of this chapter has resonated with you so far, that your brain is constantly running a commentary of what if. What if I fail, what if I'm not good enough, what if I don't get that invoice out. This constant questioning leads you to second guess your decisions and, as I said, earlier, can lead to decision paralysis or our lizard brains fight, flight or freeze kicking in.

Between 2018 and 2024 mental health issues rose significantly, figures show that in 2018 1 in 10 people were living with mental health issues (with depression and anxiety being the most prevalent) but by 2024 that figure had risen to 1 in 8. This shows just how widespread the impact of the mental health crisis is on the world population*

* https://www.who.int/health-topics/mental-health

*   https://huntingtonpsych.com/the-latest-mental-health-statistics-what-the-numbers-say-about-the-state-of-our-minds-in-2024

If you focus that research down to business owners, a survey by founder reports in 2024* found that 9 out of 10 business owners were suffering from at least one mental health issue with 50.2% struggling with anxiety. You are not alone.

* https://founderreports.com/entrepreneur-mental-health

You are the Business.

Although I've only touched this up to now, it is true that our businesses are intrinsically tied up with out identity. It's likely that you started your business because you had a passion or at least an interest and because of that you will have poured you heart and soul into it.

Putting that much into something makes it personal – it would be so much easier if we could disconnect the personal feelings from business but when it's our own business-baby that's simply not as easy as it sounds.

Your business becomes or has become a reflection of you and when the business isn't okay, neither are you. Any failings in the business: low cash months or lost clients can feel like a direct result of your behaviour – you start to internalise and blame rather than reasoning in a more unbiased way. Don't forget that as the lynch pin in your business you are also the weakest link in the chain, if you're on the point of burnout and collapse your business won't be far behind.

Always on and never off

The always on culture of the modern world is exhausting, we don't just operate in daylight hours anymore, we operate 24/7 as we move to international working and thinking. There is no off switch or down time, and it becomes challenging to put boundaries in place that protect your time.

Although we're moving away from the hustle culture that characterised the period of time between 2015 and 2020, there is still a hangover belief that hustle = good and rest = lazy. It's going to take time to re-programme the collective subconscious to treat rest as the necessity it is.

In many circles toxic productivity is still revered and that is more pressure to be performing all of the time. Even when you're not physically working your mind is on the go – either coming up with ideas or worrying about the things that you haven't done.

Success is not the cure-all.

When you create success, you often feel like it isn't enough. Often times that's because the 'success' you're aiming for is someone else's version of success, it's a what we are told we should want – whether that's 6 or 7 figure months, reduced working hours, the ability to work from a beach, a super yacht to pose on… these aren't everyone's dreams. For most people, success looks like paying the mortgage, having the freedom to do the things you want to do, having enough money to not have to worry.

Until you learn to recognise and reconcile yourself to your version of success you will never meet your goals because you will never feel satisfied. Even reaching those high performing months will leave you feeling like you need to do more.

Let me be clear, you cannot outwork your mental health- doing more, pushing yourself more will not clear the anxiety and pressure you feel. There is a point where all the productivity tools in the world, all the tips and tricks and systems will not compensate for taking time to stop, to rest and to reset.

Being proactive about mental health – before the burnout kicks in – isn't a waste, it isn't laziness, it isn't weakness. It's an investment in you and in your business. It's not a nice to have, it's a must have.

Reframing Success – Writing Your Own Definition.

Most of us have developed our definition of success from external factors – society, school, corporate life and the online world. In the business world, for example, success is often reduced down to a few factors: six or seven figure incomes, fully booked courses, 100k/sold out launches or followers and fame.

Questions to ask yourself:

• Whose version on success am I chasing – and does it feel good to me?
• What does success actually mean to me?
• What milestones do I need to hit to feel I'm making progress towards my success?

Those questions might feel a little big to start with so we can break it down even more:

• What makes you feel fulfilled? What things bring you joy and pleasure?
• What makes you feel proud and gives you that endorphin buzz of succeeding?
• What makes you feel grounded and energised, that feels just right?
• What kind of life do you want to build a business round?
• What would success feel like to you if no one else saw it?

As an exercise you can utilise your subconscious to help you understand some of those feelings without allowing external definitions of success to influence you.

Take a moment to sit comfortably, relaxed and without external stimuli and allow your mind to quiet. You are going to imagine your perfect day; assume it is 5 years from now or 10 years from now. Think about the detail – where are you, what can you see, what can you hear or smell or touch. Think about who is with you and what time of day it is. Are you warm, are you inside or outside, how do you feel.

You want to put yourself into an imagined scenario where you feel utterly at peace and content, this is your perfect day.

Try hard to put aside thoughts of images you have seen online, the preconceptions your mind is holding onto – those images of lounging on a yacht, of working from a beach in Bali or getting up at 5am to do sunrise yoga. Think about the things that you want, the things that make you happy – however big or small.

Let your mind wander through that vision – recognise all the things that are bringing you joy and peace; recognise all of the people that you are surrounded by; recognise the tangible and intangible things that you have collected.

That vision of peace and calm and happiness – that is your definition of success.

If you saw yourself on a beach, were you on holiday or working remotely? If you saw yourself surrounded by people, were they your team or your friends and family? If you saw physical things, were they ones you aspire to own?

Write out your vision with all of the things in that made you happy. That list or statement is your definition of success.

The next question to ask then is: how close is your current business model to that version? The gap between to the two is the work you need to do to create success and it might not be beating yourself up over not achieving 7 figure months, it might be celebrating the fact that you already make enough to pay all your bills and still have cash left to have fun.

Don't forget that success doesn't have to be a major life change or shift in your business, it's just as important to celebrate the smaller milestones and the micro successes such as:

* Sending the scary email you've been putting off.
* Taking a day off without guilt and enjoying it.
* Having a peaceful morning to rest and recharge.
* Turning down work that doesn't align with your values.
* Getting a client result you're proud of and want to shout about.

Micro-wins are real, valid, and often more meaningful than vanity metrics from a personal point of view.

Most importantly, remember that success is ongoing and fluid. What you are aiming for today is likely to change in two, five- or ten-years' time. Give yourself permission to change the parameters – up or down, your success is still your personal journey.

Tools to Break Free from Comparison.

Now that you have your vision and your definition of success you don't want to allow the deluge of 'success porn' online derail you.

In order to break it's hold over you it's going to take some work, and that work will be ongoing, but I promise you it's worth it.

I recommend using my STAR system:

- **S** - Stop & Acknowledge
- **T** – Tools
- **A** - Assessment
- **R** – Reflection

Step 1 – Stop and Acknowledge

You cannot change what you aren't aware of – maybe that's why leopards can't change their spots, they don't know they are there?! So, the first stage of making this change is to recognise where you have unhelpful thoughts or patterns.

Reading through this chapter so far you might have seen yourself in some of my comments, I might have highlighted behaviours that you weren't previously conscious of or shone a spotlight on thinking patterns you may not have noticed before. I strongly recommend you review the lists above and the signs I have mentioned and reflect honestly with yourself – are you tricking your brain with any of these thoughts?

If yes, that means we know where we have some work to do but, like quitting anything it's not a simple case of stopping but recognising what needs to change is the first step.

Here's some simple prompts to help you with this exercise:

Start paying attention to your comparison triggers:

- *Are they set off by certain people or certain accounts?*
- *Are you more vulnerable at specific times of the day?*

- *Are there any specific platforms or situations?*

Keep a comparison log for a few days asking yourself:

- *When does it happen?*
- *What's the story you're telling yourself?*
- *How do you feel?*

Remember, creating this awareness is not about judging yourself (any more than you already do), it's about understanding.

So, stop and acknowledge where those areas for improvement are and let's move onto the next step.

Step 2 – Tools

I am going to give you my eight top tools for helping break this cycle of thought patterns. You won't need all of them or they might not all work for you but experimenting with these to find what does work for you is important. Think of it like a pick n mix for mental health support.

1. Digital Detox

You don't need to switch off social media, stop using your mobile phone and move go off grid but you do need to be more intentional with what you are consuming online. Here's some simple tips:

- Unfollow or mute people who regularly trigger comparison (even if you like them).
- Find accounts to follow that share the messy middle, real talk, or inspiring-but-grounded content that you can identify with.

- Use timers or blockers to create boundaries around how and when you scroll.
- Ask yourself: "Does this account make me feel energised, inspired, or deflated?" and react accordingly.

With this we are removing the triggers and the causes of the comparison – making it harder for us to judge ourselves.

2. Be your own Cheerleader.

Start keeping a log of your wins – however big or small they are. Collect client testimonials, PR coverage, posts that got really good engagement, kind words from others and anything else that makes you smile. This proof of progress log will help you ground your negative thought patterns in reality, showing how much, you are doing rather than assuming you're getting nowhere or achieving nothing.

Weekly check-ins are great for staying focussed on your own success, ask yourself what you did well, what did you handle better than last time or what were your wins for the week.

Doing well deserves a celebration and everyone's milestones – just like everyone's version of success, are different. Give yourself a gold star, treat yourself to a latte or just do a little happy dance.

The endorphins you'll get from success recognition will help you combat that feeling that you're not doing enough or that you're not successful.

3. Reconnect with your Why.

Back to that vision of success, your personal guiding light, remind yourself of that vision and of why you started your business – are you meeting or working towards those goals? Well good, because those are the only ones that matter.

You can use value-led decision making to stay on your path, working towards your success – for every decision, ask yourself – is this serving my values or my vision?
To support this work, vision boards or visual reminders are a great way to help your mind stay focussed on what you do want to achieve so you can scroll past someone working from the beach in Bali and remember that sand in your laptop is a bad idea, you burn really easily and you much prefer snowboarding.

4. Create in Silence

Audiences are looking for the authentic you and they're not going to get that if you're copying what everyone else out there is doing. In order to create genuine content that aligns with your values and vision and that feels authentic, switch off.

Find a quiet space where you can create, away from external stimuli or influence. The silence and space will help your creativity to thrive.

You really don't need to know what everyone else is doing to do your thing well.

5. Find your Tribe.

I've talked a lot about knowing where you don't want to be hanging out online and finding those accounts or people that trigger you, but the reverse is true too. Finding those places where people inspire you, make you feel seen, even make you laugh are where you need to be.

Surround yourself with people who celebrate realness, not just results. Peer masterminds, honest business friendships, therapy, coaching, anywhere that feels like a safe space to you. You'll find that you thrive in a community where comparison is talked about openly helping to reduce shame, not to mention the fact that it helps you remember that you're not alone in these feelings.
Sitting alone thinking you're the only one is a one-way ticket to mental health issues – finding people who feel the same way you do combats this instantly.

6. Focus on Control

Stress is how we react when we feel under pressure, and it usually happens when we are in a situation that we don't feel we can manage or control. That feeling of being out of control is where we start to spiral.

Have you noticed though, that a lot of the time, the things you are worrying about aren't actually in your control? If you're stuck in a traffic jam and are going to be late there's really not a lot, you can do – did you leave plenty of time but there was an unforeseen accident? Did you message to let them know you were delayed? If the answer to both is yes, then getting stressed really won't help.

Think carefully about all the things that are causing you stress and then ask yourself – is this in my control? If the answer is no, acknowledge it and put it to one side. If you've done everything you can it will not serve you to continue worrying about it.

However, you can control: how you show up, what you create, the energy you bring, your boundaries, how you react to things and your behaviour. Focus on those and you'll feel a lot lighter.

7. Solutions not Stressing or Shame

One of the most important things you can do is to focus on solutions instead of spiralling into a shame cycle. If you feel like you're not doing enough stop and ask yourself these questions:

1. Name what's triggering the comparison – what have you seen, heard or felt that makes you feel this way.
2. Take a minute to ground yourself: 'I am safe, I am learning, I am enough.' Or reflect on your cheerleader record, show yourself how much you're achieving.

3. Redirect your energy: 'What's one aligned thing I can do next?' – what work can you do towards your version of success.

Taking action to move the needle is a positive thing that will create happy endorphins, making you feel more in control and able to move forward.

We are attempting to stop the fight or flight response in it's tracks and redirect the energy in a more meaningful way.

8. Prioritise You

This is probably one of the most important tools – and one that I insist you do. You are the biggest asset in your business and it's key that you look after that asset as best you can. The calmer you can keep yourself, the easier it is to treat situations rationally, to see and assess stimuli for what it is.

Practices like finding micro-pleasures, breathwork, walking and meditation, grounding exercises and morning check ins.

There are so many ways that you can focus on yourself and your mental wellbeing and it's important to find the ones that work for you. When you do, you should build them into your daily practices.

Step 3 – Assess

Step 3 is simply about taking time to look at all of the tools available to you and find which ones work for you. Not everything will fit seamlessly into your routine or feel comfortable so it's important that you take time to assess how these feel, how these work and how they can be built into your day-to-day life.

Step 4 – Reflect

The last step, step 4, is to reflect on your progress. Things change, we change and it's important to keep reflecting and reviewing where you are. Tools might need to be changed, triggers might differ over time, your support system will ebb and flow as time moves on.

Reflection is an important part of growth and of protecting your mental health. Make sure that it's a central part of your learning and development experience.

Building a Business That Supports Your Mental Health.

Everything we've looked at so far is the tools to cope with, to mitigate the triggers that can cause you to compare yourself to others, creating that stress and mental health crisis. As a business owner it is within your gift to be able to build a world that allows you to avoid those triggers, to find your own joy.

Now that you've recognised and managed how you feel within the context of the online world you should feel stronger and more able to tackle creating your perfect world.

Here are my top tips for doing that:

- Choose a structure that works for you – a business model that fits your energy levels, your style and so on. Don't just do what others are doing (5am starts aren't fun unless you don't need much sleep!)

- Build in space to your day – I always add buffer between meetings to decompress, I have time at the end of the day to wrap up and pull together notes. Building this time in gives you breathing space.

- Learn to ask for help – the community you're going to build around yourself, and family and friends in your circle are there to support you. Learn to recognise when you need help and ask for it. Even if that means taking on a team, it's an investment in you and not just a cost to the business.

- Systems, systems, systems – automation and systems are your friend. The set up may seem painful at first but long term it will make such a difference knowing that lots of elements are handled without stress or intervention.
- Feel Compassion for everyone – compassion for your team, your clients but most of all compassion for yourself. It's so important to recognise that we are all human beings and to allow for the ups and downs that that brings.

- Own your success – revisit your definition of success often, make sure it still fits that ideal vision and, if you need to, reinvigorate or revise it. Keep it top of mind with visual cues and use that as your north star.

This is about integrating mental health into the foundation of how you work, not just treating it as an afterthought or having to repair problems after they occur.

Final Pep Talk – You're Not Behind, You're Becoming.

Your brain is an amazing tool, but it is just that. A tool. Although we sometimes feel that our reactions and emotions are outside of our control, we can influence them. Building new neural pathways that send positive messages to your brain – giving you an upbeat inner voice – is an important practice.

As a small business owner and entrepreneur, you are especially prone to feeling the effects of comparing yourself to others, opening you up to feeling unworthy, feeling like you're not doing enough or are not good enough and that's simply not true. You are enough. The fact that you decided to do this, to take this journey is an amazing step that many are never brave enough to take. Whether you've been walking this path for a few months, a few years or a decade and more you are forging the way forward in a strong, ambitious way.

You are a role model, you are an inspiration and, you are an amazing person who deserves to be celebrated. The rollercoaster you are on is entirely personal and every single day you are making moves towards your goals and your version of success. Cherish the highs and lows, scream when you need to and laugh when you can but most of all, strap in and enjoy the ride.

Denise Matthews

Talent Acquisition, Recruitment, Executive Coaching, Business Coaching, Career Coaching, DISC practitioner

Team Matters: Strategic Hiring, Scaling, and Retention for Lasting Success

Dedicated to my amazing Dad, an inspirational entrepreneur whose work took him around the world, but whose heart was always at home with us.

Linkedin - denisematthewscareercoach

TEAM MATTERS: STRATEGIC HIRING, SCALING, AND RETENTION FOR LASTING SUCCESS

Introduction

As the daughter of an entrepreneur who worked internationally, and having built my own enterprises; some that succeeded and some that taught me powerful lessons through failure, I am sharing my real-world learnings about talent management with you.

Scaling a business is not just about hiring more people. It's about making strategic, well-timed decisions that strengthen your core, protect your culture, and build real capacity for growth.

I have enjoyed a long-established career in Talent Management, working initially in retail leadership before my recruitment career in executive search, agency recruitment, and in-house recruitment, giving me a 360-degree view of what it really takes to find, grow, and keep the right people. Over the years, I have had the privilege of working alongside many businesses in my roles as a Business and Executive Coach and through masterminds with inspiring leaders and founders. I have seen the good, the bad, and the ugly of scaling, and despite it all, I still love being in business and enjoy so much satisfaction from my time with senior leaders who are wondering whether they are in the right job and seek career coaching to help them decide!

This chapter will guide you through how to decide when to build, outsource, or combine your team, how to hire with clarity and compliance, and how to onboard and retain talent in ways that create long-term success.

Done well, your talent strategy becomes the foundation for everything your business can achieve next. Done badly, it can stall your growth before you even get started. My goal is to help you plan scaling with strength, confidence, and resilient staying power.

Are you scaling or are you in freefall?

Are you reaching the point where there are simply not enough hours in the day?

Are you feeling the pressure to hire because your business now takes every ounce of your energy, stealing time from your family, your wellbeing, and even your holidays?

If every project, every client request, and every message on your phone feels urgent, and you are constantly pulled back into work when you should be resting or reconnecting, you are not alone. Many founders and leaders reach a point where what once felt exciting and manageable becomes relentless and exhausting. If you are always working, always checking, and never fully switching off, it is a warning sign; not just that you are busy, but that you urgently need a smarter, more sustainable team structure.

This chapter is here to help you shift from reaction to strategy, and to build the kind of support around you that protects both your business and your life.

When to scale - & how....?

Scaling is not about reacting to pressure; it is about planfully building a business that can grow and stay competitive and successful.

"When and how" do I build my team is a frequently asked question when I am working with founders and SME's. Scaling a team is not about filling seats. It is about building a structure that serves where your business is going, not just where it is today. Before you make any decisions about hiring, outsourcing, or expanding your team, you need to invest time deciding with clarity on what you are trying to achieve.

Start by asking yourself the following questions:
- What are your business goals over the next 12 to 24 months?
- Is your focus on agility, innovation, cost control, or scaling operations?
- What type of roles will help deliver on these priorities?
- Are you hiring to solve an immediate pain point, or to build long-term capacity?
- What impact do you want these new hires to have on your customer experience, operational excellence, or market positioning?

Taking the time to answer these questions for yourself with clarity will keep your hiring decisions focused, strategic, and aligned to your bigger business goals. Without clear intent, it is so easy to stall on hiring, or conversely hire reactively, which can lead to costly mistakes and slower growth.

Once you are clear on the types of roles you need to support your business goals, the next step is to create clear job descriptions and a structure chart which shows roles and areas of accountability, which will all lead into your Hiring framework covered next.

Job descriptions set expectations, define responsibilities, and act as a foundation for recruitment, onboarding, and performance management as they are usually linked to contracts. A strong structure chart brings clarity to how each role fits into the wider business, how reporting lines work, and where future growth opportunities might sit. Taking the time to define roles properly at this stage avoids confusion later and ensures you are hiring with purpose, not just reactionary.

Financial planning for building your team

Before you start setting salaries, advertising roles, or making offers, you need a clear and realistic financial plan. Hiring without understanding the full cost of growing your team is one of the most common mistakes small and scaling businesses make.

Your budget must cover not just salaries, but also benefits, employer taxes, onboarding costs, equipment, training, and early development support. It is also wise to factor in contingency for turnover, salary progression, and potential role changes over time. Budgeting for your team is not just a numbers exercise, it is a leadership commitment. It shows that you are serious about building sustainably, not reactively. Being realistic about what you can afford now, and what you will need to afford as you grow, gives you the discipline to hire strategically rather than emotionally. It also sets a strong financial foundation that supports both retention and long-term success.

Hidden costs to plan for when hiring

- **Onboarding time:** The cost of leadership and team hours spent training and integrating new hires.
- **Employer taxes and pension contributions:** Additional costs over and above the gross salary you offer.
- **Work equipment and software licenses:** Laptops, phones, tools, and platforms needed to get new employees operational.
- **Training and development:** Early technical training, coaching, or skills development support in the first 6–12 months.

- **Recruitment costs:** Advertising fees, agency fees, background checks, and any signing bonuses.

Pay and Progression: Laying the foundations for retention

"Building a simple but strategic pay scale is one of the most practical ways to protect your recruitment investment and create long term commitment." A clear, fair pay structure is essential to attracting and retaining the right talent. It also sends a strong signal about your business values and long-term growth ambitions.

Here is a simple approach to building an effective pay scale:

Research market rates

Start by benchmarking salaries for similar roles in your industry and region. Use salary surveys, job adverts, and recruiter insights to build a realistic range. LinkedIn also has some excellent tools in Recruiter and Prime you can use.

Define salary bands

Group roles by seniority, responsibility, and skills required. Create a salary band for each level rather than setting one flat figure. This gives flexibility to reward experience, loyalty, and performance.

Build in room for progression

Make sure there is a visible pathway/scale for salary progression within roles. Employees should see that strong performance and growing responsibilities can lead to increases over time, not just through promotion.

Balance internal fairness with external competitiveness

Pay should be fair internally across similar roles and levels, but also competitive enough externally to attract strong candidates. Underpaying or major pay inconsistencies create dissatisfaction and risk poor retention.

Document and communicate clearly

Document your pay structure clearly and be ready to explain it to candidates and employees. Transparency builds trust and helps manage expectations from the start.

Rewards and Benefits: Investing in your people for growth

Choosing the right rewards and benefits is not just a financial decision, it's a strategic one. Competitive salaries matter, but the wider package options you offer, such as flexible working, learning and development opportunities, health benefits, and performance bonuses, sends a powerful message about how you value your people. When deciding on rewards, consider what is sustainable for your business now and what will remain attractive as you grow. Focus on benefits that reinforce your culture and support employee wellbeing and career development. Even small businesses can create compelling and meaningful packages without overextending financially. Well-designed rewards help you attract strong talent, motivate your team, build loyalty, and reduce the cost and disruption of high turnover as you scale.

Examples of High-Value, Low-Cost Benefits:

- Flexible working hours or remote work options
- Paid personal development days or access to online learning platforms

- Health and wellbeing contributions, such as gym discounts or mental health support
- Birthday leave or additional paid volunteering days
- Regular one-to-one career development conversations
- Team recognition awards or peer-nominated bonuses
- Clear promotion and progression frameworks
- Buy extra holiday time

Hiring frameworks and recruitment strategies

Hiring the right people starts long before you advertise a role or speak to candidates. It begins with a strong hiring framework that guides how you assess, select, and integrate new talent into your business. A hiring framework sets out the skills, behaviours, and values you are hiring for, and ensures that everyone involved in the recruitment process is aligned. It brings consistency, reduces bias, and strengthens your ability to make confident hiring decisions.

A good framework should cover:

- The technical skills required for the role
- The core competencies and behaviours that align with your business values
- Clear evaluation criteria for interviews and assessments
- Decision-making ownership at each stage of the process
- A pay scale that reflects market rates and supports fair, competitive hiring
- Opportunities for future progression and development, clearly built into role expectations

Strong pay structures and visible development pathways are not just engaging for candidates; they also play a key role in retaining talent and supporting long-term business growth.

Once your hiring framework is in place, you can build recruitment strategies that target the right candidates through the right channels. Recruitment is not just about filling vacancies; it is about attracting individuals who will thrive in your environment and contribute to your growth plans.

Effective recruitment strategies might include:

- Direct sourcing through LinkedIn or industry networks
- Partnering with specialist recruitment agencies who understand your sector
- Advertising through targeted platforms such as Indeed or CV Library - where your ideal candidates are likely to be active
- Using employee referrals to tap into trusted networks
- Engaging in proactive talent pooling for future roles

Every hire you make is a building block for your future business. Rushing the process or relying on ad-hoc methods increases the risk of poor fit and costly turnover. A clear framework, a competitive and fair pay strategy, and a mindful recruitment approach protect your investment as employee retention will create a platform for growth.

Legal Aspects and Compliance

Hiring without the right legal foundations is a risk no business should take. Strong contracts, clear policies, and compliance processes are essential to protecting your people and your company future.

When you start building a team, getting the legal and compliance foundations right is non-negotiable. Hiring without a clear understanding of your legal obligations exposes your business to significant risks, including financial penalties, reputational damage, and operational disruption. At a minimum, you must ensure that you have the right employment contracts, compliant terms and conditions, and up-to-date policies covering areas such as equality, health and safety, working hours, data protection, and grievance procedures. You should also create a clear company handbook that brings these policies together into one place. A well-structured handbook sets expectations, reduces misunderstandings, and acts as a critical reference point for both employees and managers as your team grows. It is much easier to establish good practice early than to try and retrofit it when problems arise.

If you are hiring internationally or engaging contractors, you will also need to understand the specific compliance requirements around employment status, tax obligations, and right-to-work checks.

You do not need to handle this alone. Experienced, CIPD-qualified independent HR consultants, particularly those who specialise in supporting growing businesses, can help you put the right protections in place without overcomplicating your operations. Employment law firms who offer fixed-fee packages for small businesses can also be a valuable resource, along with specialist HR software providers who bundle legal templates, handbook frameworks, and compliance support into their services. Seeking professional advice early, even for basic templates and processes, is a smart investment that protects you, your team, and your business as you grow.

Where to Find Practical Compliance Support – a non-exhaustive list!

*   **Independent HR Consultants:** Look for CIPD-qualified professionals with experience supporting start-ups and scaling businesses.

- **Boutique HR Providers:** Small HR firms often bring together specialists across recruitment, compliance, learning and development, and organisational design, offering a broader range of expertise than a single consultant.
- **Specialist Employment Law Firms:** Some firms offer fixed-fee packages tailored to the needs of growing companies.
- **HR Software Providers**: Platforms like Breathe HR and Citrus HR offer access to policy templates, handbook frameworks, and regular legal updates.
- **Industry Networks and Business Growth Hubs**: Many regional business hubs provide access to HR and legal advisory services at a reduced cost.
- **Financial Institutions:** Some banks, such as NatWest, offer access to HR support services as part of their business banking packages.
- **Professional Associations:** Organisations such as the CIPD provide templates, guidance, and compliance resources for small businesses.

Once you have the legal and compliance foundations in place, the next critical step is deciding how you will resource your growth. Building the right team structure means choosing consciously between hiring in-house, outsourcing, or blending both. Your choices at this stage will shape the speed, quality, and sustainability of your growth.

Build, Outsource, or Blend: Making the right resourcing decisions

Deciding whether to build an in-house team or use outsourced solutions starts with understanding what your business truly needs. Building your own team makes sense when you require long-term, embedded knowledge, when culture fit is critical to success, or when you are developing intellectual property, proprietary methods, or high-trust client relationships.

If you need full control over performance, development, and retention, or you are planning steady growth and want to future-proof your leadership pipeline, building internally is the stronger choice. It requires early investment in onboarding, development, and leadership, but it creates a solid foundation for sustainable growth.

Outsourcing can be the right choice when you need specialist skills on a short-term or project basis, when speed and flexibility are more important than long-term integration, or when it is not practical to build the capability internally. It is also useful when you want to test new markets, manage costs carefully, or avoid overloading your internal leadership structure too early. Business Process Outsourcing (BPO) partnerships can be a smart solution when you need to scale operational functions quickly without the overhead of building large internal teams. Functions like customer service, finance, HR, and IT support can often be outsourced to trusted providers, allowing you to focus internal resources on strategic growth activities. Outsourcing allows you to access expertise without the full commitment of permanent hires, but it requires clear agreements, strong relationship management, and careful attention to protecting your brand and service standards.

The Role of AI in scaling your business

As businesses grow, many operational tasks start to pull valuable time and focus away from leadership and strategic activities. Advances in artificial intelligence (AI) now offer real opportunities to streamline parts of your business without immediately adding headcount. Used thoughtfully, AI can create efficiencies, reduce repetitive workload, and allow your people to focus on higher-value work.

Here are some of the most common areas where AI can add value in a growing business:

- **Customer service support:** Chatbots and AI helpdesks can handle first-line queries, FAQs, appointment scheduling, and simple troubleshooting before escalating to human teams.
- **Data entry and processing:** Routine tasks such as invoice processing, CRM updates, database management, and basic reporting can be automated through AI solutions.
- **Marketing and content support:** AI tools can generate marketing copy drafts, schedule social media posts, segment audiences, and suggest SEO improvements.
- **Scheduling and administration:** AI-powered scheduling assistants can manage diary coordination, send reminders, and track key deadlines.
- **Recruitment screening:** AI platforms can screen CV's, shortlist candidates based on set criteria and automate interview scheduling to speed up early recruitment stages.
- **Finance operations:** Tasks like invoice generation, payment reminders, basic bookkeeping, and expense tracking can be automated to improve accuracy and efficiency.
- **IT and system monitoring:** AI solutions can manage system alerts, identify security issues, and support predictive maintenance for technology infrastructure.

Whilst AI is a powerful tool, I advocate that it should be seen as an enhancement to your human teams, not a replacement. The judgment, creativity, personalisation, and leadership to drive true business growth still come from people. AI can and should free up time and energy for your team to do higher-value work, but it cannot replace the strategic, relational, and cultural elements that make a business strong. Leaders who scale successfully are often using AI to support operational excellence, while continuing to invest in building strong, capable human teams.

Deciding how to resource your growth is one of the most important early leadership decisions you will make. There is no one-size-fits-all answer. The right path will depend on your business model, growth plans, financial position, and the type of expertise you need. To help you make clear, strategic decisions, use the action plan below to assess when it makes sense to build an in-house team, when outsourcing is the smarter option, and when a hybrid approach gives you the best of both.

While technology can accelerate processes and improve operational efficiency, it cannot replace leadership, judgment, or culture. The strength of your team will always come from the people you hire and how you support them. With that in mind, the next step is building a hiring framework that aligns skills, behaviours, and values to your long-term goals.

Considerations for when to establish an 'In-House Team'

- You need long-term, embedded knowledge within the business
- Culture fit is critical to achieving success
- You are developing intellectual property, proprietary methods, or high-trust client relationships
- You need full control over performance, development, and retention
- You plan to scale steadily and want to future-proof your leadership pipelines

*Building your own team requires early investment in onboarding, development, and leadership, but it strengthens the foundation and future resilience of your business.

When to consider Outsourced solutions

- The work is highly specialised, project-based, or temporary
- You need speed, flexibility, or access to expertise you do not have internally
- You want to test new markets, services, or products without full commitment
- You have the budget for short-term expertise but not long-term headcount
- Managing recruitment, HR, or compliance internally would slow you down

*Outsourcing provides fast access to skills and scalability, but it comes with less control over culture and integration.

When to consider a Hybrid (Combination) solution

- Core roles are built internally while non-core or specialist work is outsourced
- You want to scale back-office, technical, or niche functions without diluting leadership or customer-facing teams
- You are growing fast, but your internal infrastructure cannot yet support a full team
- You want to de-risk hiring by using contractors or consultants before offering permanent roles

*Smart businesses protect their leadership and strategic capability by building these roles in-house, while outsourcing for flexibility, cost-efficiency, and specialist expertise where appropriate.

Key questions to ask yourself before deciding:

- Is this role critical to our long-term competitive advantage
- Do we have the internal expertise and capacity to develop this skill

- What is the cost of delay if we do not act fast enough
- What is the risk to quality, brand, and culture if we outsource this work
- How will we measure success, and who will own the outcome – be prepared to revisit this on a regular basis to stay aware of your outcomes and ongoing results

*Asking these questions before you commit will help you scale intentionally, building a business that is both resilient and ready for future growth.

In summary scaling is not about moving faster; it is about moving smarter; every decision you make 'now' is either strengthening or weakening the business you are building.

Scaling successfully is not just about making the right hires. It is about setting your team of people up for success from the start and building a culture together that they want to be part of long-term. A strong onboarding and retention strategy gives you a critical edge as you grow.

Interviewing and candidate decision-making: Hiring with Purpose

Interviewing is not just about assessing skills. It is about uncovering whether a candidate can deliver in the role, respect and live your values, and strengthen your business as you grow. Every interview should be structured, consistent, and aligned to your hiring framework. Unstructured conversations create hiring mistakes, waste time, and expose your business to bias risks. The goal is to create a process that is fair, insightful, and decisive.

Strong interview techniques to use:

- Structured questions: Ask the same core questions of every candidate for the same role to allow fair comparisons.
- Values based interviewing: Include questions that uncover how candidates have demonstrated key behaviours like resilience, collaboration, leadership if relevant, initiative and adaptability in the past.
- Real scenarios: Present practical, role-specific challenges or examples and ask candidates how they would approach them. This tests not just what they know, but how they think and solve problems.
- Skills testing (when relevant): For technical or critical roles, include a short, relevant task that reflects the real work they will be doing.
- Consistent scoring and debriefing: Use scorecards aligned to your hiring framework to rate each candidate immediately after the interview, based on evidence, never gut feel!

Managing applications, Data protection, and candidate communication

Managing candidate data responsibly is not just good practice; it is a legal requirement. Under GDPR and similar data protection laws, any personal information you collect during the recruitment process must be stored securely, accessed only by authorised individuals, and kept no longer than necessary. You must also be transparent with candidates about how their data will be used.

Create a clear process for storing CVs, interview notes, and communications, and document your data retention policy. Good candidate management goes beyond compliance. It is also about building your employer reputation. Communicate respectfully and promptly with every candidate, whether they are successful or not. Set clear expectations about timelines and next steps at every stage.

When you show professionalism and care during the hiring process, you not only protect your business legally, you also enhance your brand, strengthen your talent network, and show your values in action from day one.

Best practice summary for Candidate data:

- **Collect only what you need:** Limit data collection to information relevant to the role and decision-making process.
- **Be transparent:** Inform candidates how their data will be used, stored, and for how long, ideally at application stage.
- **Store data securely:** Use password-protected systems, not personal drives or unsecured spreadsheets.
- **Restrict access:** Only allow those directly involved in the hiring process to access candidate data.
- **Set a clear data retention policy:** Typically, retain unsuccessful candidate data for no more than 6–12 months unless specific consent is obtained.
- **Communicate outcomes:** Always close the loop with candidates after interviews, whether they are successful or not.
- **Delete data responsibly:** Remove candidate records securely when the retention period expires or if the candidate requests deletion

Making hiring decisions

In my experience good hiring decisions come from clarity, discipline, and the ability to stay focused on what really matters.

Before making a final decision:

- Revisit your original hiring criteria. Does this candidate meet the critical skills, behaviours, and values you set at the start?
- Balance short-term needs with long-term potential. Hire not just for today's workload, but for tomorrow's leadership and business plans.
- Do not settle for "good enough" just because you are under pressure. Hiring the wrong person costs far more time, energy, and money in the long run.
- Trust evidence over instinct. Personal chemistry matters, but measurable alignment to role requirements and your company values should come first.
- When in doubt, keep looking for the right fit. A delay in hiring is better than a bad hire.

Strong hiring decisions are not about finding perfection. They are about finding the right person for the right role, in the right business, at the right time — and being confident enough to hold that standard.

Onboarding, Retention, and Culture: Your Growth Foundations

Onboarding processes
The quality of your brand and company onboarding experience will shape how quickly and confidently your new hires settle into the business.

- **Pre-planning:** Before a new employee joins, ensure that contracts, systems access, training plans, and first week schedules are fully prepared. A clear roadmap shows professionalism and creates early momentum.

- **First Week and Month:** Focus on supporting them to integrate, not just allocating them tasks! Introduce them to key people both clients and internally, communicate business goals and help them understand how their role fits into the bigger picture. Early feedback conversations matter. If you have worked with a third party to hire, stay in touch with them too for any feedback they gather.

- **90 Days:** Set clear performance expectations and milestones for the first 90 days. Schedule regular check-ins to review progress, address challenges, and reinforce strengths. A strong 90-day plan accelerates confidence and performance.

Hybrid and Remote Working Support

If you are scaling with hybrid or remote roles, onboarding must be very focused. Clear communication, structured check-ins, and access to the right tools are essential. Remote team members need to feel included, not isolated or feel there is no guidance. Set clear expectations around availability, communication norms, and outcomes from the start, and create opportunities for discussions and connection beyond task-based online meetings.

Remote work offers flexibility, but it is recognised that it also brings real challenges when it comes to motivation, connection, and performance. People who work from home most days of the week can quickly feel isolated, disconnected from the wider purpose of the business, and unclear about their impact if communication and engagement are not handled well. Leaders must be proactive. Regular one-to-ones, clear goal setting, visible recognition, and opportunities for development become even more important in a remote environment. It is not about constant supervision; it is about creating rhythm, structure, and belonging.

Remote employees need to feel trusted and supported, but they also need to see how their work fits into something bigger. A strong culture of communication, accountability, and shared wins is essential if you want your remote team to stay motivated and contribute at their best and enjoy their role.

Practical ways to keep remote teams motivated

- **Weekly check-ins:** Schedule short, structured one-to-ones focused on progress, challenges, and support, not just task updates.
- **Visible goals:** Set clear individual and team goals that are visible and regularly reviewed so everyone sees how their work drives business results.
- **Recognition and wins:** Celebrate achievements publicly, no matter how small. A culture of regular recognition builds momentum and belonging.
- **Learning and Development opportunities:** Offer remote workers clear access to training, mentorship, and career progression discussions.
- **Virtual Team Connection:** Create informal touchpoints such as team huddles, project showcases, or skill-sharing sessions to strengthen team bonds.
- **Clear communication:** Set and model clear expectations for responsiveness, collaboration, and information sharing across platforms.
- **Build regular** weekly, monthly and quarterly meetings to establish in-person connection, make certain meetings compulsory in person such as annual or quarterly planning sessions.

Retention strategies

Keeping great people is just as important as hiring them. Retention starts even before the offer letter by creating an environment where people feel valued, supported, and able to grow.

Focus on:

- Career development pathways and visible progression opportunities
- Regular, meaningful one-to-one conversations focused on growth, not just performance
- Fair and competitive reward structures
- Recognition of contribution, both formally and informally
- Creating a sense of belonging and shared purpose

Cultural anchors & Values

Culture is not 'what you say', it is what you consistently do and how you demonstrate your values. Cultural anchors are the behaviours, values, and practices that hold your team together through growth and change.

How to live your values in the business

Values only count if they are visible every day in how you lead and how you run your business. You cannot expect your team to act on values they only hear about in a presentation or read in a handbook. The team need to see them lived through your decisions, your behaviour, and the way you treat people, (& especially when the pressure is on!).

To embed your values into the business:

- **Hire for values alignment, not just technical skills:** Ask interview questions that test not only what candidates can do, but how they behave under pressure, with clients, and with colleagues. Choose attitude and approach as carefully as you choose ability.
- **Communicate your mission and values clearly and consistently:** Your values should show up in onboarding, in team meetings, in performance reviews, and in everyday

conversations. Make them part of the rhythm of the business, not a special event.

- **Model the behaviours you expect:** Leadership sets the tone. If you want accountability, own your mistakes. If you want collaboration, show it openly. Every action either reinforces or undermines the culture you are trying to build.
- **Reward values-driven behaviours:** Do not just reward end results. Recognise and celebrate when someone shows the right attitude, builds trust, or makes a decision that reflects your principles.
- **Link values to growth opportunities:** Promotions, bonuses, and leadership roles should go to people who live the values, not just those who deliver numbers.

Embedding values is about consistency. If you are inconsistent, your team will quickly understand that the real rules are different from the written ones.

The real test of culture happens when you start to grow quickly. It is easy to hold your standards when you are small. It is so much harder when you are hiring at pace, entering new markets, or facing pressure to deliver faster results. Growth will test whether your values are real or just words.

To protect your culture through scaling:

- **Make values part of every major decision:** Hiring, partnerships, client selection, and internal promotions should all reflect your cultural standards.
- **Select cultural champions deliberately:** Identify people at all levels who consistently live the values and empower them to influence others.
- **Build feedback loops into the system:** Regularly check whether the team still feels connected to the values and whether behaviours on the ground match what you stand for.

- **Act early when behaviours slip:** If someone undermines your values, even if they are technically high-performing, deal with it quickly and directly. Protecting your culture is more important than protecting individual short-term results.

When you invest early in onboarding, retention, and culture, you are not just building a team, you are building the foundation for a business that can thrive for the long term.

Growing your team: The role of Performance Reviews and one-to-ones

As your team grows, regular performance reviews and one-to-one conversations become essential for maintaining alignment, momentum, and standards. Reviews are not just about tracking results. They are leadership tools that reinforce expectations, recognise strengths, surface development needs, and keep individuals connected to the business and its goals.

Build in a review process which addresses different aspects of performance:

- **Regular weekly/monthly reviews should be focused on results,** progress against goals, and immediate problem-solving and information sharing. These sessions help keep projects on track, maintain accountability, and quickly address any emerging issues.
- **Six-monthly and annual reviews should go deeper.** These sessions should cover broader topics such as teamwork, attitude, values alignment, leadership potential, resilience, and career aspirations. They are an opportunity to step back from day-to-day tasks and have meaningful conversations about personal growth, contribution, and future opportunities within the business.

A strong performance management rhythm shows your team that growth is expected, supported, and rewarded. It gives individuals clarity and motivation; while giving you the visibility and leverage you need to build a stronger, more capable team over time.

One-to-one agenda suggestions

For regular one-to-ones, keep the structure simple but intentional:

Progress review:
What goals or projects have been completed or progressed since the last meeting?
Where have results been strong, and where is support needed?

Challenges and barriers:
What obstacles are getting in the way of performance or wellbeing?
What decisions, tools, or resources are needed?

Feedback exchange:
What feedback do you have for them, and what feedback do they have for you?
Keep it two-way, honest, and constructive.

Development Focus:
What skills or behaviours need building for their next stage of growth?
Agree one practical development action they will take before the next session.

Values and culture check-in:
How well are they living the company values day-to-day?
Recognise good examples and discuss any gaps openly.

Future goals:
Set clear next steps and confirm what success will look like by the next meeting.

Common mistakes to avoid in Performance reviews

Focusing only on results, not behaviours:
- High performers who undermine culture still create long-term damage. Review how goals are achieved, not just whether they are met.

Letting feedback pile up or avoidance:
- Waiting for six months to address issues makes small problems bigger. Address concerns early and often through regular one-to-ones.

Turning reviews into task updates:
- Reviews should focus on development, values, and the bigger picture, not just a list of completed tasks. Separate project updates from real performance conversations.

Avoiding tough conversations:
- Avoiding feedback to keep things comfortable weakens standards over time. Lead with honesty and respect, even when the message is tough.

Failing to link individual goals to business goals:
- People are more motivated when they understand how their work contributes to the bigger mission. Make the connection visible and meaningful.

If you are serious about scaling, you must be serious about leading. Strong teams are created through the daily discipline of coaching, feedback, and clear standards, not hope or good intentions.

Setting and reviewing key statistics for scaling

When you are scaling a business, relying on instinct alone is not enough. You need clear, measurable data to track progress, spot risks early, and make confident decisions. Key statistics should cover both operational performance and team dynamics. At a minimum, set and regularly review metrics such as revenue growth rates, client acquisition and retention, project delivery times, and profit margins. On the people side, track employee turnover, time-to-hire, onboarding success rates, and internal promotion rates. Pay attention to team engagement measures as well, such as feedback participation rates, wellbeing surveys, and voluntary exit reasons.

Good data gives you early warning signals when systems are under pressure, team morale is slipping, or customer experience is suffering. Keep an eye on Glassdoor and Indeed for employee reviews so you can respond if you wish.

Succession planning: Thinking beyond today's team

As you scale, it is not enough to think only about the team you need today. You also need to prepare for the future leaders your business will require. Succession planning is not a corporate luxury; it is a vital part of responsible growth. Identify early who shows the capacity to grow into bigger roles, not just based on technical performance, but based on values alignment, leadership potential, and resilience. Create clear pathways for development and stretch opportunities. Building a strong internal leadership pipeline reduces the risk of critical gaps, improves retention, and helps your business maintain momentum even as key players move or progress.

Key people metrics to track

- Employee turnover and voluntary exit rates
- Time-to-hire for new roles
- Cost of recruitment
- New hire onboarding success rates (first 90 days retention and performance)
- If in a sales or £performance role track their ROI
- Internal promotion rates and leadership pipeline health
- Engagement survey participation and sentiment scores

- Reasons for employee exits captured through exit interviews

Data does not replace leadership, but it strengthens it. The businesses that scale successfully are the ones that measure what matters and act on what they learn.

In summary:

Scaling a business is one of the greatest leadership challenges you will ever take on.

It demands clarity, consistency, courage, and a deep commitment to building something bigger than yourself.

Every hire, every conversation, and every decision you make shapes the future of your business.

Build with purpose.
Lead with intention.
Protect your culture as fiercely as you chase growth.

When you scale with strategy and strength, you are not just growing a business — you are building a legacy.

Sarah Hands

I provide small businesses with a finance department that fits their budget, is bespoke to their needs, jargon free and can grow as their needs change.

Cashflow – how to predict, prepare and prosper

To all the awesome women I know creating amazing businesses

Linkedin - Sarah Hands

CASHFLOW - HOW TO PREDICT, PREPARE AND PROSPER

Finance is my passion. As a child I had a little book where I tracked my pocket money and what I was spending it on. It was natural that I would end up in a finance career. My parents had told me to 'choose a useful degree' and because I had an irrational dislike of marketing (too fluffy for my black and white brain) I chose to pursue an Accounting and Finance degree which had an industrial placement year. The rest is history. That placement opened my eyes to working in large organisations and the variety of finance roles on offer and I loved it and then spent twenty-five years working across finance honing my skills. Always happy to take the roles no-one else wanted, the roles talking to the business and translating the world of finance into something meaningful to non-finance people.

Inside these big organisations, the people I worked with had a passion and expertise for different business areas. They then found themselves promoted and with the extra responsibility came a budget to manage. In the majority of cases, that promotion didn't come with any finance training. It was my role to help, guide and show them what the numbers meant and how they supported what they felt was happening or helped them to understand why the profit number wasn't quite where they expected it to be.

I now have my own accountancy practice specialising in supporting small businesses to be more confident with their numbers.

Introduction

If you are reading this chapter, I'm going to guess that finance is not why you got into business. You had a passion for something or saw that your skill could benefit many people and the financial bit is just a necessary evil when running your business.

When you started your business, I doubt you started it to worry about bookkeeping, tax deadlines and accounts. You do what you do because you love it, but now there are all these hats to wear, some of which don't suit you, and some don't fit. Finance could well be that awkwardly shaped hat where you can't even figure out which is the front and which is the back.

Finance is not often a space that new business owners are comfortable in. When numbers are not a strength, finance can quickly become stressful. Business finance can feel like it is full of impenetrable jargon, and a lack of understanding can leave you feeling like an impostor in your own business. You should know this stuff, right? I think you would be surprised by the number of business owners who know very little about their business finances and are happy to have an accountant at the end of the year who does all the tax stuff, leaving them to carry on what they were doing.

In this chapter, I will tackle what I think is the ONE FINANCIAL ACTIVITY all business owners should do and why, I will break down some barriers and help you become financially confident.

Most business owners focus on sales, and some may watch their costs to ensure they maximise their profits. While both measures are important, I would suggest that cash flow is the most important thing to focus on when running a small business.

Let's start by busting some myths:

- **"If I'm profitable, my cash will take care of itself."**
Not necessarily. You can make a profit on paper, but you could be waiting weeks for payment when bills are due today.
-
- **"Forecasting is only for big business."**
Forecasting is more important for small businesses. Since they don't have the same financial buffer as a large company, predicting the future is their superpower.

- **"You can't predict the future, so what's the point?"**
True, you can't predict the future, but that's not the point. Forecasting is all about preparing for likely events and giving yourself early warning of potential problems.

- **I'll sort this when I've got more time."**
In that time, you could be making poor decisions with a longer-term impact. Cash flow forecasting helps you make better decisions before things get too urgent to ignore.

I want you to finish this chapter feeling empowered to own your business's finances, taking back control, having a clear vision of what's coming, and having a plan to handle it.

Over the next few sections, you'll learn how to:
- Understand the basics of cash flow and how it differs from profit.
- Recognise the common traps that cause cash flow crunches.
- Build a simple, clear cash flow forecast - even if you hate spreadsheets.
- Use your forecast to spot problems early and make confident decisions.
- Avoid sleepless nights and frantic last-minute scrambles for cash.

This is not about you becoming an accountant; it's about making finance something you understand and can use to make better decisions, not something you avoid.

Cash Flow Basics

Cash flow is money in and out of your business, it as simple as that. At any one time, the money in your bank accounts is your cash position.

Think of your business as a leaky bucket. The cash coming into your business is like the water going into your bucket from the tap. The money you spend on wages, bills and with suppliers is like the money trickling out of the holes. The amount of money in your business is the water level in that bucket. The point of a cash flow forecast is to ensure that you never run out of money, or in my analogy, you need to make sure your bucket never gets empty.

Many people confuse profit and cash in their business, so let me give you an example to illustrate the difference.

You do a job in April for £1,000, but don't get paid until May. You have wages and overheads to pay in April of £600. On paper, the profit will look like you made £400 (£1,000 less £600). The reality is that you could not pay those bills at the end of April, as the cash hadn't arrived. This is how businesses get into a tricky situation, as they know their business is profitable, but they haven't realised that their bank account is showing a different story.

To support you in managing cash flow, start by tracking your cash inflows (income). Sales will generate the most significant inflow for your business, but remember that it only counts as cash flow when you get paid. Other inflows could be grants, loans, and affiliate income.

Cash outflows (outgoings) are anything you spend regularly, such as wages, rents, utilities, materials, subscriptions, subcontractors, insurance, tax bills, and the not-so-regular, like a new laptop, equipment, or van.

Please note, that just because you are tracking this it does not mean that you can't still run into cash troubles. Let's look at a few scenarios:

- **Cash goes out before it comes in.** Sales are healthy, but the cash comes in later, often over a month after that sale. Then you have customers that don't pay, or can't pay, and it slows or stops the cash flow inwards.
- **You grow too quickly.** Your business starts to take off, and you hire staff or bulk buy materials, but it takes a while for the sales generated to catch up with the cost outlay.

- **Tax bills.** You didn't put the money aside for VAT or Corporation Tax, and the bill comes due.

- **Seasonality.** Sales fluctuate with the seasons, leaving dips in the year that leave you short of cash.

- **Personal Drawings.** You take out more cash than the business can afford, leaving you short of cash to pay the bills.

Some of these may sound familiar to you, but don't worry, that's normal business life. The good news is that all these challenges can be managed by understanding your cash flow and giving yourself visibility through a cash flow forecast.

Cash is an emotional subject, not just a financial one. Stress in business can occur because you don't know if you have enough money to pay the bills. The stress builds and tips over into family life and friendships. The good news is that you will make decisions from a knowledgeable position once you gain clarity and confidence with numbers. You will have space to plan. The stress will ease, if not slip away.

Cash flow forecasting should not be seen as an admin task to do when you get time; it's a powerful business tool that gives you control and confidence, making you a better business owner.

Common Cash Flow Pitfalls

Cash flow issues rarely occur without warning. In most businesses, patterns help us predict what will happen and, most importantly, help us spot the warning signs of issues so we can swerve them!

Here are some common issues that crop up in businesses and how we can reduce their impact.

* **Waiting too long to get paid.**

Most businesses, especially service-based businesses, have credit terms. You will agree to do the work, complete the job, send the invoice, wait to be paid, and sometimes wait some more.

Taking some steps to be more in control of this aspect can have positive benefits for your cash flow.

Make sure you are clear about your payment terms. The terms should be stated on your contract, and those terms should be clearly stated on the invoice that is sent.

Follow up persistently on late payments. Most bookkeeping software will have automated reminders that you can set up, but beyond those reminders, don't be afraid to pick up the phone and ask why you haven't been paid. Remain polite but firm. You deserve to be paid for the work you have done.

For larger projects, you may wish to consider deposits or stage payments. Be clear about what triggers the payment request.

- **Spending during busy periods.**

Business is going well. The bank balance looks good. You decide to upgrade the website, hire staff, sign up for that subscription to that software that will save you so much time. The problem with that approach is that what you have today may not be what you have tomorrow. Business fluctuates, and without understanding how a change in sales could impact your ability to pay bills in the future, you could over-commit.

If you are in a growth phase, consider flexible and short-term commitments to help you stay in control.

Always check your forecast before taking on additional commitments. Be sure you can still afford the additional costs if sales dip in the future.
It's a bit of a juggling act when you are in a growth phase and there is always a compromise between the speed of growth and ensuring your business isn't starved of cash.

- **Underestimating the tax bills**

The bank balance looks amazing, and you treat yourself because you've been working hard. Then the reminder pops in about the VAT that's due or the Corporation Tax you'd totally forgotten about. The resentment builds because taxes never feel fair.

This is one of those events that requires preparation! Set aside the tax monthly in a separate bank account. Ask your bookkeeper or accountant for an estimate to understand what you need to save. Do not touch that money unless it's an emergency.

Not understanding the lumpy nature of your income

You could be seasonal or have low-volume, high-value contracts. Your business can feel a little bit like being on a rollercoaster. For businesses with more up-and-down income, planning is crucial to ensure you have a buffer in the lean times and don't spend what you need later in the year.

Look at your monthly sales for the last 12 months and understand when the quieter periods may be. Start creating a cash buffer for the lean times in the busy periods.

Where you have larger projects spanning longer time periods, consider a retainer model, or stage payments to help manage the cash. Forecasting will help you feel like the rollercoaster is suitable for children and not a high adrenaline version!

Paying yourself what and when you like

You deserve to be paid for the hard work you put into your business, but that business money is not all yours; you can't just dip in and take cash when you feel like it. You must balance what the business needs to be sustainable with what you need to live.

Treat yourself like an employee with a fixed salary. Agree with yourself how much you will take out each month and stick to it. The amount you take out of the business should be in the forecast, like all the other wages and bills. Review the "salary" regularly to ensure it's sustainable and growing in line with business growth if desired.

Forgetting the annual bills

It is easy to forget the annual insurance or the software licence charged once a year. Review last year's accounts and ensure you have a list of those less frequent items, when they are charged and the previous cost. Make sure all those items are in the forecast.

Maintain that list. If you forget one this year, put it on the list so you don't forget it next year. That list will also help you look at the renewal options with enough time to switch if necessary rather than having to renew for another year because you have left it too late to research.

Not looking ahead

If money and finances make you uneasy, or it's a job you loathe, ignoring it won't make it go away. Be intentional. Plan the time each month that you will set aside to review what's happened and reflect any changes in the forecast. Make an appointment with yourself as if you are a client – it's not OK to cancel a client at the last minute unless an emergency, same goes for your finances.

It doesn't have to be perfect. Trying and improving it in small steps is way better than not starting at all.

You don't have to do this alone. If you need help, ask a trusted friend or a professional, but don't struggle.

What is a Cash Flow Forecast

You've been reading along, nodding your head, acknowledging a few of the examples as things you do yourself then you are ready to take action and this is where the fun starts!

By understanding how to forecast, you can turn cash chaos into a clear picture of the future. The Cash Flow Forecast is a simple tool that allows you to see what is coming up in the future and plan – think of the weather app on your phone. Before you leave for a day of outside activities, you would check if you need an umbrella, waterproofs, or to reschedule. It's the same with a cash flow forecast, but we look at money in and out to ensure there are no nasty surprises you aren't prepared for.

I'm turning it a little on its head and starting with what a forecast isn't.

- It's not a set of accounts or a tax return
- It doesn't need to be perfect
- It doesn't need to be complicated
- It is not a guarantee

Think of your cash flow as a guide to the future.

The forecast will start with your bank balance, show all the cash expected to come in for the period, and show all the cash leaving the accounts in the same period, giving you what you expect your bank balance to look like at the end.
The forecast should be separated into timeframes that suit you. If cash is tight, weekly may be best. You may do a combination of the immediate month in weeks, moving out to months when things are less certain.

Let me give you a simple example,

	Week 1	Week 2	Week 3
Opening Balance	£1,000	£2,500	£1,500
Money In	£2,000	£2,000	£1,000
Money Out	£500	£3,000	£3,000
Closing Balance	£2,500	£1,500	-£500

You can see a shortfall in week 3, which is two weeks away. You have time to take action rather than let it be a surprise.

Keeping on top of your cash flow forecast is vital for all businesses. This is not just something large companies should do with their teams of finance folks; small businesses don't have the size of safety net that larger companies have, so I'd argue it's even more critical for a small business to have a cash flow forecast in place.

Here's what a cash flow forecast will help you do:

- **Spot shortfalls before they happen.**
If you know you will be short of cash, you can take action. You can chase up payments, delay expenditure or secure an overdraft or loan.

- **Make confident decisions.**
The cash flow forecast lets you see if an investment such as a new laptop is affordable.

- **Sleep better at night.**
With the forecast laid out in front of you, there is less guess work. You can plan for the quiet periods and see what is coming in and out, giving you peace of mind.

- **Communicate better.**
A cash flow forecast demonstrates that you are thinking ahead and are in control of your business. If you need that loan, the lender will look favourably at a business that can show its cash position and demonstrate that it can repay the loan.

There is no right or wrong answer regarding how far out you should forecast. The further into the future you forecast, the less accurate it will be, and the more unknowns will come into play. These are your options:

- Short-term – 2 to 3 months into the future is needed when cash is tight. Usually forecasting in weeks makes more sense for this time period.
- Medium-term – 3 to 6 months is useful for planning day to day activities.
- Long-term – 6 to 12 months is useful for growth plans, major decision making or investment decisions.

If you have never forecasted before, start small. Just the next month can make a big difference. Remember, small steps are better than no steps.

To get started, a spreadsheet, either Google Sheets or Microsoft Excel, will do the job. Specialist software is available, but I find a well-organised spreadsheet works just as well. You will need your bank balances and a list of upcoming payments and income.

The first step is building the forecast, which we will do in the next section. The real value comes from updating it regularly, being willing to make that appointment with yourself to spend time updating and improving. This is not a one-off exercise.

Building the forecast

You've made it this far - you understand why it's important, and you want to feel in control, so let's build one together. I promise this will not be scary. You don't need to learn any new complicated software. You need your current numbers, a bit of time, and a willingness to take a look and be honest with yourself.
Step 1: Open up a spreadsheet

Start by putting in the time periods as columns, like my example previously. This could be weeks or months, depending on how tightly you need to manage cash flow. I suggest you start with three or four columns of time.

We will now start to populate the rows.

Step 2: Bank Balances

Open your bank account and check the balance now. Don't guess and don't go off what your bookkeeping software says is in there.

Remember, cash flow forecasting is all about actual money, not guesswork or accounting.

In the second row, add a header called opening balance and in the first time period, add what your bank account said.

Step 3: Expected income

Make a list of all the invoices that have been sent, but no payment has been received. If you use bookkeeping software this information will be available as a report – it could be called aged creditors, or aged receivables.

In the third row, add a header called invoiced sales.

Look at when those payments are due and add the value into the month you expect to receive the money. If you have a customer who always pays a week late, reflect that. Remember, we are forecasting what we think will happen, not what should happen. Think about the work you know will be invoiced soon and when that will be paid. Have a separate line called forecasted sales; this will help you see that this is not guaranteed yet. Over time, this will help you get more accurate with your sales forecasting.

Finally, consider any other income you may receive, such as grants, one-off payments, and interest, and add them to a line called "other income." If it's easier for you, have them on separate lines.

Step 4: Outgoings

Go through your regular business spending and note all upcoming payments. Group similar things together and add lines into the spreadsheet to reflect when that money will be paid.

Include wages, pension payments, rent, electric, software subscriptions, loans and repayments, insurance, training, VAT and other tax payments, your drawings.

A good tip here is to go through last month's bank statement and check you have included everything.

Remember that list we made of the less regular payments, grab that now and see if any of those payments are due in the time frame we are doing the forecast for. Add the necessary ones in.

Step 5: Calculate the closing balance

Take the opening balance (from the bank account), add the income lines, and deduct the outgoings. This will be your closing balance. Do this as a formula in the closing balance line, so any adjustments you make will be automatically updated.
Make the opening balance of period 2 equal the closing balance of period 1 and so on. Your last entry should be a closing balance.

Step 6: Build it out

Carry on adding the income and expenditure into the periods you want to forecast. Don't worry about it being perfect, it's so much better to get something rough down than spend ages worrying about small amounts.

What does your closing balance look like? Are there any months when it goes into a negative number? This is the magic: you can see those problems ahead of time and take action now.

Step 7: Keep it alive and relevant

By its very nature, a forecast will never be 100% accurate. That's OK. Things will change, but what matters is that you keep it alive and relevant to what you can see. Add notes and comments about why you're adding numbers the way you have – for example, Client A always pays 2 weeks late, Ms B is back from maternity leave, pay back to full. These will help remind you why the numbers are moving.

It's your tool. If you need to break income down into more lines that make sense for your business, then do it.

The key is to then start using it as a live document:

- Update the just-finished period with what happened. Try to understand if you need to change anything in the future months based on what you know now.

- Change the income and expenditure as you have new information – so the sales forecast will become sales invoiced, new supplier bills will come in.

- Use it to make decisions. If you can see a period when cash gets tight, delay a spend or chase a payment.

It may feel hard when you start and you may miss some things. This is normal. A forecast is not about perfection, but more progress. As with most things in life, making it a habit is the hard part; the forecast will get easier every time you look at it. Just make a start! Complexity and software tools can come later if you want them to. Cash flow forecasting is a core skill separating reactive from resilient businesses. Before you know it, you'll wonder how you managed without a cash flow forecast.

Real Life Scenarios

If you are not a numbers person, then trying to understand how cash flow forecasting can fit into your business may be hard to visualise. I'm going to give you some examples of real-life business owners, just like you, who faced challenges in their business and used cash flow forecasting to overcome them and feel confident in their decision-making.

Case Study 1: *A service business with a small growing team*

Meet Louise, owner of a social media management company, with five employees.

The Problem
Client work is consistent and profitable, but at the end of each month, Louise panics about payroll and sometimes has to dip into her personal savings to meet the shortfall.

What changed
Louise sat down with her bookkeeper and mapped out a three-month forecast using a simple spreadsheet. She mapped out known income from client contracts, fixed and variable costs, and weekly cash balances to check for future dips. Louise looked at the forecast before making decisions such as new spending or taking on larger projects.

The result
With a clearer picture, Louise could negotiate better terms with a couple of clients and chose to delay hiring a new team member until the cash position felt stronger. No longer relying only on gut feeling, she felt more in control.

Louise's win
"Before, I was guessing. Now I make decisions with facts. It's a game-changer."

Case Study 2: *Art Teacher with seasonal income*

Meet Sonia, an arts teacher who runs after-school and holiday clubs, as well as pop up events at festivals. Her bumpy cash-flow is giving her sleepless nights.

The problem
School holidays provide Sonia with more income than during the school terms. Towards the end of a term, cash dries up, and she has to use her credit card to bridge the gap until the holiday club income starts again. Sonia doesn't know how to break out of the cycle of boom or bust.

What she did
With the help of her bookkeeper, Sonia mapped out a full school year in Excel, month by month, splitting her income and expenses by the three areas of her business:

- After School Clubs
- Holiday Clubs
- Festivals

For each area of the business, she looked at average attendance and associated income, costs associated with each of her three business streams and what her personal drawings would be.

The result
They saw that the festival work was well paid and the same format could be run each time. Sonia realised she could afford to bring in additional support to run the festival workshops and therefore not have to limit the holiday clubs, overall increasing the income during the summer holidays. By putting aside money from the summer work, she could use that to support the leaner months when only after-school clubs were running.

Sonia's win

"I feel back in control of the business and have clear sight of what part of the business makes what money. I don't have to worry in term time about paying myself; it's such a relief."

Case study 3: *Freelance designer working on projects*

Meet Rachel, a brand designer who works mainly on projects. The nature of the work means some months her income is £5,000 and others less than £1,000. She doesn't know what to pay herself, if she can take a holiday and feels insecure despite being busy.

The problem

Rachel was stuck making decisions. She knew she was profitable, but it never felt like that; the bank balance always felt like one late payment could create a cash crisis. She would take on more work to stay ahead, meaning she felt burnt out and wasn't sure if getting a job would just be easier.

What she did

Rachel created a simple 12-week rolling forecast in Google Sheets. She listed her confirmed project values, adding estimated payment dates with a two-week buffer for late payments. She logged her business expenses and what she would like to pay herself personally each month. It was important to Rachel to understand when not to worry, so she looked at what the minimum bank balance would need to be, so she didn't panic.

The result

Rachel realised her quieter months were nothing to worry about, as payments from earlier projects would arrive. Having this breathing room meant she stopped overbooking herself and started a savings pot to cover the leaner months, so her bank account didn't dip below the comfort zone.

Rachel's win

"Instead of fearing a quiet spell, I now plan for it. I feel more in control and am sleeping much better".

These three people had one thing in common: They used forecasting to move from firefighting to forward planning. There was no need for them to become accountants or use specialist software. They took a small amount of time to look ahead in their business and gained clarity, enabling them to become calm and confident in their businesses.

Tips to stay on track

You've stuck in and created a forecast - that's a huge step completed right there. Like any new habit, we have to nurture it. Carry on making those appointments with yourself to keep it up to date. You've come a long way, and we don't want that spreadsheet gathering dust and not being used.

The real power of forecasting is those small adjustments you make as things shift a little in your business or you understand more about the trends happening in your numbers. So, how do you make sure it's not a once-and-done exercise?

Make a date with your numbers

Make that date with yourself - treat yourself like your favourite, most important client so you won't be tempted to break it.

If you do your own bookkeeping, it's good to update the forecast once you know your bookkeeping is complete. Updating the forecast will get quicker the more often you complete the job.

Compare your forecast with reality

Review what is happening regularly. When you first start, it may be easier to do the weekly. Compare what happened to what you expected and understand if there is anything in the future periods you need to adjust.

- Did your clients pay on time?
- Were all the costs as you expected?
- Were there any surprises?

Remember, this is not about perfection; it's getting better each time. You may want to build in buffers for some uncertainties, but you will soon spot patterns and estimate more accurately.

Use it to make decisions
Proving to yourself that the forecast is a valuable tool will motivate you to keep it updated. You can start asking questions such as:

- Can I afford to take on a new employee?
- When would be the best time to buy this new equipment?
- Do I have enough to pay the VAT?

The forecast will guide you, rather than dictate to you. You are in control!

Spotting the dips early
The most significant benefit of a forecast is understanding when you will have a shortfall with enough time to take action. If you see your cash balance dropping below a comfortable level, can you:

- Delay a purchase?
- Speed up income by invoicing earlier, getting a job finished quicker, or chasing up a client who hasn't paid yet?
- Speak to a supplier about delaying payment?
- Reduce your own drawings for a short time?
- Would a loan be a good option?

Options are the key here; by understanding you have a shortfall, you have time to explore different ways to overcome the dip and plan for it to happen.

You don't have to do this alone

Consider completing it with someone else if forecasting is boring, dull, or a drag. It's OK to ask for help.

- You could talk it through with your bookkeeper or accountant
- Pair up with another business owner – keep yourselves accountable, perhaps have a regular co-working session where you work on your numbers

The more you talk through numbers, the more natural it will feel and the more confident you will become. You will own the numbers and be comfortable with the forecast; it will come as a tool rather than something to fear.

Remember, forecasting means freedom. You can stop second-guessing yourself, plan with certainty, reduce stress, and start enjoying your business again.

What do you do when things are tight?

Forecasting is a superpower; you can look into the future so you have time to take action. Many businesses will face times when cash becomes tight. The benefit of a cash flow forecast is that you have the time to act. Knowledge is power.

So, your forecast shows you that you will not have enough cash in the business in three months. What do you do? Well the first step is not to panic. Accept this is a normal part of business and give yourself a little pat on the back because of the time you have put into your cash flow forecast. You have the knowledge ahead of time and can get a plan sorted.

Step 1: Quantify the problem

Looking at the forecast, understand how big the gap is and how long it will last. There are different actions for a £1,000 issue lasting a week and a £5,000 problem lasting three months.

Step 2: Understand if you can bring income in quicker

The first place to look is your income. Can you get money in quicker, or boost income? Some options to consider:

• Invoice straight away. If you normally send invoices at the end of the week or month, get them out as soon as the work is complete.
• Chase up late payments. Be polite but firm, you are entitled to be paid on time for work completed.
• Launch a flash sale or offer to increase sales quickly.
• Don't be afraid to ask for a deposit for new work booked in.

Step 3: Reduce or delay expenditure

The good news about having a forecast is that you can see all your outgoings.

• Review subscriptions – can any be downgraded, paused or cancelled?
• Delay non-essential purchases
• Ask for extended terms from suppliers – the earlier you can do this, the more likely you will be successful
• Review marketing, networking or training spends to see if you could reduce the cost here temporarily

Small amounts add up and it can be quicker to reduce costs than generate additional income.

Step 4: Talk to people early

If a shortfall is still likely, talk to people as early as possible so you remain in control.

- Talk to your bookkeeper or accountant – fresh eyes may spot something you have missed.
- Call HMRC - they may be willing to set up a payment plan. This is not an unusual request, and the earlier you ask, the more willing they will be to help you. HMRC will have confidence in you, knowing you have a forecast, and you know how long the shortfall will last.
- Speak to your bank - there may be options for short-term credit, such as an overdraft. As with HMRC, showing you have a forecast, and the time period of the gap will be in your favour.

Step 5: Update your plan

Make sure to update the forecast to reflect your plan, which is likely to be a combination of the above steps. This will help you remain in control and ensure you have the right information to make sure the path ahead is clear.

Final thoughts and action steps

If you have got to the end of this chapter, well done. You've taken time to learn something that many business owners avoid. Learning a new skill is not a small thing; it's a sign of genuine care for your business.

Cash flow forecasting isn't about numbers in spreadsheets; it's about giving you peace of mind, knowing that you are in control and can see what the future holds, and helping you to make better decisions.

Let's recap what we have covered:

- Profit is not enough on its own to keep a business afloat
- Common pitfalls that catch business owners off guard
- How to build your own forecast, step by step
- Real-life examples of how other entrepreneurs have used forecasting to stay in control
- Tips for sticking with it and building a habit
- Steps to go through when your forecast shows a shortfall

You now have everything you need to get started or improve the process if you've already started.

Get started while it's fresh in your mind:

1. Open a blank spreadsheet
2. List your expected income and costs for the next 4-12 weeks
3. Work out the closing balance for each time period
4. Review it weekly to start with
5. Get help if you need it

You started your business because you had a passion for your craft, something you knew others could benefit from. Forecasting ensures you will be able to carry on doing what you love by ensuring you can pay the team, keep the lights on, the taxman happy and earn an income all while continuing with the business ambition.

You don't need to be a finance expert to forecast. You just need to be a business owner who wants clarity, confidence, and control.

And now, you are.

Sarah Bolitho

Supporting behaviour change and healthy habits

Burnout Be Gone

Whether you want to change the world or tweak your life, you need to start today and keep moving forward. Even your smallest steps are part of your journey.

Instagram - @fabnewlous_active_lives

BURNOUT BE GONE

Sarah Bolitho helps people to change their lives and achieve their dreams. She does this by working directly with clients to identify their habits and promote positive behaviour change, and also by training fitness and health professionals to support sustainable behaviour change in their clients and patients.

Has Sarah experienced burnout? Absolutely. Her field can be a bit feast and famine which increases the risk of burnout, so she has developed ways to support her physical and mental health and maintain a balanced life. As a solopreneur this is vital as if she can't work, she doesn't get paid. Knowing that prevention is better than cure, Sarah shares her Burnout Prevention Strategy in this chapter. This is as important a strategy as your marketing or sales one so do read it.

Part of Sarah's BPS is creating routines, whether this is walking every morning at 5.30am, prepping lunch for the whole week, getting her clothes ready the night before or taking regular breaks from the computer. This doesn't mean missing out on fun as she creates nothing time (read the chapter to find out more) so she has space for enjoyable activities or the odd game of Candy Crush.

When not working, you will find Sarah walking, hiking, or just being in nature so if she doesn't answer your email immediately, it's because the mountains called, and she had to go!!

Find out more about Sarah's offers and grab a couple of downloadable information sheets at www.fabnewlous.com. If you want to get in touch email sarah@fabnewlous.com

Introduction:

Seriously, I'm reading a book about business and all of a sudden, Sarah is wittering on about making your bed, watching the clouds and cooking soup. What's that all about?
I'll tell you what this is all about.

Burnout.

And how to avoid it.

If you are reading this book, you probably know someone who has 'burnout'. You may even have experienced it yourself. It is an issue for both employed and self-employed business people so we need to be aware of the signs and symptoms so we can manage risk.

So, what is burnout?

The World Health Organisation (WHO) (1) considers burnout an occupational phenomenon, (not a medical condition) and their definition is:

"Burn-out is a syndrome conceptualised as resulting from chronic workplace stress that has not been successfully managed. It is characterised by three main symptoms:

- Feelings of energy depletion or exhaustion.
- Increased mental distance from, or feelings of negativism or cynicism related to one's job
- Reduced professional efficacy."

These may present differently in people, but if you notice even minor issues with any of these then this chapter is for you.

Some research indicates that burnout rates may be lower in entrepreneurs, possibly due to having a stronger vision and mission, a greater sense of control over working life and the feelings of achievement that success brings, but other studies suggest not.

What we do know is that running a business of any size carries responsibilities to yourself and others. Long working days, up to or over 60 hours a week in the early stages leave little time for anything else. The combination of inconsistent income and financial pressures can cause anxiety; having to deal with everything and anything alone is overwhelming and on top of that, it can be isolating.

Recently, the financial company Xero published a report called Small business, Big Stress, (2, 3) identifying issues that increase stress and decrease wellbeing. They found that wellbeing scores in the UK were lower than any other country. Mental Health England's Burnout Report (4) and the Deloitte Report, Mental Health and Employers, (5) found that many UK workers report feeling unable to cope with workplace stress, showing the need for more support, particularly for younger employees (16-24) and women. Signs of burnout are also becoming more common, with 63% of UK employees now showing symptoms like exhaustion and disengagement, up from 51% two years ago.

In May 2024 , Deloitte (6) found that:
- 88% of entrepreneurs struggle with their mental health
- 41% of women struggle with imposter syndrome
- 46% struggle with high stress
- 39% worry about money
- 34% experience burnout
- 27% have poor work-life balance
- 27% struggle with loneliness and isolation
- 22% have insomnia or other sleep disorders

This shows that burnout is a real risk, and prevention is vital for the Unshakeable Entrepreneur.

Before we consider prevention strategies, let us look at the type of entrepreneur at risk of burnout and why. You probably fit into one or more of these categories, so it is even more important to look at the burnout prevention strategies later in the chapter!
Solopreneurs, sole traders, and freelancers. It should be no surprise that I've put you at the top of the list as it's all on your shoulders and if you don't do it, it doesn't get done. You may work in any of the following categories and all I will say right now is creating a healthy balance is essential. You need to do this asap as if you burnout, the whole business falls down and if that goes, so might your security.

Other at-risk fields or roles include the following – if you're a sole trader in any of these see above! If you manage a small or even a medium size team, you not only have responsibilities for the business but also for your staff, which can add considerable pressure to your already substantial load. This list is not exhaustive so if your category isn't here, choose the closest fit.

Coaches and therapists: You are often so busy looking after others that you forget about yourself. It isn't just the appointments; it's the notes and admin as well. There is also an emotional toll to coaching which may lead to a sense of overwhelm and burden.

Creatives: You may be anything from a caterer, cake baker, to a graphic designer and many more in-between! Your issue is often working on a one-off basis, so you need to attract a regular stream of clients to bring in income. This means constant marketing and selling on top of the creative side, so taking time off is hard as no clients means no pay.

Start-ups: The start-up phase carries huge pressure to succeed, fear of failure, responsibility to investors (if applicable) and the need to scale as soon as possible which leads to working all hours to drive forward.

Consultants: Consultants and strategists need regular clients to bring in consistent income and that can result in working long hours to keep everyone happy. There may also be a sense of responsibility for the success of the client's business so time off is not an option.

Fitness professionals, physios and other therapists: I bet you long to sit at a desk for part of the day instead of running with clients, massaging people, fixing injuries don't you? These are physical roles and take a toll on the body as well as your time. People often want sessions when they aren't working so early mornings and late nights are common. It is also hard to create a more passive way of working as many clients want in person training.

Perfectionists: OK so you may be in another category as well as this one! If this is you – have a word with yourself! Sometimes good enough is, err good enough! And by that I don't mean shortchange your clients, I mean set realistic standards, don't overdeliver, delegate as much as you can (and don't micromanage) so you can reduce the pressure on you and your business.

Scalers: Not an official term, but scalers are those who are moving from solo operations to having staff, employed or freelance. This brings a whole new level of responsibility and accountability as the income of others relies on us so we end up working even harder so we can pay our staff.

Working from home: Finally, who works at home? You definitely need a burnout prevention strategy as it is too easy to check on emails at 7am or 8pm, finish that document before bed, work through lunch, fire up the laptop at weekends – sound familiar?

As you can see, burnout is a risk for all of us whether we are entrepreneurs, solopreneurs or small business owners. If you get to burnout stage, then unless you have a strong support or secession strategy in place everything could collapse, bringing a whole new set of problems.

The Burnout Prevention Strategy

So, can you protect yourself from burnout? Yes!
A few simple strategies make up the Burnout Prevention Strategy (BPS) which is part of your futureproofing plan.

The BPS includes several simple things to do to reduce your chances of burnout. However, like anything it is best to start small and integrate into your schedule gradually. If you manage staff, employed or freelance, make sure they are part of this strategy, so they avoid burnout as well.
This is a three-step process, and you can take it as fast or as slow as you need.

Step 1: Check in with yourself regularly.

There are several signs and symptoms of an impending burnout, but we may be too busy to notice them so a regular check in is vital. This should be part of your business strategy – just like checking your bank balance.

Schedule time once a month (more often in times of increased pressure) to go through your BPS checklist. Think it sounds a bit daft? WHY - you probably have checklists and systems for other aspects of your business, so this is just another one!

Create your personal checklist. What this contains is personal to you. It might be simple tick boxes, 0-10 scales, or something else, whatever works for you. Do keep it simple though as you are more likely to complete it. What areas to check also depends on you, but here are some suggestions:

Mood	Muscle tension	Headaches	Appetite	Libido
Exercise	Tiredness	Energy	Activity	Self-medication
Learning	Reading	Fun	Hobbies	Socialising

Another method is to use the following statements, adapted from the Xero report, to create a simple checklist:

On a scale of 0 – 5 (0 = never. 1 = hardly ever. 2 = occasionally. 3 = a few times. 4 = most of the time. 5 = all the time) how do you rate each of the following over the last week?

1. I feel cheerful, calm and in good spirits
2. I feel active and energetic
3. I wake up refreshed and rested
4. I am productive and positive at work
5. I have made time for physical activity
6. My day includes non-work activities that I enjoy

Track these regularly and if your scores start to drop it's time to reflect on your life balance.

Brandon Burchard suggests checking the following ten areas on a weekly or monthly basis. He uses a 1 (awful) to 5 (excellent) scale. Note, for partner/love, if you are happily single score that highly. The spirit section could mean faith, energy, joy, or something else.

Add up the numbers and multiply by 2 if you are using 1 – 5 to get a score out of 100. Monitor this over time and see which areas need to be improved.

Health	Mental/Emotional	Partner/Love	Family	Friend
Mission	Experiences	Spirit/Energy	Finances	Learning

You can create your own checklist – and this could be a productive activity for a quiet day.

Step 2: Prevention is better than cure.

Just as you have systems and processes in your business to prevent problems, you need strategies to support your health and wellbeing, and that of your employees if you have them. Good health, physical and mental, underpins everything we do in life. If your health is poor, it is hard to give 100% to your business, and harder to focus on yourself. And that is when burnout becomes more likely.

Self-care, me-time, time-out – whatever you call it is important but if you haven't done this before, start small. You won't go from zero to an hour a day in one leap. Start small. Take five or ten minutes a day to do something that is not related to your business. Try reading, meditation, a brisk walk, sitting with a hot drink, making your bed. Whatever helps you to get used to including non-business activity into your daily life.

Like all habits, you need to start small and build gradually so don't rush. Create an enjoyable time out that you anticipate as that makes it more sustainable.

Back to making your bed. This might sound strange, but it starts the day with a completed task. Some research says we should throw back the covers to let the bed breathe for a while so do that while you dress. Then go back and make the bed. This simple task starts your day with an accomplishment, a tick on your to do list. It also means that at bedtime, you enter a tidy environment which can promote sleep and help you see tomorrow more positively. Admiral William H McRaven gave a speech about this titled 'if you want to change the world, make your bed'. Now you may not want to change THE world, but one small positive habit can change YOUR world.

Put simply, if you can do the little things, the big things become easier. Consider a task that you put off for ages because you didn't know where or how to start or thought it would take too long. When you eventually got round to it, it was probably quicker and easier than you thought! All tasks are like that. Start with one tiny step and complete that. Then do the next step. Soon you will be halfway or have completed the giant task because you broke it into small steps that were manageable.

Now take a break, make your bed then sit with a drink and look at the sky. Bonus points for recognising different cloud types.

Step 3: Futureproofing

Now for the pillars that underpin your health and wellbeing and support the roof – your business. Mine are Movement, Nutrition, Wellbeing, Environment, and Working Well is the roof! Yours might be different but these are good to start with.

Some suggestions for each pillar will work for you, others not so much. But as these areas are important for your current and future health, start with one as that will naturally lead to the others. And as with everything, you need to actually start, so choose the one that appeals to you or will fit into your day and build from there.

A. Movement

With my background, physical activity has to be first on the list! However, there are well-evidenced reasons why though, so it's a good place to start.

The weekly health-related activity recommendations are 150 minutes of moderate aerobic activity, two or three strength training sessions and daily flexibility and balance.
Be honest, do you meet these? If you do, well done and keep going, but if not then we will start with some simple steps. And remember, **some is better than none** so even a five-minute walk, ten squats or stretching one muscle counts.

Go for a walk: The average daily step count in the UK is around 3000, meaning many people are way below the level that will boost our health. If you do 150 minutes of aerobic activity a week your step count is probably around 8000 so well done! (By the way, the 10000 number was a marketing ploy to sell pedometers!). If not, you need to move more but here is no way you will go from 3000 a day to 8000 a day. Tracking steps can add pressure to an already intense day so start with a couple of ten-minute walks before or after breakfast or lunch or when it suits you. You can walk while on a phone call, listen to a podcast, course or document (word does audio versions!) or have a walking meeting with someone.

Aim for a brisk pace that gets your heart beating a bit faster, breathing a little harder and feeling warmer. Do this once a day and you are halfway towards the recommendations.

Sit less: Wearable trackers can notify you to move or stand each hour. This nudge is great as sedentary behaviour (sitting or lying with minimal movement) is a risk factor for many medical conditions. No tracker or don't like them? No problem, just set an alarm a set time and get up and move for a minute or two. Shake yourself, walk to another room, dance – doesn't matter what just move!

Strength is your new strategy: If we are inactive and as we get older, particularly women, we lose muscle mass and strength and if we do no strength training the loss is quicker. The benefits of strength training include:

- Stronger bones and joints and reduced risk of falls
- Improved strength, endurance and general stamina
- Better posture, balance and flexibility
- Improved metabolism and weight management (strong muscles use more energy!)
- Improved gastrointestinal transit time – how long it takes food to exit from eating it! This improves gut health and increases production of serotonin, one of our feel-good chemicals.
- Improved or regulated mood, and body image leading to better self-esteem and confidence.
- Better sleep patterns

I could go on, but you get the picture. Strength is not the new anything, it's the always something!

Yes, you are busy and going to the gym for an hour seems unworkable. But there are many exercises you can do at home, with or without equipment. Here are four you can do at least twice a week. Start with one set of 10 – 12 and increase when they are easy.

- Squats or sit to stand from a chair
- Calf raises (stand and rise up onto the toes then back down)
- Wall press ups
- Triceps dips off a chair seat or the stairs

There are many others you can add, and it is worth booking a personal trainer for a session to teach you a whole-body strength workout that fits into your day.

Stretch: Are you more flexible in your business than in your body? When we sit in the same position all day our muscles are working hard to keep us in that position. If they weren't you'd slide off that chair! Yet few people bother to stretch at the end of the day. Also if we don't stretch regularly muscles become tight which affects posture, walking gait, and strength and can lead to physical tension. Plus, if are at a desk for long periods, your body becomes almost chair shaped – tight hip flexors, shoulder and chest muscles, saggy glutes, weak and loose back muscles and tight ankles. This is not only unhealthy, but also means your body is less efficient, affecting your health over time.

Build a stretch session into the middle and end of your working day. It doesn't need to be lengthy; even five minutes will benefit your muscles. Focus on the muscles that are shorter from sitting a lot – chest, hip flexors, hamstrings, calf and the front of the shin (tibialis anterior). Yes, there are other good stretches, but these are good ones to start with. That PT you hired for strength advice can help with this!

While you are at it you are sitting for several hours a day so get a top-quality chair that promotes good posture and supports your back. Remember to claim it as a business expense.

B. Nutrition - You are what you eat

A huge part of self-care is getting the right nutrition. Be honest, how does your eating stack up? When was the last time you planned (and implemented) your meals? Have you skipped a meal (or two) recently?

Are you grabbing whatever is to hand just to get some energy? Are you hydrated or dehydrated? Nutrition is our cellular strength so as well as moving more, you need to look at what you are eating and drinking as this impacts on our overall health and function.

Diet: A healthy balanced diet is what all the books, websites and research tells us we need. Unfortunately, as a busy entrepreneur it is often way down our to-do list. There are many reasons for this – lack of time to prepare meals, minimal knowledge about nutrition, not prioritising food, or even just not being bothered about what you eat!

If this is you, stop right here.

You need to eat. And you need to eat nutrients to fuel and support every single cell in your body, especially your brain!

Now, you aren't going to change your eating patterns overnight – that Is neither sensible nor sustainable. But you do need to start somewhere. So, grab a piece of paper and create a table like the one below. Then fill it in for a few days to track what and when you eat.

Be honest, no one else will see this but it will give you an idea of where you can make simple adjustments. There are examples so you can see the sort of thing to write.

Time	What I ate	How I felt afterwards
7am	Bowl of cereal and fruit	Fine but got hungry an hour later
7.30	Coffee	Energised
10am	Two corn cakes with butter	Still hungry
11.30am	Bowl of vegetable soup	Good but got hungry around 1pm

Time	What I ate	How I felt afterwards
7.30	Coffee	Energised
12.30	White toast and butter	Felt really hungry and irritable before I ate then felt sluggish afterwards and couldn't concentrate on work.
7.30	Large pizza with two glasses of wine	Was really hungry and ate fast. Got indigestion and felt thirsty
10.30	Chocolate and another glass of wine	Woke feeling thirsty in the night and couldn't sleep. Really tired in the morning

Then make one or two small changes. Example 1, add some protein at breakfast and lunch to stave off hunger pangs and boost satiety (feeling full for longer). Example 2 lacks protein and good quality carbohydrates, and meals are erratic, which affects physical and mental function. Swap white bread for wholegrain and include protein, even cheese or peanut butter, to help balance energy. Wine will always affect quality and quantity of sleep so swapping the third glass for a large glass of water instead would help. Yes, there are other improvements to be made but start with one small change at a time for simplicity and sustainability.

Hydrate more: And that brings us to another important factor: Hydration!

How much water or other fluids do you drink during the day? While there is no specific amount to drink (despite what you may read) it is important to keep yourself hydrated. Key signs of dehydration are feeling tired or fuzzy, having chapped lips or skin that doesn't bounce back when you pinch it (back of the hand is best) or dark yellow urine (it should be a pale straw colour).

If you spend a lot of time in front of a screen, live at altitude or in a hot country, or work in centrally heated or airconditioned environments you almost certainly need more fluids than you are drinking.

Treat yourself to a beautiful jug, around 1.5 to 2 litres. Keep it on your desk and aim to get through it by the end of the day. This not only keeps you hydrated, but it benefits your muscles and your brain as well as every cell in your body. Tea, coffee and other juices also count but in larger amounts can be dehydrating so make water your preferred option.

C. Wellbeing

Moving on to ways to boost your mental health and wellbeing. Again, don't try these all at once as none will stick. Pick one that sounds interesting, manageable or fun and do that.

- **Meditate:** If you think meditation is about staring at a candle while chanting for an hour, forget it. Apart from anything else, you'll get bored! Meditation is a skill and like any skill, learning it takes time, so you need to start small. Here are a few suggestions:

- Sit outside and watch the clouds or trees for a minute or two.

- Spend one minute focusing on breathing in and out rhythmically.

- Walk at a slow pace outside for at least five minutes noticing your footsteps, the surroundings, the temperature, look for something you haven't seen before.

- Focus on your breath for a few minutes – box breathing is an easy way to start. Inhale for a count of 4, hold for a count of 4, exhale for a count of four then pause for a count of 4 before inhaling. This is a good technique if you are nervous or anxious.

- Doodle. Grab a sheet of paper, a pencil and just doodle whatever comes to mind. Make it messy, neat whatever – just scribble away for a few minutes.

- **Mindfulness:** Mindfulness in its simplest form is being fully present in the moment, being aware of what you are feeling or thinking. This can be through meditation or while doing an everyday task like washing up, dusting, washing your hair, exercising, or even cooking. Give your full focus to what you are doing, notice any thoughts and let them pass through your mind to be dealt with later.

- **Get creative:** There is something so rewarding about creating things isn't there? In fact, evidence shows that any creative activity has positive effects on our mental health and wellbeing so give yourself time each day to get creative. Not sure what to do, here are some suggestions:
- Knitting
- Embroidery
- Sketching
- Painting
- Colouring in
- Journalling
- Writing (poetry, prose, limericks, whatever!)
- Dance
- Play

Remember that nothing needs to be perfect – in fact the messier the better as that means you are letting go of perfection! So yes, you can colour outside the lines!

- **Socialise:** Whether you are an introvert or an extrovert, you still need some social contact. For the sole business owner or freelancer, loneliness can be an issue as we often work from home, online or offline, and often with long working days. This means the opportunity and energy to socialise is missing and that leaves a gap in your lives. Belonging is an important need for us as humans, (check out Maslow's hierarchy), but working alone means we often lose that connection. Socialising with others, both fellow entrepreneurs or friends and family, gives us not only that connection and sense of belonging, but also much needed time out and support. Schedule at least one social activity a week so you get away from the desk and into a community. Simple ways to ease into this are: find an accountability buddy you check in with once a week. Join a networking group - on or offline for a business and social connection, go to a class – anything from dance to exercise to art will do. Join a local walking group. Meet a friend for coffee or a walk. The actual social activity doesn't really matter, what is important is connecting with others. Just make sure you are connecting with positive and uplifting people, not drains!!

- **Relax:** Honestly, learning to relax took me a very long time. This was not only because I found it hard to switch off, but also because I felt guilty if I wasn't working. Now I love it. Relaxation is about releasing tension and anxiety or stress. It can be physical or psychological – but good relaxation involves both! How you relax is up to you and as with any new habit or behaviour start small and build gradually. No-one ever went from never relaxing to drifting mindlessly for an hour overnight! Start with five minutes in a quiet and soothing environment in which you feel safe, and at a time of day that suits you and choose something that reduces muscle tension and calms your mind. There are so many ways to switch off, including meditation, mindfulness, creativity, lying in the sun, reading a book (not business!), breathwork, visualisation, chatting with a friend, walking, stretching or simply dozing in the fresh air. Listening to soothing music or ambient sounds may also help you to get into a flow state. If you aren't feeling it, not a problem, just get back into your normal day and try again later.

D. Environment

The final pillar is your environment. Do you love it? Hate it? Feel a bit meh? The environment we are in can have a big impact on our productivity and stress levels.

Let's start with your office. Take a look around your work area – is it clear or cluttered, calming or chaotic? A chaotic and cluttered office can add to stress levels particularly if you are working on several things at once and need to have paperwork to hand.

Invest in a bookcase or shelving to organise your filing systems. Use trays, magazine holders or lever arch files for any physical resources you need for current projects and file away anything not needed now. Not only will this create a less cluttered office, but it also means you can easily find what you need.

If like me you have a dozen notebooks on the go but can never find the specific notes you are looking for, consider investing in a digital note taker so your notes can be stored, sorted and sourced efficiently. If funds don't allow, there are physical notebooks you can use to write notes and then scan and send to different destinations.

Schedule time at the end of the day to tidy your workspace. I allow fifteen minutes to clear my desk, organise paperwork and review my actions and achievement for the day. Then I set my agenda or actions for the following day, stretch, close my office door and leave 'work'.

Are you sitting comfortably? No, I'm not going to tell you a story, but if your office chair is not comfortable, it will negatively impact your posture and muscle tension and that can lead to reduced comfort and efficiency. Schedule a time to go shopping for the most ergonomic chair you can afford as that muscle tension won't be helping your stress levels or productivity.

Now let's look around your home. Is it calming and efficient or is it another stressor as it is so disorganised? As with your office, create systems that improve how your home functions. If you can afford it, get a cleaner weekly or fortnightly (or even monthly for a deep clean) as that is one less task for you and means your home will be clean and tidy for a few days at least.

Schedule time for laundry, shopping, cooking or delegate chores to other family members. Minimise clutter as there is less to tidy or clean. Create storage for toys, books, clothes, shoes – anything that can create clutter – and keep it organised. This will keep things tidy and means you can find what you need more easily.

You are aiming to create a home environment that is calming at the end of your working day so start with one room, or corner of a room, and get decluttering and organising so you have a sanctuary.

E. Working well

Now for the roof - it might surprise you that work comes last but honestly, you need everything else in place first as those are the often-neglected pillars that support a successful business.

Start by making a list of all your tasks, systems, and processes. Then think about the following:

It's SMART Jim but not as we know it!

SMART was created to help achieve outcomes in business and as such it can be helpful. However, we often need a more flexible approach so let's recreate it to suit the needs of the Unshakeable Entrepreneur.

Dream big, plan small: It is said we overestimate what we can get done in one year but underestimate what we can do in ten years. Do you have a big five or ten-year dream? Can you visualise it in detail, from how your day will run to what you are wearing, eating or living. Yes, then start to plan small steps towards your big dream. And by small I mean tiny steps to take each day that motivate you to keep moving towards your outcome. To help with this, I have reimagined SMART.

Ask yourself, either for the outcome or the first step...

- **Skills:** What Skills do I need to hire or acquire to achieve my desired outcome?
- **Meaningful:** Is the outcome Meaningful for me? Why? How will it change my life?
- **Accountable:** How can I create Accountability and find support to keep me on track?
- **Relish:** Is the path to my outcome enjoyable, something I will Relish doing?
- **Time:** Do I have the Time to take the necessary and regular steps to move me forward?

It is different way of looking at goals and it's not science, but it might help you to create and work towards your desires in a more sustainable and successful way. Remember that your key steps are not the ones you take on a good day, but the ones you take even when it's a bad day.

Time management: If only there was more time... So little time, so much to do...

You need to prioritise working ON your business, as well as IN it. This means making time for strategy and growth and it can be hard to balance the ON and IN at first, but it is vital.

There are dozens of time management systems out there. Some will work for you; others will add to your stress levels! It doesn't matter if you use pomodoro, Eisenhower matrix, eat the frog, 80/20 (pareto) principle, 1-3-5 method, 3-3-3 method, time blocking or any other method – it just needs to work for you. (By the way, a quick online search will tell you what each is and how to use it.)

For example, I find that starting work at 7.30 am means I get all my admin and marking done and out of the way before 9 am when my official workday starts. I finish around 3pm and head out for a walk, checking on any urgent emails around 4.30pm before I 'leave' for the day. You may find starting and finishing later works for you. Or two longer blocks of work with a two-hour break in the middle of the day. Maybe you prefer a longer day over four days with a three-day weekend. Try different methods to find what works for you – and adapt them to suit your needs, energy levels and the demands on your time both during and outside working hours.

Whatever method you choose or create, the key is to stick to it. There is no point in creating a brilliantly organised method, matrix, or whatever then ignoring it! And that brings us to:

Routine: The dictionary defines routine as 'a sequence of actions regularly followed' and in business establishing a regular routine can help with organisation, time management, productivity and success. Go back to your task list and start to create a routine for your routine tasks.

This can be anything from setting fixed times in your day to check and respond to emails, time each month to update your accounts, an hour a week for networking or accountability, one day a month for professional development or a business retreat once a year. It also relates to what you do outside work, regular lunch times, physical activity, socialising, or anything you want to do!

Routine doesn't need to be rigid though, have blank space in your calendar in case something comes up (more on that later) so

343

you can either do it then or move something else into that time slot to free up time for the new activity.

Delegate: This is such a hard skill to develop and even more so if you are a one-person business. But it is essential if you want to grow and to prevent burnout. Alongside delegation you can add ditching – is the task in hand one that needs doing or is it a procrastination activity? If it is truly unnecessary then ditch it and use the time for something that will move your business forward.

You really can't do it all so stop trying, go and look at your list and see what you can delegate.

I do love an acronym and created one to help you decide what to delegate. Using your list, ask yourself the following questions to help you COPE:

C – Does it need my Control?

Yes – do it. No – delegate it.

Some tasks need your input and for you to be in control, and these are priorities for your time. Others you may like doing (see E) but ask yourself if they actually need you or it's a micro-control thing.

O – Can I Outsource or automate this?

Yes – find someone to do the task. No – schedule a regular time to do it.

There are tasks that need doing but are time consuming and low-income generating. This includes tech, social media scheduling, bookkeeping etc. Can you delegate these to someone else who can do them more efficiently? There may also be tasks that need a qualified expert such as accounts, tax returns, or legal contracts, which you should delegate.

P – Am I using it to Procrastinate?

Yes – delegate or ditch. No – set a time to work on these tasks.

Do you do tasks that really don't need doing just to put off something that seems overwhelming? Typically, these get in the way of productivity or growth so need to be ditched or delegated. Are you guilty of any of these - tinkering with your brand colours, rewriting your sales pages every day, waiting for that course to be perfect, creating schedules but not implementing them yet...

E – Do I Enjoy it?

Yes – keep doing it but create a fixed timeslot. No – delegate it!

This final question is important as sometimes there are simple tasks we could delegate but really enjoy. You can keep doing these but allocate specific time slots for them, so they don't impinge on other more important tasks.

Boundaries

If only I could go back in time to set (and stick to) stronger boundaries. Well, I can't, and neither can you, but we can start now. Boundaries protect your time, energy and business and are important. These can be a simple as having set work hours, not responding to emails outside these, taking at least one full day off a week or setting out an out of office when you are away. It is hard at first, and people who are used to fast responses from you may take time to get used to a different way of working but it benefits everyone in the longer term. You are less likely to burn out and your clients will still get a speedy response, just not immediate!

One thing you definitely need to ditch is the 'can I pick your brains for a minute' calls. It's never a minute. Often it takes considerable time, and the advice is something your regular clients have to pay for. Set up a payment link and give that out to anyone who asks if you have a minute for a quick question. It doesn't have to be expensive, but it puts a value on your time and knowledge on both sides!

A final boundary tip – if you work from home, set up a 'commute'. Go for a short walk (outside ideally but round your house is fine) before you start work to put yourself into work mode. Then at the end of the day, tidy your work area, set actions for the following day, close your office door or put up a screen, and go for another short walk. This bookends your working day with a clear start and finish. It also gets a bit of activity into your day!

Nothing time

Every day in my diary, in every course lesson plan, in all my planning I create what I call nothing time. Nothing time is simply blocked out space in my schedule. Why do I do this? Having a half hour or hour of blank space factored in means if something comes up I can do it then or move something else into that space. If something overruns I have time to catch up and if I'm overwhelmed I have time to take a breath and regain my sense of balance and control. It's like setting boundaries for me!

It has taken me a long time to realise both the importance and value of nothing time in my schedule but now it is invaluable in keeping me on track with both work and my wellbeing.

Imposter syndrome

Finally, let's have a quick look at imposter syndrome. I don't know anyone at any level who hasn't experienced this at some point or several times, however, we are going to look at it from a different angle.

Yes, it is an issue, but what if we reframe it as development syndrome? One good thing about imposter syndrome is that is keeps us working on our skills and knowledge, so we develop and grow instead of stagnating. So next time you find yourself feeling inadequate or inferior, flip that thought from *'I wish I was that good'* to *'What can I do to get as good'.* Then go and do it!

And finally – is it burnout or boredom?

I am going to leave you with one last thought – are you experiencing burnout or is it boredom?

Often the feelings of frustration, overwhelm, irritability and fatigue are not because we are burning out – but because we are bored. If you have lost motivation, interest or enjoyment in your business, feel tired or exhausted at the thought of another workday, ask yourself if perhaps you are just bored. If it is boredom, think about what you can do to reignite your passion, or ask yourself if it time to close down or sell up and move on. Only you will know the answer to that one, but you will definitely need to take time out and seek advice before making any decisions. This is where that social and support network is so important.

And If you aren't sure, go back and read this chapter again and see what comes up for you.

Summary

Burnout is a real risk for any entrepreneur, regardless of the size of your business. By putting strategies in place to prevent it, you will be futureproofing your business, supporting those who work for or with you and creating a better life balance.

Do I follow all my own advice? Mostly. I am getting better as I know it makes sense to prioritise my health and wellbeing as I don't want to, nor can I afford to burn out. Luckily I love what I do which makes it enjoyable. Well, apart from admin and cleaning which I'm about to outsource!

References

https://www.who.int/news/item/28-05-2019-burn-out-an-occupational-phenomenon-international-classification-of-diseases

Xero report: https://www.xero.com/content/dam/xero/pdfs/FINAL%20-%20April%20 2023%20-%20The%20global%20state%20of%20small%20business%20owner%20wellbeing. pdf

Xero and Unmind report: https://www.xero.com/content/dam/xero/pdfs/Brains-of-the-Business-May-2022.pdf

https://euc7zxtct58.exactdn.com/wp-content/uploads/2025/01/16142505/Mental-Health-UK_The-Burnout-Report-2025.pdf

https://www.deloitte.com/uk/en/services/consulting/research/mental-health-and-employers-the-case-for-employers-to-invest-in-supporting-working-parents-and-a-mentally-health-workplace.html

Domzalski, D. & Andre, M. (2024) Navigating entrepreneurial mental health: insights from the trenches. Founder Reports. https://founderreports.com/entrepreneur-mental-health-statistics/

Ashley Lexine

Artist management and coaching, live event booking, social media management, podcast production, fashion, music and wellness.

She Was Found in Overwhelm

"Well don't you listen to what they say, 'cause we're a little different anyway!" The B-52's

Instagram - @HealthyMetalHippie

Healthy Metal Hippie Group (Healthy Metal Hippie Podcast, Heavy Metal Hippie Music & Subscription Box)

SHE WAS FOUND IN OVERWHELM

Ashley has been looking at ways to combine all the things she loves into one bigger way to connect with people. It all comes down to being a lover of the arts and a lover of wellness. She knew there had to be a way that they all fit together, even though it seemed unconventional at the time. This is where the Healthy Metal Hippie was born. Out of the wellness work she had been doing, along with the work with musicians and artists. She now hosts the Healthy Metal Hippie Podcast while running a rock 'n' roll wellness subscription box. Ashley continues to work in a coaching capacity with a variety of authors and artists and provides additional services such as podcast production and social media management. She is a strong believer that your passion has a purpose and that every single person can change the world.

Introduction

Everything came crashing down for me all at once. I left Canada in 2019 and I expected an idyllic life to begin to develop when I moved to the UK to join my then husband. Hey – I needed a shakeup! I left a stable environment, a lovely home, a long term secure job, and all my family and friends behind. I was ready for it.

I was ready for this beautiful life I had been dreaming of and planning in my head. I'd rejoin the insurance industry here in London and live this glamorous (read – super corporate) life among my peers in the industry I had excelled in for my entire working career to that point. Well, to cut a long story short, it took me a long time to find a job, my marriage was a massive disaster, and I lost my job several months after leaving the marriage, and I knew I just couldn't go back to it. That was in early 2022 and I knew I needed to begin to carve a path out for myself on a path that I'd find fulfilling; I was looking to uphold a promise to myself that I'd made so many years before.

I always knew that I wanted to run my own business and what I've wanted that to look like over the years has completely evolved but always has seemed to come back to the core things that I love in my life. Music, writing, fashion, makeup and wellness. It's pretty simple stuff – but how does it work together!? Well, I am living proof that it can work together and that it is working and building as time goes on.

Listen though, I was absolutely drowning through it. I was suffering from PTSD (still am) and I had no idea of where to turn next. I knew it couldn't be back to the industry I've known so well over the years. I wanted to be authentic. I didn't want to have to hide who I was anymore. I didn't want to be this ultra polished businesswoman. I wanted to be real and authentic, be strong, throw my cards on the table and connect with the people I worked with more than just a quick lunch, small talk.

I had taken music industry courses throughout lockdown and I wanted to see how things could be different. I dreamed to help the emerging artists in the world. How do you make it on your own as an artist anyway? I had these ideas of tapping back into my Feng Shui education, my time as a body piercer, and all the training I'd done in massage and natural wellness... despite insurance being my main work. I had been busy working hard behind the scenes figuring out what I really wanted to be when I grew up.

Coming out on the other end of losing my job and trying to find my way back into the world with this new layer of PTSD was a struggle for me. It never is just one thing is it! I had to face my fears of being in the world, being around men I didn't know, feeling, looking completely broken after everything that happened in the six months prior. So off I sent myself, teetering my way into the business world. I wasn't really ready to be honest, but at the same time, much like children, are we ever really ready?

I'm a single mother, with no family nearby, a very small support net around me. This adds to the overwhelm at times when I don't have the support nearby that I would have if I was doing this in Canada. Add this aspect to everything else I've had to work through and it's been a big leap of faith. I would like to take this time to shout out to my mum, who has helped me put things back together over the last few years and encouraged me to follow my dreams.

I told my son, who was just ten at the time and having to work through some pretty big things himself that I was going to start focusing on my business. I told him that we were going to build something that would give me more time with him, a lot more happiness and the things we want from life. I started planning, I built my website, I decided I'd focus on Heavy Metal Hippie Music but also start a wellness subscription box since I was an expert in both areas! I set to work creating some social strategies, getting products together, crafting pieces – you know… getting down to business.

I wasn't expecting how difficult it'd be to get customers though. I wasn't expecting how terrified I'd be to simply turn up for myself and the things I believed in and was dreaming of. I didn't expect that I'd be working longer hours than the twelve plus hour days I had been putting in previously. But here we were. Tremendous pressure to prove it to myself, and prove to the people who said I couldn't, that I could. My mental health suffered along the way. I excelled when I was working for someone else, so why was I falling down here?

Truth be told, I was learning. I had some more to learn about running my own businesses and I had to really start to look more at my past. I had to go back and deal with some really heavy shit that I allowed to hold me back along the way. There was trauma to release and a lot of baggage to unpack about how I viewed myself, my abilities, my strengths, what things I needed to learn, and what other things I needed to ask for help with.

It was hard to ask for the help when I needed it and it still can be difficult. Trying to figure out what to do when it comes to figuring out which tasks are the most important at any given time can be a heavy load to take on!

The past year has been extremely helpful in organising my thoughts, streamlining my businesses and finding focus in what exactly I wanted to do. Instead of a ton of baskets that I kept building, how could I find a way to have less baskets, but ones that provided more impact and value to my customers and more fulfilment to myself. Along the way, there have been additional mental health, and physical health issues that have risen up and it has thrown me for a loop but ultimately I have come back stronger and more prepared to take on the challenges I have thrown at me.

What do we do when we're hit with these unexpected roadblocks though? No matter where you are in your business journey, everybody has been thrown off by something at some point through life. Overwhelm can come through strictly business related events and pressures or a combination of business and personal stresses and it can seriously cause us to shut down depending on the severity of it.

I believe there will always be an element of overwhelm with looming deadlines, or that extra sales push for the last quarter or whatever the case may be. Those are the normal stresses though.

The ones that should be used as fuel to continue full force. We are talking about the paralysis of overwhelm that prevents us from moving forward on our path.

It leaves us with the question of what to do when we experience overwhelm and where do we go when we have no choice but to carry on even though it feels like we're drowning.

There are two paths that we can take. We can choose to admit defeat and go find a so-called simpler way forward… or we can evolve and come out on top. This all comes down to the attitude we want to come at it with. Trust me when I say that sometimes my attitude about it flips back and forth. Sometimes I go "okay Ash, give up… on everything" and then I have to go stand in front of the mirror and say "No, you need to keep going because of this and that reason." So sure, it can be wavering at times, but overall the answer has to be YES I CAN! Even if that means it's 55% yes I can and 45% I cannot to start with, it's a start and I want you to use that as the propeller to keep you on that forward trajectory.

Eventually, how we manage it will evolve, and the dial will move. I've noticed for myself that the dial is moving too. This means that the periods of overwhelm and treading water are far shorter. I can pull myself out of the water more quickly and get back to running.

First things first, I suggest that you take some serious time to reflect. Take yourself to a place where you can relax and let your thoughts flow freely. I want you to take apart your life on the page. Look back at various points over the last couple of years, both from a personal and professional perspective. I want you to really dig deep down, maybe look at old journal entries or posts on social media, photos or whatever else you can muster up! This will help transport you back to the space in time so you can really see what was happening. Not just with the rose tinted glasses of the "good ol days" but instead, with a layer of honest reflection and wrapped completely in love for yourself.

Going into this exercise without judgement can be the most difficult part of the whole thing. It's really easy to be critical of ones self but I am going to challenge you to look at this with love and compassion because I bet you were going through some shit then just as you may be going through some different shit now. Here's the reminder that it is all part of the process in your evolution. When you've got that frame of mind securely in place, let's start putting down what was going well then, and what you were perhaps struggling with at that time. I want you to get real, down and dirty and put out all the feelings you had at that time. Not only the feelings, but the facts of what was going on at the time. Maybe you had goals then that haven't quite been met, or maybe you smashed everything out of the park and now it's become so big you've hit the place of overwhelm, and you're figuring out the next step.

Go through it all, get every last detail out onto paper. From there, pull out all the key pieces and put that on another page for easy reference. It can be overwhelming in itself to go through all of it. So if you need a break, that's okay too. Once you've got the key pieces pulled out, set it aside and let's move on. The next piece is repeating the whole process, but with your current situation. And then pull out all of the pieces that are important and relevant right now.

This is a huge help because sometimes there are just too many thoughts and ideas swirling around in our brains that become overwhelming in themselves. From here, we can begin to organize our thoughts and really pick down to the nitty gritty of what is overwhelming us. It helps us quickly decide what can we easily shift, what is going to take some extra work, what we need to outsource and what we should keep close to us.

I know for me it helps when I can split things into these different categories and it also helps me reflect about what is important and pick out things that perhaps we feel overwhelmed with and aren't of much substance in the bigger picture. These things could even be simple daily home tasks and your life admin never ending to do list. So just pulling those aside out of the brain muddle can make a massive difference already. It helps you break it down into manageable areas that you can make decisions on in each area.

Once I've organised each area, I can work on each one independently and decide what is important and what isn't from each categories. I want you to be brutal here, dump the stuff that really doesn't matter. Don't hold onto ideas, things, or processes that you'd be better off without or things you'd bet better off having someone else handle for you!

I know we're all superstars and I know "nobody can do it better than me" but that kind of thinking will hold you back in the long term. We have to delegate to other people, we have to outsource for help, we have to drop off the things that aren't doing anything for us and don't align with the path we've mapped out.

While you're dropping things off those lists, I want you to look for themes and progress. Are there places that you always get overwhelmed? Or are the challenges you face different than they used to be? When you look back at this time, do you see the progress you made along the way? Say five years ago you were at one point in your business and now you're much further ahead. Sometimes that reflection does make all the difference to really accept how far we have come. I want you to sit in it, and relish in it. Even if it's not quite where you meant to be in five

357

years, you've still moved the dial, and that takes some massive celebration.

There can be hard truths that we have to face within this reflective space. We recognize the struggles that we had to face and get ourselves through but we cannot dwell on them. The best thing is to look at what we learned from them and what knowledge we can take forward to better our future. I remind myself often that I cannot let the past things continue to hurt me, I need to use them to make myself better and the world better. If you can use the overwhelm or the hurt as part of your strength, it does help in the long term.

After you've had your reflection time, and you've organized all of your thoughts… Take a break. That is some seriously heavy mental load to take on. When you're feeling refreshed, I want you to sit down and organize your thoughts, your ideas, and set your priorities up first thing. What are the things that you're giving to others to handle? What are you keeping close? What goals have you redefined?

What comes from this practice is getting more clarity on what you want and the roadmap forward. It helps to calm down all the thoughts and feelings going 100mph through your head. It helps reset us to a calm headspace and make sense of all those thoughts. It grounds us and helps us care for our overall well being in the process.

A lot of my overwhelm has come from a trauma space that I carried for a long time, and I see the changes that have taken place over the years to grow stronger, more resilient, more compassionate, more understanding. So I know I always look for the positives in these times that have added strain and endless pain. It is the only way I've been to come forward without crumbling. Forcing myself to do the difficult, step out of my comfort zone when I REALLY do not want to.

Let's talk about self care for a moment while we're here. I want to break the idea that self care is simply fluffy socks, bubble baths and having your nails done. It can certainly include those kinds of activities – I absolutely encourage a treat yourself moment, but that's not all that it is. Sometimes my self care includes going to a concert, sometimes it could be doing a deep clean of my kitchen, or sometimes, it could be journalling, it could be workouts, setting routines, and it could be therapy too. Sometimes self care is getting your dishes cleaned and your laundry done. It is all relative. And

Taking care of our body, our mind and our soul is incredibly important. I know that I need a few things to start my day out right. Most if it comes from getting myself into the right mindset for the day and the most important part for me is getting some movement in. I am much better once I've had some time to exercise and walk. It plays a bigger part to my mental health more than my physical health in many ways. No matter what the right activity for you is, I suggest scheduling time for movement in the morning. Even if that is only five or ten minutes.

Make sure you are properly fuelling your body and taking any supplements that you may need. I've found several major deficiencies after blood testing that have helped me get back on track after starting supplements. We then have to make sure that we're giving our bodies adequate sleep, and time for things that we enjoy (outside of work! that round out how fulfilled we feel. Taking care of these little things daily, really helps us overcome the long term state of overwhelm and helps us accomplish our dreams. It can be okay to get a little bit close to the line of overwhelm from time to time, but living in a perpetual state of overwhelm will slowly drive us into the ground. If you can develop systems right now and your own trigger points where you know it's time to take action, you'll be left in a much better state.

My biggest lesson that just seems to be taking hold recently is that you need to be a stubborn bitch. You need to be unrelenting in going after what you believe while not giving up on yourself and your needs. Be stubborn. Be strong and believe in yourself and your vision. Allow yourself to delegate and ask for what you need to be successful. Don't be afraid to speak up and advocate for yourself. It doesn't mean you can't listen to outside advice, but it does mean that you are the visionary and the driving force. The strength has to come from you believing in yourself and having the faith to push forward.

Every year reminds me that as we grow and evolve, things will get easier. We gain wisdom, we gain perspective and we gain compassion... mostly for ourselves! We'll certainly unlock new challenges along the way, but that is the exact proof that shows us that yes, we are making progress. You've come a lot further than you think that you have so set out to work through the emotions that surround overwhelm. I am so proud of you!

Be sure to check out the Healthy Metal Hippie Podcast on all streaming platforms for weekly stories, art, wellness and overcoming trauma. We may be able to help you take a load off in other ways too, so check out Heavy Metal Hippie Music and drop me a line if you'd like to connect!

In the meantime, I'll be here cheering you on every step of the way. I can't wait to connect with you! You can reach me at info@ heavymetalhippiemusic.com

Gillian Airey Goodwin

Educationalist, Psychologist, Mental Health and Wellbeing Entrepreneur.

Be Kind to Yourself, It's Tricky Being Human

To my husband Steve, for everything.

Linkedin @GillianAireyGoodwin

BE KIND TO YOURSELF, IT'S TRICKY BEING HUMAN

Burnout is a real thing. It is happening daily to all kinds of people, not just those who work in stressful environments such as the military, police, doctors, and nurses but those of us who are struggling to juggle the difficulties and stresses of everyday life. As the term suggests, burnout is like a slow burning candle, the constant daily grind chipping away at confidence and, self-worth. The ability to recognise what we are capable of, slowly diminishes until there is no fuel left to burn, resulting in breakdown.

As an entrepreneur, wherever you are in your business story, you will experience problems, you may already recognise some of the tell-tale signs of burnout and feelings of being overwhelmed, such as: difficulty sleeping, eating or drinking too much and stopping your exercise routine. The trick is to recognise, identify and manage those factors that indicate a wellbeing issue is just around the corner, and to put in strategies that support you and help you overcome the difficulties you are inevitably bound to face in your business, in your families, in juggling finances and in supporting others. This is where I can help. I've been there and I hope my experiences and the strategies I adopt will be of use to you.

I managed to avoid a breakdown, but I suffered burnout and when I look back it is frightening how close I came to a breakdown without realising it at the time. I was working long hours, I was feeling exhausted, I started to miss meals and instead ate chocolate to keep me going, my work took over my life and I was choosing to work rather than spend time with family and friends – does this sound familiar? When building a business spending time on creating your ideal company is time well spent, but you also must put your needs above your company's needs on occasion, otherwise you may find yourself on the path to

363

burnout and breakdown. It is very difficult in today's climate to not feel overwhelmed but there are strategies that can help you to create boundaries, stay in control of your health and be successful in your endeavours.

I was fortunate in that I was asked by my employer to become the Senior Mental Health and Wellbeing lead, and this is where my entrepreneurial story begins. I began to learn about wellbeing, about mental health and about the need to be mentally well to thrive. A love affair began….my love of psychology and my absolute passion for providing wellbeing support using positive psychology and solution focused therapy. I love fostering a feeling of empowerment, developing perspectives, helping others to identify what they control and developing in others an attitude of kindness, forgiveness and a love of thyself. I am currently a psychologist in training at Wolverhampton University, graduating in September 2025, the founder of Goldfinch Enterprises, and I am living my best life so far.

To ensure you are mentally well and you avoid burnout there are some key issues you need to be aware of and take control of, first:

Wellbeing:

Your wellbeing is your responsibility. I don't mean to be harsh and it is difficult to put yourself first when demands are being made on you from all directions, but as the common psychological analogy of putting your own oxygen mask on first, before helping others dictates, you need to be well to be your best and to support others in your teams, in your family and in your business. The World Health Organisation outlines wellbeing as:

"A state in which the individual realises his or her abilities, can cope with the normal stresses of life, work productively and fruitfully, and is able to make a contribution to his or her community."

There are various ways for you to look after your own wellbeing. There are only so many hours in a day and identifying priorities for each day and week will help you feel in control. Create a work diary or calendar, where deadlines are noted and the activities and tasks that need to be completed before that deadline are identified. Always plan some flexibility for those unexpected jobs that appear at the busiest of times.

Rest! Yes, sleep is important, but rest is vital. Take a moment to switch off mentally, emotionally and physically throughout the day. This could be taking a short walk around the block, spending 15 minutes listening to music or reading. It is amazing how creative the brain is when you relax and stop using it. Sleep issues are common especially for hard working individuals who are focused on building a business and are overwhelmed with the demands and difficulties associated with entrepreneurship. It may sound obvious, but you need to plan a bedtime routine that helps you to switch off. So, stop looking at devices thirty minutes before you want to sleep, keep paper and a pen by your bed so any great ideas can be written down rather than play over and over in your mind. Relax, focus on your breathing, practice mindfulness or have a bath, whatever will help you close off the day.

You need to eat and drink. Not drinking water regularly and skipping lunch, were factors in my burn out experience. You need fuel to help you build and maintain a business. When working hard there is a tendency to eat energy rich foods to give you a boost, but the sugar rush is short lived and eating properly will help sustain you for longer.

Ask for support. When unexpected events happen, which they frequently do, having a support network you can rely on to help you is vital. Your family, friends and colleagues will want to help. People feel they do not want to burden others but helping others is a fundamental social aspect of being human. It allows others to show how much they care and gives others permission to seek support from you if required. There are so many social media networks available with likeminded people learning and sharing, which can provide a wide range of ideas and suggestions to support you – join them.

Know, accept and activate boundaries. As said previously, your wellbeing is your responsibility, and you may need to put your agenda above the agenda of others. If you decide to finish your working day at a certain time, keep to it. Don't answer any work-related calls, emails or text messages after this time. You can politely inform your clients that you are unavailable during these set times, but you will be one hundred percent focused on their needs the following morning.

So, remember:

- Your wellbeing is your responsibility
- Put your own oxygen mask on first
- Prioritise – create a work calendar – add some time flexibility too
- Rest during the day and have regular short breaks
- Sleep
- Eat and drink properly
- Ask for support
- Know, accept and activate your boundaries.

Task:

Choose one or two of the above suggestions that you are going to work on next week. A small step forward is still a step forward.

Stress:

To be mentally well and avoid burnout you need to manage your stress. The amount and type of stress an individual encounters in a day can be very different. From small irritations to major catastrophes. Give your stress a number between 1 and 10. Being stuck in traffic and being late for a meeting may not feel at the time as a 1 or 2 but compared to a broken bone caused by rushing up stone steps outside your office, the traffic jam is minor; everyone experiences traffic jams and understands it's not your fault. Perspective is important along with recognising what you can and can't control.

Stress has a purpose, and recognising that purpose helps reframe your thoughts regarding stress. Instead of something to fear it becomes something to welcome. Stress and anxiety are emotions. They are data about your feelings. Stress and anxiety do not define you. The psychologist Dr Susan Davies, in her book Emotional Agility, reminds us that we perhaps should refrain from saying 'I am stressed' instead say 'I am feeling stressed'. The feeling can go away just as quickly as it arrived. Stress is way of keeping the body alert. Certain physiological reactions to stress occur which prepare the body for fight or flight. In stressful situations you are more likely to focus on the issue at hand, to plan your reaction to the issue with clarity, be motivated to address the issue head on, to listen more attentively - in the words of Billy Ocean stress means "when the going gets tough...the tough get going."

Breathe through the stress and actively focus on calming your emotions. Identify what triggered the feelings of stress. Often stress triggers are more to do with us than the source of the stress. As someone who dislikes conflict and upsetting others, one of my stress triggers is when someone has a criticism of my work or a complaint, or I feel I have disappointed someone by not fulfilling their expectations of me. I have learnt to accept

I am not perfect, to listen attentively to the complaint without automatically assuming the complaint is valid. Keeping a stress journal has helped me identify my sources of stress and often I am my own worst enemy. It is also worth noting that complaints and criticisms are not about you they are about your work, the decisions you have made or a mistake. You learn from them and so they are invaluable for growth. Use them to improve your work or the services you provide. Explain why you made the decisions you did and if you feel on hindsight (which is a wonderful thing), that you made a mistake – own it. Accept it, apologise and move on.

The language we use to speak to others is important but the language we use to speak to ourselves inside our head is invaluable. Think of a dear friend and imagine a conversation you would have with them if they were feeling stressed about something. Think about what you would say. How you would remind them of the skills they have, that they are human, that although they are feeling stress, you have confidence in how they will successfully deal with the issue. Why don't we talk to ourselves in the way we talk to our loved ones?

So, remember:

- Put your stress into perspective, give it a number, 1 to 10
- Recognise stress is there for a reason – listen to it
- Breathe
- Identify your triggers, where did they come from and why
- Keep a stress journal to aid understanding
- Listen attentively to yourself and others
- If you've made a mistake – own, it
- Talk to yourself as kindly as you talk to others.

Task:

Think about the last time you felt stress, what happened? Write it down and try to identify where the stress came from and why did you feel it.

Control

To avoid burnout and the feeling of being overwhelmed, one must recognise what they do and don't have control over. You can control you; you can't control others. Other people's opinions of you, what they say about you, how they treat you – that is their business. How you react, what you write, and how you treat others that is on you. Your values, your views, your opinions and the way you have chosen to conduct your business is a reflection of you, that you alone control. It is so easy to take things personally, but I ask that you keep an open mind and be above all things be kind. You never know the battles someone is fighting. A top tip that I am currently working on is an idea from 'thecriticalthoughtlab.com' which is 'observe not absorb.' This is reminding me that I am not responsible for others' actions, only my own.

You decide on your business plan, you decide how you are going to represent yourself in the business world, you decide on your content, your targeted audience, how you are going to develop the business and the type of reputation you would like to build. You choose who you work with, which assignment to accept and how you are going to implement the service or goods you provide. You choose what you walk away from too.

So, remember:

• Identify what you do and don't control
• Other people's opinions are not your business

- Keep to your standards, values and beliefs – stay authentically you
- Observe don't absorb
- Choose wisely who you work with
- Walking away is an option.

Task:

Make a list of the things you currently control.

The art of saying no

Saying no in business is surprisingly hard, but on occasion necessary. A contributing factor to my burn out situation was that I found it hard to say no to things I was being asked to do. I continued to take on more and more responsibility and tasks. My reputation was one of, 'getting the job done' and as such I felt pleased when I was asked to take on another leadership role or project. This began to take its toll as I was feeling more and more pressure, and I was putting more pressure on myself. I ended up being my own worst enemy.

Entrepreneurs especially find it hard to turn down work and worry about where the next project is coming from, but you can't provide services and goods if you are burnt out.

There are many ways of saying no, and actually explaining your own perspective is surprisingly easy and very readily accepted. Saying 'I would love to work with you and will be available in one month's time, does that work for you?' demonstrates your interest and also how in demand you are. Planning workloads so you can provide a valuable, unrushed and bespoke service to your clients is much better than being rushed, tired and then unavailable due to other demands.

Be honest about what you can and can't provide. If you are not interested in the role or job, say how kind the offer is but on this occasion it's not the direction you want to go in, at the moment. Try not to cut off opportunities that may be useful in the future but take control of what you put your valuable time into.

So, remember:

- Ask yourself if you honestly have the resources to do what you are being asked at this time
- Prioritise your tasks, how important are they? Can you say no to some of them
- Plan your workload – what you are going to do and when
- Be honest about what you can and cannot do
- Remember saying yes to a task means you may have to say no to something else
- Your time is valuable – use it wisely.,

Task:

Make a list of the things you feel you could say no to.

Social comparison

Social comparison and competition are prime factors of feeling stress, overwhelm, burnout and imposter syndrome. Firstly, social comparison is a natural human behaviour that can be useful or damaging to our well-being. We compare ourselves with others to get a perspective of who we are, and where we are in societal groups. This can spur us on to do things or become a better person, to be inspired and create. Social comparison can also intimidate and confuse and be a factor in negative self-talk.

There is a lot of competition in the workplace, but no one is like you. You are unique. As there is no one like you, comparing yourself to others can be a wasted exercise. No one will deliver in the same way you do; no one will support your customers as you do. Providing goods and services is intrinsically down to how you present yourself, market yourself, how you support your clients, how you charge for the goods and services you provide. You can learn from others; you can compare your business with others but do this in a positive manner – to improve what you provide and to learn. Keep to your authentic self and your business values regardless of what others are doing. You will obviously need to keep ahead of business trends and demands but remember what you are in control of. You may need to adapt and change your business model, or you may reach a decision that you need to say no and completely change your business. Remember -you always have options, and you always have a choice.

Imposter syndrome is a common feeling of not being good enough. It is when you doubt your abilities to do a job. It develops when negative self-talk begins to take over and changing your mind set can help you battle that doubt. Remember everything you can do, remember your skills and achievement, remind yourself of why you began your business in the first place – what were your goals? Instead of thinking of what you can't do, remember what you can do. If you need training in a specific area sign up for a course and develop your skills. There are so many opportunities to learn and extend your knowledge so take them.

So, remember:

- Recognise self-comparison is natural, it has a purpose
- Remember you are unique
- Learn from others
- Be positive and honest about your achievements
- Develop your skills
- Make the most of opportunities that come your way.

Task:

Make a list of your skills, talents, unique selling point and achievement.

Negative thoughts and talk

The way we talk to ourselves in our heads can make the difference between coping with life and feeling overwhelmed with the responsibilities and workload our businesses and family life create. Being positive does not mean you ignore the difficulties you encounter, it means having a positive attitude towards how you deal with those difficulties. Reminding yourself that you are a capable, intelligent and resourceful person will help you to face stresses, deal with issues and recognise what you do and don't control. Saying a daily mantra to yourself is one way of changing the language you use when referring to yourself.

We support our friends and family all the time with positive comments, we allow others to make mistakes and praise others for having a go; for attempting something new and we forgive them if things go wrong. Yet, with ourselves we are more likely to revisit mistakes over and over in our heads, feel embarrassed and give ourselves a bad time for being human. Reframe your thoughts, actually write your thoughts down if it helps you and speak to yourself the way you would a friend. Be kind!
So, remember:

- Recognise and identify negative thoughts and talk
- Ask yourself if the negative self-talk or thoughts are helping you
- Talk to yourself the way you would a friend or family member
- Recognise challenges for what they are
- Reframe your thoughts – what can I do about this?
- Be kind to yourself.

Task:

Think of a mantra that you can say every day to remind yourself that you are capable, resourceful and in control.

Forgive yourself

To avoid the feelings of being overwhelmed and burnt out it is essential to forgive ourselves when we make a mistake. We are human, and as a waitress in a hotel in Victoria, Vancouver Island, Canada once said to me and my husband, "You are human and therefore innately flawed." I don't know her name to be able to cite her properly, but I will be forever grateful for her comment, it has helped me to forgive myself.

We do get tired, we do get overwhelmed with tasks we have to do, we do put pressure on ourselves and on occasions we snap at our loved ones, treat a customer in a way we regret, make a poor decision or forget to pay an invoice. If you make a mistake, I suggest firstly you forgive yourself, own the mistake, recognise and identify it, then put it right any way you can. Accept you snapped, apologise, explain and do something kind for your loved one. Apologise to your customer, accepting the service you provided was not at your usual standard and correct the error. Pay the invoice as soon as possible and write invoice deadlines on your work calendar so the mistake does not happen again. It is hard to hold a grudge when a genuine apology is given, and people do understand when you explain your mistake.

So, remember:

- Accept you are human and not perfectForgive yourself
- Accept and take responsibility for mistakes
- Correct the error
- Genuinely apologise

- Remember we have all been there, everyone gets things wrong on occasion.
-

Task:

Think about a mistake you made recently; how did you handle it? How would you handle it now? What could you have done to forgive yourself?

Guilt, let it go

We feel guilt when we have acted in a way that is below our own values and expectations. Guilt is closely linked to shame. As the previous section said, we are all human and we make mistakes and feel guilty. Guilt can eat away at our self-worth and self-esteem, contributing to feelings of being overwhelmed, adding to feelings of stress and guilt is a factor in burnout. One of the signs of burnout is constantly feeling guilty and another is resentment.

Guilt is a natural emotion that has a purpose – listen to it. Why are you feeling guilty? Write down what caused the guilt? Try to identify the triggers and reasons for it. Once you understand where the guilt comes from, why you are feeling it, how you can learn from it, then…. let it go. The guilt is no longer productive; it has done its job so put it in the past and leave it there.

Hindsight is a wonderful thing, but you cannot change history. You make decisions at the time you make them, based on the situation you are in at the time. If we could see the future repercussions of our decisions life would be so much easier, but we can't. You weigh up the pros and cons and using your experience, knowledge and skills at the time choose a path – if it was the wrong path on this occasion feeling guilty won't change it. Learning from the guilt will add to your knowledge and help you make better decisions in the future.

So, remember:

- Guilt is a natural emotion everyone experiences
- Guilt can damage self-esteem and self-worth
- Try to understand why you feel guilty
- Let it go, leave it in the past
- You can't change the past only learn from it
- Guilt may help you make better decisions in the future.

Task:

Do you still feel guilty about something you said or did? Write it on a piece of paper, screw it up and throw it away.

Self-belief

As entrepreneurs believing in ourselves is important. If you did not have a genuine desire to start your business, and a belief in your own abilities and the services you can provide I doubt you would have begun your entrepreneurial journey. Self-belief was probably a factor in your decision to do what you do. It can be easily eroded however in the competitive world we live in. So, keeping it can help with wellbeing, goal making and decision making.

Remember your skills, remember why you decided to become an entrepreneur and the unique talents you have. Having self-belief does not mean that you think developing your career is going to be easy and stress free, it means you believe the effort required, the difficulties you experience and the mistakes you make are worth it for you to grow in your business and to achieve your life goals.

Being overwhelmed, stressed and exhausted can chip away at your self-belief so looking after yourself will help you to retain that determination you began your business with. Take part in self-reflection and remind yourself of the reasons why you began your business. Working hard is a requirement of success in all endeavours and positive self-belief is a contributing factor to success too. Visualise where you want your business to be in two, five- and ten-years' time, and 'one step at a time', work on getting there.

So, remember:

- Self-belief is important
- Self-belief can be easily eroded, keep working on it
- You have unique talents
- Remind yourself why you started this journey
- Be determined
- Visualise your successes

Task:

Write down where you want to be in the future and the steps you need to take to get there. Visualise your success and believe you can make it happen.

Once you realise that you are in control of your wellbeing, and you recognise some of the factors that lead to feelings of being overwhelmed you can avoid burnout. You are important to your friends, family and business so you need to put yourself first sometimes. Having priorities and boundaries can help you feel in control of events, tasks and demands being made on you. Creating a business plan, having clear goals, knowing your audience and believing in the services or goods you provide aids positive thoughts and action. Remember what you can and cannot do and think of solutions to problems rather than letting problems overwhelm you. This is all easier said than done and we all have a default setting so give yourself time to reframe your thoughts. Thoughts lead to emotions and emotions to actions. Emotions are important as they provide information, but they can get in the way of logic and lead to emotionally fuelled behaviours. Take your time, breathe, and journal your emotions so you can understand them, learn from them and put them aside allowing logic to take over.

But finally, I invite you and encourage you to be kind to yourself and remember it's tricky being human.

Gillian provides wellbeing workshops, training and support for educators, entrepreneurs and everyone looking for prevention of, rather than cure of mental illness.

LinkedIn: @GillianAireyGoodwin
Email: contact@goldfinchenterprises.co.uk
Please visit her website: Goldfinchenterprises.co.uk

Now your brain is filled with Unshakeable ideas the best thing you can do is to give yourself permission not to worry. Some of the themes we have touched upon will be things you experience and some of them may never ever be an issue. Please do not dwell on the things that can go wrong. Let this book be your survival guide when you need it, dip into it and out of it but do not absorb heavy weights that are not yours. I hope many of the things we have touched upon either will never be needed or that you sail through them with the confidence of a mediocre white male world leader.

You were made for great things and great things do not come easy to those who deliver them to the world. It's your burden and your gift.

Take what resonates and build a beautiful life around each opportunity that you create for yourself, ignore the passages that hold no baring for you and perhaps in an act of becoming part of our village that take care of each other, share this book with a friend. Or leave it in the waiting room or coffee shop where others may enjoy it.

Like the sentiment of together, the sentiment of supporting each other to win - pass it on and continue the ripple effect of what was started here, you become a handprint in the legacy by doing so.

A Massive thank you to Danielle Thompson, Dee Airey, Sandra Ten Hoope, Maria - Ines Fuenmayer, Anna Payne, Ashley Lexine, Denise Matthews, Hayley Baxter, Amber Doughty, Nic Davies, Gillian Airey Goodwin, Sarah Hands, Sarah Bolitho, Kellie Williams, Heidi Williams for your dedication to this project but moreso the purpose of it, the message behind it and the dedication to others that you have shown by being part of it. You make the world a better place and we are all better for having you be part of ours.

Go forth and become your own version of an Unshakeable Entrepreneur - you are strong and we believe in you.

Printed in Dunstable, United Kingdom